MILLENNIALS: OMG! LIKE SO OFFENDED RIGHT NOW

Kevin J Mervin

Published by

Foot in the Door Publishing

All rights reserved

First Edition published 2020

A catalogue record for this book is available from the British Library

Chapters

Millennials

Acknowledgement

A huge thank you to my children for growing into responsible and sensible adults whilst many others succumbed to our modern social disease. I would also like to thank too many Millennials to mention for telling me about their trials and tribulations growing up in precarious and difficult 21 Century world, highlighting my discovery as to where the Millennial Generation came from and where it is heading.

Other books by Kevin J Mervin

Weekend Warrior: A Territorial Soldier's war in Iraq
PTSD: Living Comfortably numb

Introduction

Arguably the term Millennials has been around since 1991 although not really used as a definition until the late 1990's. Born in 1980 this generation started to leave school and enter adulthood by 1996. It was only then that the term Millennials was globally perceived to be a perfect title describing the next generation heading towards the forthcoming Millennium. But why are they perceived to be completely alien to past generations?

Studies tend to lean towards believing Millennials display a different social attitude to previous generations due to growing up in a 21st Century world of science, virtual technology and digital communication. Totally reliant upon computers, tablets and smartphones, yet have very little comprehension, care or understanding of past technologies that created their devices. But these particular studies fail to explain what Millennials represent, where they came from, why they portray themselves to be completely different, where they are heading, or if they actually existed at all.

Born in 1966 with a childhood through the seventies and starting my working life in the early eighties, I never realised what a massive impact the next generation would have upon my country, let alone the world. I grew up in an era still recovering from the Second World War. Even in the 1980's unexploded bombs continued to be discovered on wasteland, new housing estates, commercial building developments and on occasion dug up in gardens.

Bomb damaged factories and warehouses were still playgrounds 30-years after the Luftwaffe created them. And there was a very good reason for this: the United Kingdom was skint due to cost of war. Not forgetting having to repay an enormous lend/lease loan of a zillion trillion dollars to the United States – finally paid in full by July 2006. In the meantime United Kingdom (UK) Government had to spend a fortune of yet more borrowed money on defence just in case those pesky Soviets made plans for an uninvited visit, or went completely mental and nuked us all.

Due to enormous cost of the Cold War, and whilst still paying for the Second World War, UK government struggled to keep its head above water for decades. Whilst all this was going on, latter part of the 1960's and through a decade of industrial disputes in the 1970's the nation endured a 3-day working week and power cuts. In return, families struggled to make ends meet. This meant – to coin a modern phrase – expendable cash was for them rich folk down in that there London, whilst the rest of the country simply had to do without.

My old fashioned view of the world was kept very much alive with a make do and mend attitude thanks to my parents, who in turn had no choice but make do and mend whilst their parents did their bit for the war effort. This particular culture came with many other attributes: being polite to others, having good manners, never swear (or at least be heard swearing by your teachers or parents), and to never answer back when being told off – take it like a man. Not forgetting to keep a stiff upper lip when times were hard – just get on with it. Bottle emotions, never show weakness, and not forgetting the all-time favourite: do your household chores, before and after school, let alone weekends.

Of course moaning about chores and cursing under ones breath goes without saying. And not getting caught voicing an exceptionally loud opinion saved you from receiving a thick ear. But mum always had the last word and children were there to exploit: washing clothes in a tin bath – also used to bathe the family – sweeping the yard, washing-up, clearing soot from the hearth, taking out rubbish, so on and so on. Daily chores were simply part of growing up.

These morals and cultural disciplines were past down from the Greatest Generation to the Baby Boomers and most certainly evident within my Generation X – last of the realists. Since, old-fashioned values have been diluted somewhat, if not disappeared altogether. But why is that, and what has all this got to do with Millennials?

As an amateur historian my interest matured into an investigation – borderline obsession, almost – of our modern Millennial era. During my eye-opening yet entertaining years watching my own children grow into adulthood, I extended my fascination further still with a 5-year study of Scandinavia and other European countries to discover if there is a common understanding between different cultural perspectives and our own-grown Millennial frustrations.

In doing so I found myself having to dig deep into history to unravel the true origin of modern society where I came across some remarkable and fundamental global events dating back as far as 200-years that support my discovery. All of which had a profound effect upon our Millennial Generation, placing past studies into question as to why technology is a forgone conclusion for their unusual behaviour.

From basic moral standards and disciplines, patriotism, socialism and government intervention, political division to radical extremism, an ever-expanding social jigsaw of past key events grew larger and larger. Many questions quickly materialised as I painstakingly joined each piece that influenced the Millennial era, eventually giving way to answers as the picture slowly clicked into place, revealing why modern society behaved in a manner to which it had no choice but grow accustom.

Why we found it difficult to address, complain or feel compelled to give Millennial tantrums a wide birth, and why past generations had an unnatural fear of becoming condemned and pigeon-holed by Millennials should others dare contradict their behaviour. Answers to why they adopted a lesser understanding of certain nouns not realising the true definition yet emphasised its importance believing the interpretation is designed for them and them only, such as Catastrophe: unable to find a WiFi connection or losing a mobile phone signal. Or used to describe and exaggerate a situation because dad disallows sole use of the driveway.

Gay, Nazi and Fascist are further examples used loosely and without thought. Again, having little or no understanding as to what the words really mean or there impact and effect they have upon elders that do. Not forgetting the huge concern that Millennials fail to recognise key events in history. Simple dates such as 1066 and the battle of Hastings, June 6th 1944 and D-Day, and more recent, 11th September 2001 – globally recognised as 9/11 but scarily not to young Millennials.

Answers to why history is becoming less and less important and why we continue to allow modern social ignorance evolve without guidance and control. So strap in, buckle up and hold tight, you're in for a bumpy ride. I'm going to take you on a fact-filled, fun-packed and somewhat fast and incredible journey, with the odd example thrown in, which I'm sure you will have never experienced before and most probably never will again.

I first take you back to a time when life was hard and brutal, the very creation of our own modern existents. The original footings that support not only Millennials but all previous generations in our modern world. For

what I'm about to reveal may come across as outrageous,
dangerously profound, definitely cruel and most probably
offensive. But then again, who said life was going to be
easy.

Chapter One

Where did it all go wrong

USA believes a generation stretches to a rigid, unequivocal 15-years. Japan believes it is every 10-years. But they're both wrong. The correct definition is when socially accepted by people born between a certain period where such social change, cultural or global events and circumstances influenced a new generation.

Millennial Generation, however, is believed to be a collective of micro generations starting from 1980 ending in 2015 by endorsing enough evidence – wherever that came from – to support further generations in between Generation Y, Z and iGen respectively. Although iGen is apparently the latter part of Generation Z and there's a whisper of an even newer generation, Generation Alpha – wherever that came from, and what does it mean? Of course, cramming in as many demographics as possible within a short period of time is simply bonkers.

To add a little more confusion, between Generation X and the Millennials, Xennials squeezed into a 10-year gap starting in 1975. Last of which were born in 1985. And this is where total chaos begins. Latter births of Xennials were born within the Generation X era, where Generation Y supposedly started with its first born in 1980 creating, as I see it, the birth of a semi-synthetic culture 5-years inside the last generation, ending in 1994. Try to keep up.

Then came Generation Z – or iGen in latter years – the fully synthetic culture, just in time for Windows 95. Could there be a connection? This extremely confused gaggle supposedly ended in 2012 lasting a closer realistic 17-years, with Generation Alpha in hot pursuit starting in 2013. You see, total chaos. But where did this sudden deluge of duplicitous, ignorant, narcissistic, exaggerating, arrogant, obsession with Soya, outrageously demanding, completely inconceivable self-important modern culture come from? Is it new, or has it been around for a while?

Teenagers, for instance, at a transitional age between childhood into adulthood are a natural target for ridicule; casting aside their ugly yet naïve demands on social or even global revolution – in their favour, of course. In fact, teenage attitude hasn't changed throughout the ages, and we will certainly never see any change in the foreseeable future. After all, they know everything, don't they? Grown-ups understand this because they too were once young and relied upon elders to sometimes intervene and teach them about life's perils and frustrations.

Certainly today's modern society has been inundated with television, print and social media headlines covering almost every aspect of Millennials and their every day issues. BBC Radio two presenter, Jeremy Vine, constantly goes on about how hard the Millennial Generation has it. But their constant finger pointing, refusal to take responsibility, blame everyone and everything other than themselves, has been incredibly exhausting to listen to, including the Jeremy Vine show, let alone frustrating to the point of suffering a migraine. And yes, I did mean Jeremy.

Whether its politics or house prices, university fees or Brexit, Millennials have this seemingly unstoppable impulse to shout – not debate – but shout their must heard unequivocal correct opinion. And should there be the slightest of contradiction from anyone, they're not only wrong, it is perceived to be a personal attack. Instantly defending their position with radical accusations of either being a racist, Nazi, or both for daring to have a different opinion or corrected by those that actually know what they're talking about.

My Generation X youth didn't care less about current affairs, political debate or house prices, let alone contemplate discussion or debate amongst themselves with such subjects. As far as we were concerned life was too short. All that mattered was to leave school at sixteen, get a job, give a few quid to mum for board, constantly repair our first clapped-out motorbike or car, get pissed and try out cheesy chat-up lines down a night club. Reaching our late teens to early twenties it was time to fly the nest and continue with a busy singles social life – worry about bills and rent later.

Throughout previous generations young adults have always ignored parents on various issues, only to learn the hard way. Enduring mistakes, hard knocks and life changing decisions. Our own choices led to our own mistakes; it was no one else's fault or blame. We accepted that and took it on the chin. Nevertheless, something radically changed modern society's way of thinking. A particular event that somehow fundamentally changed cultural belief of an entire generation that can only be described as a disaster. And it must have happened recently to create such catastrophic repercussions upon today's society, perceived to be nothing more than a quagmire of cultural differences resulting in a consequential collapse of beliefs and morals on a global scale.

Recent history shows that a huge chasm of misguided differences quickly appeared and the catastrophe that at first went unnoticed hit us all with a surprising yet incredible force, whilst indoctrinating a belief that previous generations were wrong.

Consequentially a synthetic confidence ensued a new generation, where they were, without debate or question, correct in every way. A new generation eager to start from the top by enforcing demands, destroy an old, fusty, arrogant, outdated government, and support a brand new revolution spearheaded by a deluded, yet manipulative opportunist desperate to exploit a delicate situation and gain control. A leader determined to undermine a society that usually held a liberal belief of life and social structure yet forced to renounce it.

Nonetheless, with loyal disciples, a new political party emerged from underneath the radar spreading social unrest throughout the masses. Gaining huge support from a young population eager to toss aside an outmoded and outdated establishment seen nothing more as turncoats. Allowing rule by foreign political outsiders, caring not a jot about its people, blamed for destroying their own country. They simply had to go.

Political campaigns are part of the course when running for government. Spreading the word and gaining support in a, let's say, unconventional way, is a very different animal. But if followed by a group of young activists – easy pickings that haven't yet had the chance to live in the real world but have a very loud voice – and an older traditional follower from a certain persuasion with a grudge to bare – national support quickly gathers momentum. Media organisations soon take an interest, and those with a biased view jump on board for the ride. The carrot has been dangled.

For a radical political party to excite a new generation, however, needs a particular leader. A leader that can only be described as a tad dodgy with an even dodgier history, yet charismatic and genuine to a hard-fast deniable believer. Someone who appears to be a great leader for the masses but has a more sinister agenda for his country and yes, Europe. A leader that isn't afraid of gossip towards his xenophobic attitude of the Jewish community, and a brilliant speaker that can almost hypnotise an audience at rallies with his radical philosophy.

A contagious passion would erupt arousing an emotional and dangerous support from followers, developing tough boundaries of acceptance within the party and a zero tolerance towards disagreement by exploiting an extremely delicate and volatile political climate. Loyalty is mandatory, where disloyalty and support of any opposition will result in immediate expulsion, ridicule and an unsavoury public hatred.

But what about those that didn't agree with these new policies, did they have a voice? Well no, not really. It's too late; the die has been cast. Any contradiction towards anything this mighty leader says will be shot down in flames by naïve extremist followers and a biased media, to the point of contradicting opposition parties on every debate, discussion or disagreement. This leader, with an army of loyal disciples, is correct in every way. All other political parties, including its members and supporters, are simply and unequivocally wrong.

The age of debate and democracy was destined to come to an abrupt and violent end with this leader, allowing followers to spread mayhem, if only to exploit attention. Could you imagine, a society led by a maniac, where everyone has to have the same views? Denied self-determination, freedom of speech, even arrested for expressing an otherwise previous accepted opinion, only to suddenly become illegal just because it no longer favoured a new political belief that everyone must obey?

At this point I must ask if you have someone in mind to whom I refer. If it's Hitler, you are wrong. For those who think I was referring to Tony Blair or even

Gordon Brown, well, you're not far wrong. I was actually referring to Jeremy Corbyn, but they do all have one thing in common: radicalisation with a mandate of total control of a nation by implementing National Socialism to defend their own selfish agenda. Not unlike the very beginning of our modern society, but with a freakish twist, as you are about to discover.

Nevertheless, those that were at school during these latter eras won't have childhood memories of eating mud, constantly playing outside in all weathers, and treated junk fast-food or takeaways as a rare treat. Those from an older generation, however, will understand the meaning of free speech, being offended doesn't actually hurt, or feel compelled to shout murderer at someone squashing an insect and start a peace concert in its memory. To you I say peel back the following pages and unravel the true origin of our modern society, the very template of our 21st Century existence.

For those that are disgusted by meat eaters, never take blame because it's always someone else's fault, still live with their parents beyond the age of forty, cry at weddings and demand a benefit concert for a squashed insect, first, get a grip. Second, best you don't read on. Because if you do, boy, are you going to be so offended.

Chapter Two

Genuinely, like, OMG!

Once upon a time a brother and sister lived with their single mummy in a modest three-bedroom semi-detached house in a quiet leafy suburb of Perfectville. Diane, the elder sister of Jeremy, was sat at the kitchen table scratching her head thinking hard what to do for mummy on mother's day, which was tomorrow.

'I'm stuck.' said a disgruntled Diane Googling what to do for mother's day on her smartphone.

'So am I.' Jeremy added, not really interested as he continued to scroll through his messages on WhatsApp.

Diane tapped a pencil on her lips, staring into space. Suddenly she let out a screech, making Jeremy jump. 'Oh my god, I've, like, got it! Like, genuinely, let's, like, make mum, like, breakfast in, like, bed.'

'Breakfast in bed? Like, totally sounds a bit, like, boring.' Jeremy said, as he continued scrolling through his smartphone uninterested.

'Oh, c'mon, it'll be, like, brilliant. But we'll have to actually, like, start, like, early. Gonna be, like, six o'clock.'

'Bit, like, late for breakfast.'

'OMG! No, Jeremy, like, six in the, like, morning. Totally, like, genuinely.'

'Six in the morning! Like, does such a time, like, exist?' cried a surprised Jeremy, 'and why should we?'

'Oh my god!' shouted a bemused Diane, 'because it's, like, mother's day, and it's only, like, fair that we, like, do something for her.'

Jeremy wasn't happy about the whole task, let alone waking up at 6am just to make breakfast for mum. Suddenly he raised a smile. 'I have, like, an idea for mum's, like, breakfast.'

'What?'

'Genuinely, like, cornflakes. Like, quick, easy, and, like, we won't, like, need to get, like, up early.'

Diane shook her head. 'OMG! Like, no, Jeremy, it will actually, like, be a, like, full English.'

'A full English?'

'Yeah, you know, like, genuinely, like, eggs, beans, mushrooms, tomatoes – '

'And bacon!' Jeremy interrupted.

Diane let out a gasp. 'Oh my fucking god, Jeremy! Like, genuinely totally offended, like, right now. Are you, like, serious? Bacon? That's, like, actually so racist.'

'How can bacon, like, be, like, racist?'

'Oh my god! Are you, like, totally serious? Bacon is, like, so offensive, and like, only racist and Fascist. Like, genuinely symbolises, like, hatred against, like, religion and, like, Muslims.' Jeremy shrugged his shoulders, not really understanding what Diane was barking on about, but conceded to her outburst. After all, Diane is the big sister, so she knows best. 'So, like, no bacon,' Diane emphasised.

'What about, like, sausages?'

'OMG! Have you, like, genuinely, been listening to, like, a word I've been, like, saying? Sausages are, like, made of, like, meat. And meat is, like, eaten by, like, Nazis. Like, so offended right now.'

'Nazis?' questioned a now very confused Jeremy.

'Duh, like, yes, because they're, like, genuinely nasty people, like the government and, like, UKIP. They only eat bacon and meat. Genuinely.'

Jeremy was completely confused. 'So, like, Nazis are in our, like, government?'

'Oh, my, fucking god! For fuck sake, are you, like, genuinely totally out of, like, fucking touch with, like, life and stuff?' an even angrier Diane questioned, 'of course the government are, like, Nazis. They hate, like, nurses, all students, Europe, children, Muslims, and, like, teachers. That makes them to be, like, Nazis.'

'Even your teachers?'

'Duh! Genuinely, like, yes, they hate, like, totally, even my whole, like, school.'

'Where did you, like, learn this crap, at school?'

'OMG! You are, like, genuinely totally not, like, fucking real, like, right now. Why can't you, like, understand? My whole school were actually, like, taught about Nazis from the, like, olden days, and now they, like, genuinely run the government.'

Jeremy lost interest, but was intrigued to know something. 'So, what about, like, McDonalds?'

'What about it?'

'What about McDonalds for breakfast? That's, like, meat, isn't it?'

'OMG! Are you, like, being, like, so genuinely, like, serious right now? McDonalds isn't meat. They have, like, chips and, like, burgers, and they're actually, like, allowed right now.'

Jeremy shrugged his shoulders again. He'd had enough of sociology and politics for one day. 'So cornflakes are, like, out of the, like, question?' hoping for an easier option.

'Well yes. 'We'll cook, like, mackerel. That's okay.'

'Yuk,' Jeremy whispered under his breath, as he didn't want to upset Diane any further, but felt an urge to react because he hated the taste of fish.

After Diane calmed down from waving her arms around and shouting at Jeremy's lack of social unawareness, she had another fantastic idea. 'Oh my god! What about, like, a mother's day card to go, like, with, like, her breakfast?'

'I don't have any, like, money for a mother's day card, and neither do you,' Jeremy added.

'No, but we can genuinely, like, make one out of, like, cardboard and, like, things. And, like, draw a picture on the front, or attach, like, an old fashioned photograph of us with, like, a nice message inside.'

Jeremy shrugged his shoulders again. 'But I'm not allowed to use scissors, remember?'

'Oh yes, forgot. Never mind, I can, like, cut the card for you, then you can, like, sprinkle glitter on it. I know you're, like, capable of doing that.'

Diane and Jeremy went into their bedroom's to find card, crayons and glitter, then settled down at the kitchen table to make mum her card. After a few hours they'd finished their masterpiece.

'Right, cards done, ingredients for breakfast, like, in the fridge. I think mum will, like, be actually blown away when we give her, like, surprise tomorrow,' said a pleased Diane, then looked around. 'Where is mum?'

'Gone out to, like, get some things for her, like, special night in.'

'Oh, wine.'

'Yeah. Mum seems to, like, have loads of, like, special nights in lately,' muttered Jeremy.

The following morning Diane was first up. In fact she didn't really sleep at all, but not through excitement. More so because she was on her mobile phone most of the night texting friends and updating her social media accounts with whatever the latest gossip was. So getting up at 6am wasn't ever going to happen. Nevertheless,

Diane was up, dressed, and made her way down stairs at ten-past nine, where hopefully, Jeremy will already be in the kitchen. Of course, Diane should have guessed, he was still in bed.

Annoyed with her brother, Diane made a point of stomping up stairs, forgetting – or rather not really caring – if she woke mum, and stormed into Jeremy's bedroom. The stench almost made her gag. And there he was, curled up under his stain covered bare quilt. The ironed cover mum gave him ten days ago was still on the floor, along with a pile of fresh laundered clothes, knowing mum would eventually cave in and put them away.

'Oh my fucking god! Like, genuinely, how can you, like, possibly sleep in this pit of, like, shit? Totally, like, so grossed out right now. Genuinely.'

'Your room is no different,' Jeremy muttered.

'C'mon, get up!' Diane shouted into Jeremy's ear, ignoring his reply.

Jeremy stretched out a leg from under his filthy quilt, poking a dirty half-socked foot out of the bottom.

'Ah! Genuinely, you've actually, like, still got your, like, socks on, and your feet, like, really stink! I'm, like, actually so totally going to throw up, like, right now.'

'Leave me alone. I'm, like, so tired.'

'OMG! Tired? Genuinely, like, get up, like, right now! We have mum's breakfast to actually, like, make.'

'You'll wake mum with all that, like, shouting.'

'She'll, like, totally be asleep after one of her, like, special nights, remember?'

Climbing over piles of casually discarded urine-stained pants, dirty socks, jeans, trainers, X-Box games and magazines amongst freshly folded clean laundry, Diane managed to exit the pit from hell. Half an hour later Jeremy finally made it down stairs only to be met by a busy Diane cooking mum's special breakfast, with the frying pan sizzling away full of plumbed tomatoes, mushrooms, beans and mackerel.

'What can I do?' asked a yawning Jeremy, scratching his long matted greasy hair.

'You can, like, make the toast.'

'With what?'

'Duh, with, like, bread and the toaster,' Diane replied with a tone of sarcasm.

Reluctantly, Jeremy placed two slices of bread into the toaster. 'Now what?'

'Like, boil the kettle, and, like, make a pot of tea.'

'Do I have to? I've, like, already made the toast.'

'Oh, my, fucking god. Are you, like, being genuinely serious right now?' shouted an annoyed Diane. 'It's actually not, like, a lot to ask, is it. Like, just get on with, like, boiling the kettle. You can then, like, butter the toast when it's, like, done, Jeremy. Jeremy?'

Jeremy was out of view, but when Diane turned around from the contents of the frying pan, there he was, head in arms, slumped over the kitchen table.

'Jeremy!'

'What.'

'Genuinely, like, totally get the fuck up and, like, fucking help. And are you, like, actually going to get dressed, like anytime? You look, like, so gross in your dirty piss-stained pants and filthy tee-shirt.'

Dragging himself up, clearly disinterested in doing anything, let alone getting dressed, he offered a token gesture by flicking the switch on the kettle – not checking first if there was any water in it – before resuming his position slumped over the table. Diane emptied the contents of the frying pan onto a plate, which was a mess to say the least.

Jeremy raised his head. 'Genuinely, that looks like shit.'

'Oh my god! Are you, like, totally fucking joking? This is going to be the best breakfast mum has, like, ever had. C'mon, we'll take it up to her. Where's the toast and tea?' Of course, two slices of bread stood in the toaster un-toasted, boiled water remained in the kettle and the teapot was bagless because Jeremy couldn't be bothered. 'Oh, for fuck sake, Jeremy!

'What have I done now?' he mumbled.

'That's the problem, you haven't, like, done, like, anything!' Diane screamed.

'In that case I'm, like, going back to, like, bed,' he replied dragging himself upright before attempting the effort to climb the stairs back to his pit.

'Oh my god! I'll actually, like, do it all, then! Like, on my fucking own, and take all the credit that it was all, like, my idea!' shouted Diane from the kitchen.

Pleased with her effort, Diane finished brewing the tea, placed the pot and breakfast on the tray with her card – throwing Jeremy's token effort onto the floor –before carefully making her way upstairs. Without knocking she burst in shouting, 'happy mother's day!' At first mum didn't move a muscle, so Diane shouted again to grab her attention. 'Mum, like, happy mother's day, mum. Mum!'

Lying face down under her quilt, mum finally responded. 'Go back to bed, Diane, it's too early.'

'Oh my god! Genuinely, you can't be, like, fucking serious. Like, you will not believe, like, what I have done to, like, prepare this for you. And, like, is that all I fucking get? You actually genuinely, totally fucking serious? Like, so offended.

Mum let out a sigh, sat up and allowed her eyes to focus on what was about to present her. 'Oh, wow. Breakfast in bed. Thank you, Diane,' she muttered with a hint of sarcasm.

'Well, I should fucking think so. Show some, like, respect, because I've been, like, genuinely slaving away, like, totally making this fucking treat for you for hours, just for your, like, special fucking day.'

'Okay, Diane, calm down, and stop swearing. It's not nice coming from you.'

Diane tutted as she placed the surprise breakfast on mum's lap. Eyes now in focus mum stared at the breakfast wondering what on earth was staring back.

'Tuck in, and happy mother's day! I'm going back to, like, bed, because I've been up, like, hours making this especially for you, and I'm now, like, actually totally amazingly fucked.'

Before mum could say anything Diane left, followed by a bedroom door slamming, quickly followed by loud thumping music. Mum sighed, looked down at the plate of mess, stared into the ether sighing once again, knowing the mess that awaits in the kitchen. She placed the inedible breakfast to one side, dressed, and made her way to the kitchen to, as always, clear up after her children.

Predictably there were bits of fish, baked beans and tomato juice scattered over the work surface, floor, cooker and remarkably on the ceiling and down the cupboard doors. Empty packets and tins were left on the floor next to the recycle bin rather than placed inside it, and one of the cooker rings was left on.

'Happy mother's day,' mum mumbled to herself, scanning the carnage before her. Without hesitation mum set to work clearing the mess and cleaning the kitchen. Within half an hour it was spick and span with a gleaming cooker, wiped down ceiling and cupboard doors, clean work surfaces and a mopped floor.

Mum took a breather leaning on the mop handle surveying her completed challenge, rewarding herself with a smile of satisfaction. But then she noticed washing in the machine. The same washing belonging to Diane and Jeremy. In fact the same washing mum asked Diane and Jeremy to hang out yesterday once the cycle had finished.

Just one simple task; not too much to ask, is it? After all they were certainly old enough to help with the washing whilst mum drove into town to collect their dry cleaning, pick up Diane's laptop from the repairers – pay for it – and withdraw much needed cash Jeremy needed to buy X-box games. Not to mention do the weekly shop, including treats and goodies. But no, it was left, conveniently forgot, because mum will do it, as always.

Mum switched to auto mode once again and set the washing machine to carry out a quick cycle before emptying the now full recycle bin. In doing so she noticed another conveniently forgotten simple task that Jeremy should have accomplished the day before – dog poo patrol. Not the best chore in the world, nevertheless, important. But no, it wasn't done, as usual. Instead mum set about clearing the mess off the lawn.

Returning to the kitchen mum decided that whilst still in cleaning mode other tasks needed to be done such as dusting and vacuuming before grabbing a well deserved cuppa. Kettle boiled and tea bag brewing nicely, mum leant against the worktop and started to sob. She was exhausted. Completely tired of constant cleaning and clearing up every day – before and after work – let alone weekends. She simply needed a break. Brushing aside a tear, mum made her tea and was about to sit down at the kitchen table, hoping to rest on her special day.

'Take me to my friends house, mum, like, actually now.' Diane insisted as she ran down stairs staring into her smartphone.'

'Which friend?'

'Val's.'

'Oh, not Vals's, on all days, not today, please.'

'Oh my fucking god! Like, you're being, like, totally selfish right now. I'm, like, so genuinely offended. I make you, like, a special, like, breakfast, and this is, like, how you, like, repay me. For fuck sake, mum, like, you're so fucking unbelievable. I need to go to Val's because I need, like, all the homework she's, like, done for me.'

Mum couldn't be bothered to ask why Val has completed Diane's homework, or mention her foul language, so she left her tea and drove Diane to Val's house 25-miles away – an hour and a half round trip through heavy Sunday shoppers traffic. When Mum arrived home she was greeted by a scruffy Jeremy slouched over the kitchen table flicking through his smartphone.

'Got my money, mum?' he asked, without lifting his head, 'I need it, like, right now.

'Oh yes, of course, I almost forgot.'

'Good. I need you to take me to Dave's, like, straight away.' He demanded as he snatched the money from mum's hand.

'Dave's?' Why Dave's?'

'For fuck sake, mum, genuinely, don't you, like, totally ever listen? I owe Dave two-hundred pounds to pay him back for the X-Box and games he sold me. Best we go, like, now because you know what the traffic is like on a, like, Sunday with all those shoppers clogging up the roads.'

Yes, mum was well aware of Sunday shoppers. She'd just been driving amongst them. And now she has a further half-hour journey taking Jeremy to a friend he owes money, knowing he wasn't in a position to pay her back. When she finally returned home it was near as damn it lunchtime. But she never had the chance to prepare a Sunday roast. So with the house empty she decided to take advantage of this rare opportunity and grab a few hours sleep before the mad free taxi rush later.

Mum's phone sprung to life playing its merry tune. It seemed she placed her head on the pillow for a few moments, then noticed the bedroom was in complete darkness.

'Hi, Diane, what's up?'

'What's up? Duh! Are you, like, genuinely fucking serious, like, right now?'

'Why, what's the matter sweetheart? And please, don't swear, it's not nice,' mum replied, still half asleep.

'OMG! For fuck sake. Like, just actually fucking listen to me. I, like, genuinely so need collecting from Val's immediately! So offended right now. And it's all your fucking fault.'

Mum checked the time. It was almost half-past-eight. 'Oh my god! I'm so sorry, sweetheart. I'm on my way right now.' Without hesitating mum jumped out of bed and into her car to collect Diane, then onto Dave's house to collect Jeremy. By the time they returned home it was almost ten-thirty.

As soon as mum opened the front door Jeremy pushed past and went straight to his bedroom whilst texting a mate without saying a word of thanks, unlike Diane. 'I'm off to bed. Thanks to you I, like, genuinely haven't, like, finished my, like, work for school, and it's, actually, like, all your fucking fault, mum!'

Mum chose to ignore her comment, walked into the kitchen, grabbed a bottle of red from the rack, sat at the table and sobbed once again as she poured herself a large one.

The following morning mum's alarm sounded like an air raid siren as it screeched its warble at precisely

6am: time to get up and start a new day, although no different to any other working day. She showered, fixed her hair and make-up, then made her way to the kitchen and to prepare breakfast.

'Diane, Jeremy, breakfast is ready.' mum shouted as she placed their hot buttered toast next to glasses of orange juice and bowls of cereal. Half an hour later, 'Diane, Jeremy, your breakfast is ready. Hurry up or you will make me late.'

No reply. Instead mum had to repeat the school morning ritual by going upstairs and physically shake them awake, only to face a barrage of abuse and obscenities. As always, mum ignored them. Instead she carried on making lunch boxes and finding shoes to polish. Twenty minutes later they finally made an appearance, followed by moaning about the cold toast and blaming mum for not waking them early enough for breakfast before climbing into the car.

As usual, mum never had time to eat her breakfast, and most certainly no time to clear up after Diane and Jeremy. Instead she endured the daily morning ritual knowing she'll be late for work as she stopped first outside the gates of Diane's school.

'Genuinely, I don't want to, like, go to fucking school, like, today. Text them and, like, explain, I'm, like, genuinely so totally poorly. In fact, I, like, think I'm going to, like, genuinely throw up right fucking now.'

'I can't do that. Anyway, you're here now, outside the gates.'

'OMG! Genuinely, like, I haven't, like, finished my work, and, like, I'll be actually told off by the, like, fascist head teacher, which isn't, like, fair, because its, like, totally all your fucking fault, like, why I haven't finished it. So you have to actually, like, tell school I'm not well, and, like, won't be in today.'

Mum was getting agitated because she was going to be later for work than usual. 'Now look, you have to go in. You have got to start learning from your own mistakes and stop blaming others, including me.'

'O M fucking G!' You're so, like, genuinely unbelievable right now. You have, like, no fucking idea –'

'Arrrrrrrrgh!' mum screamed at the top of her voice, instantly stopping Diane halfway through one of her rants. 'Enough! Now go to school, take the punishment for not finishing marking your class homework and just get on with it. You have responsibilities. You're a fucking history teacher, and you're almost twenty-nine years old. It's time you acted your age and grew up!'

Diane was dumfounded, in complete shock. Mum had never spoken to her in such a crude and direct manner before. But she'd had a gut full. And her supposedly special weekend was the straw that broke the camel's back.

'As for you, Jeremy,' mum sternly said, turning to face him as he squirmed on the back seat, 'you're twenty-seven with a physics degree. But for the past five years you've done absolutely nothing with it. You're a spoilt lazy piece of shit!'

'But mum, I've, like, hurt my wrist. I can't write or type anything,' he replied pulling on his dirty tangled bandage in a feeble attempt to justify his laziness.

'Bollocks! You slightly sprained it when you fell of that stupid skateboard of yours, which was months ago. And why do you still have a fucking skateboard at your age? It's pathetic. You're pathetic. So take off that bandage, get out of the car and go and sign on. Whilst you're at the job centre, find a fucking job!'

—

'Okay, I will, I will. God, stop, like, going on.' Jeremy muttered, hoping mum didn't hear.

'Go on then, get out. You can walk from here.'

'What, from here? But I'll, like, miss my, like, early appointment, which is, like, so unfair, and won't, like, get paid, and it will be all your fault.'

'Paid? You don't know the meaning of the word. You've never worked, even during the six months or so you were home between studies at Uni. You just sat around, as you do now, slumped on the settee watching telly or in your filthy flea pit of a room playing video games and wanking.'

'Mum!'

'Shut the fuck up, Diane. You're no better. Neither of you has ever lifted a finger to help around the house. I do everything. I'm nothing but a free on demand taxi, cleaner, cook, gopher, launderette, moneylender – for both of you – but never get it back. I pay the mortgage, WiFi, and all the bills. I'm expected to drop everything in an instant to help you because your lives are much more important than mine. Neither of you have ever offered to pay board. I put up with constant moaning, complaining, swearing, disrespect and your relentless bad attitude. So if you miss your signing on time, Jeremy, that's your fault, not mine. And if you get a bollocking for not finishing marking homework, Diane, which is your job, that's your fault, no one else. Now fuck off, both of you!'

Without hesitation they both frantically scrambled out of the car to escape mum's fury. As soon as the doors closed she screeched off like a formula one driver, deciding not to go to work. Instead, went home, phoned in sick, and started to do what she wanted to do for years – pack Diane's and Jeremy's possessions into bin liners and throw them out of the house. In doing so a huge weight lifted from her shoulders. A whoosh of relief surged through her body like an orgasm as she collapsed on the settee totally satisfied with her efforts. All she had to do now was wait.

Jeremy was first to arrive home. 'What the fuck, is, like, going on, mum? Why are all my, like, clothes and stuff on the, like, front lawn?'

Mum couldn't help but spread a huge smug grin across her face as she took a sip from her large glass of morning red. She didn't need to acknowledge him; the look on Jeremy's face was well known to her when he's upset. Instead, she carried on drinking at the kitchen table, waiting for the confused scruffy looking lanky piece of shit to appear into view.

'Did you manage to sign on?'

'No, I fucking didn't. I was, like, genuinely, only twenty minutes late, that's all, but they, like, told me I actually, like, missed my appointment so my money will be, like, put on hold whilst they, like, investigate for the next, like, thirteen weeks! Until then, I still have to, like, sign on but won't receive any, like, money until they've done, like, checks. And it's all your fucking fault!'

'Oh dear,' replied a cool, sarcastic mum, 'whatever will you do?'

'OMG! It's, like, totally obvious. You'll have to, like, lend me money until I get my, like, benefits back, beings it's actually all your fault. And why is all my, like, stuff on the front lawn?'

Mum got up to pour herself another large one, then started to laugh. 'You haven't a clue, have you. And still you think I will give – not lend as you put it – but give you money just because your benefits have been stopped.'

'Well, yes,' replied Jeremy, not really understanding mum's attitude.

'Jeremy, how can I put this,' mum calmly said, 'you missed your appointment because of you, not me. You assumed I would drop you off at the job centre, and it was you that didn't give a fuck if I was late for work. I also told you that I'd had enough of both of you. So I'm not going to give you any more money – ever. And your stuff is on the lawn because you and Diane no longer live here.'

'I don't, like, understand. What have I done to, like, deserve this?'

'You haven't done anything, Jeremy, that's the problem. So you need a little tough love, a parental kick up the arse to make you realise I will no longer wipe it. You're old enough to start your own life, and I'm tired. Do you get it, I'm so fucking tired.'

Of course Jeremy didn't understand. After all, why would he? He'd had his arse wiped for the past 27-years. Never needed to lift a finger around the house because mum did it all, even when dad was around, until he left because mum refused to cut the apron strings. Unfortunately she now reaped the consequences that she'd sewn.

Slowly turning around, Jeremy walked towards the front door, seemingly in shock, struggling to comprehend what had just happened as he stepped out into the cold brisk air, closing the door gently behind him.

'One down, one to go,' mum said without a care.

It wasn't long before the front door burst open, only it wasn't Jeremy. 'OMG mum! Like, genuinely, what the fuck is, like, going on with you today?' Yep, Diane had arrived. Mum didn't acknowledge her and continued to watch television, accompanied by another large glass of red. 'Mum, genuinely, why is, like, my stuff spread, like, all over the front fucking garden? And why is Jeremy,

like, actually sobbing in the middle of it surrounded by his, like, stuff? You've, like, so genuinely
lost your fucking mind, and you, like –'

'Diane!' mum interrupted, 'shut the fuck up.' She knew Diane would throw a wobbly and was ready for her. 'Jeremy is sobbing on the front lawn because he no longer lives here.'

'What? Why? That's so –'

'Ah, ah, let me finish,' mum quickly said, looking Diane right in the eyes, wagging a finger, quietly adding, 'and neither do you.'

'Oh my god! Are you, like, actually totally fucking serious right now?' You genuinely can't throw me out. I totally have, like, fucking human rights, and I will, like, text Childline and, like, get you, like, totally arrested, and it's, like, so genuinely against the law. How, like, fucking dare you! I'm so totally offended, like, you will not fucking believe –'

'Diane! I'm not going to argue. I really can't be bothered. I've heard it all before, a million times, so you need to know something. This is my house, not yours. Childline won't listen because you're almost thirty years old. You have also, like Jeremy, never lifted a finger to help around the house, ever. Your attitude stinks, and just like Jeremy, you have never ever respected me or anyone else. I've had enough, so I've chucked you and Jeremy out of my house. Not your house, mine. That's why your things are on the lawn too. So just, like, gather it all, like, up, and like, get the fuck of my, like, premises, because you both, like, so offend me right now!'

So there you are. And I'm sure you will agree there's a lot going on there, eh? And the incredibly annoying impulse Millennials have with the overuse of adverbs and nouns such as totally, like and genuinely (listen to students, they do it all the time. Especially those from that incredibly cringeworthy programme, Love Island) when conversing with the simplest of sentences.

Some may say Diane and Jeremy's story comes across as being far fetched and maybe a little extraordinary or even offensive. Some may say racist, Fascist, feminist, homophobic, and with a little ageism thrown in. Maybe even according to Jeremy Vine. Yes, really. Oh, come on, let's face it, that bloke can stir mayhem and cause a national division over an empty room. Yes, that trivial. But I'm confident the story resonates with thousands, if not millions of parents up and down the country, even around the world. Question is, can you relate to it or recognise any similarities?

Whether it is fault of past or present generations, parents with or had teenage children most certainly experienced similar issues. But for some reason young Millennials seem to have developed a somewhat disjointed over-sensitive social attitude, where they simply cannot or will not accept in any shape or form contradiction or instruction from parents, teachers, in fact anyone.

Any kind of discipline is perceived to be illegal and blaming others is their god given human right. Young Millennials also have an unstoppable urge wanting to become adults as soon as possible, only to believe themselves as being adults far sooner than previous generations. Yet their child-like mentality remains well into their late twenties and remarkably into their late thirties and even early forties.

Unfortunately there seems to be a media-led frenzy – print and airwave alike – encouraging this mind-set by renouncing previous generations for thwarting many issues and topics that – as they relentlessly report – ruined Millennials future. Education, pensions, politics,

NHS, exorbitant house prices, unreasonable rent increases, global warming, even human rights. All ruined, according to the likes of Channel Four, ITV and the BBC, by previous generations. But why do they all do this, and is it true?

When the media supposedly report what is happening around the world, they cannot resist interjecting their own, as it blatantly appears, scripted, instructed, or personal point of view. But to us elder and wiser generations it is nothing more than a way of brainwashing a vulnerable naïve next generation into their way of thinking. But for what purpose? Millennials are certainly easily persuaded, offended and cry a lot, yet love criticising – everything.

Previous generations, however, tend to look at later generations whilst shaking their head, knowing they're talking bollocks simply because they're older, wiser and vastly more experienced. But can you feel that niggling doubt? That annoying itch you cannot reach. A thought of something outrageously different with Millennials miles apart from previous generations?

Chapter Three

Natives are getting restless

Hard to believe, I know, but to have any understanding of Millennials you have to start from the beginning – the real beginning. A time when fighting for better employment conditions, human rights and a healthier life style actually meant something. A time of real protest and real concerns, where disputes and accountable demands caused ripples throughout the decades that followed, effecting, if not over-spoiling today's generation.

In fact, you need to dig a rather deep hole to expose the foundations of yesteryear that supports our modern world. What we did with it afterwards can only be described as building a house with equally strong walls but now has a badly fitted roof due to ignoring the original design but blaming the previous generation because it leaks.

It is a documented fact that ancient Greece and the Romans debated, created and passed rules to control the masses, often with a rod of iron, thus preventing society collapsing into chaos. Much can be said for the church and how it spread, literally, the fear of god during the Middle Ages. But these societies are way too far back in history to reflect any connection or behaviour upon our modern digital life. After all, what did the Romans ever do for us?

Well, yes, I know, the aqua-duct, and so on, but I'm on about modern society. So forget about them, and the dark ages. They just went backwards after the Romans legged it in 410BC, leaving us with a bunch of bearded maniacs ruling the land. You have to fast-forward to the early 19th Century for some credible influence upon our modern way of life. The industrial revolution seems a good place to start.

Although it technically started in 1698 with the invention of Thomas Savery's steam pump to remove water from mine shafts, consequences of the revolution remained stagnant for quite a while. It would be a further 150-years before countless steam powered improvements, invention and innovation would see an inevitable tarnish to its romantic ideology.

The poor, being the majority working for many national industrialists, gradually fought back for better working conditions but with little success at first. The only improvement to an otherwise meagre existence came from Philanthropists with fat wallets and a wealthy liberal attitude towards their fellow man. Employment Rights were virtually non-existent during most of the industrial revolution, and much to the annoyance of parliament, some liberal-thinking Members of Parliament managed to pass the odd law or two protecting the ever-expanding working poor.

Starting at the bottom of the social pile, in 1834 introduction of The Poor Law Amendment Act of Workhouses was reformed, superseding the outdated Poor Houses Act. This particular reform supposedly protected those in real need, rather than perceived to having a want of need. In other words, sort wheat from the chaff, as it were, encouraging beggars that refused to work in any shape or form to actually find real work. Not dissimilar from a certain class of society today.

Rich and influential liberal minded pressure groups continued their quest demanding change for the poor, giving way to new laws supposedly designed to save the poorest from starvation and disease. However, the amended Poor Law Act soon revealed itself as nothing more than a political pawn; a legal tool to deal with the poorest of the poor and exploit as cheap labour in return for food and shelter.

The Poor House was nothing new in the early 1800's. They had been around since 1576 and remained until 1930, with a few festering for a while under a different guise until the 1940's. Nevertheless they were still a Workhouse of some kind, taking in the poorest of the poor. Even a young Charlie Chaplin, the famous comedy actor of the silent screen era, resided at the Newington Workhouse in London for a few weeks. He once recalled, as a child the punishments endured included caning for no reason at all.

Conditions inside the Workhouse were deliberately harsh so that only those desperate and with nowhere else to turn were at their mercy – the Department of Work and Pensions of the early 1800's. Should an entire family knock on the door they were immediately segregated where men, women and children were used for various tasks in different parts of the Workhouse.

Strict rules and regulations quickly followed: everyone wore a uniform and subjected to hard labour, be they man, woman, young or old. Children young as four were even sold and used as slave labour for outside businesses such as factories, coal mines and chimney sweeps. Remember Mr. Bumble selling Oliver twist to the Undertaker? Charles Dickens lived close to the Workhouse in Cleveland Street, London, where he was inspired to write a story about a young orphan boy called Oliver forced to live in a Workhouse.

Criminals found guilty of certain crimes were sentenced to hard labour as a punishment, but paupers in Workhouses were succumbed to similar tasks. An educated person falling on hard times due to redundancy and desperate for work easily found themselves in a Workhouse crushing rocks or painstakingly unravelling rope for ship builders. Both a punishment whilst serving sentence, yet simple work for paupers. And for all this hard labour, a weekly wage of nothing more than a few pennies to buy simple rotten food from the Workhouse owner.

Food, if you can call it that, was deliberately kept to a minimum to keep workers alive – just – from starvation. Some workers, also known as inmates, became so desperate they would eat putrid flesh from bones before crushing them to make fertiliser. Paupers of all ages were subject to unscrupulous masters and matrons that treated the poor with relentless ridicule and abuse. Remarkably periodic inspections and even basic medical care to look after the inmates welfare was enforced by local authorities, albeit in the interest of Workhouse owners to sustain their income.

Punishments were incredibly popular, where inmates were subjected to beatings on a daily basis, and children often whipped with stinging nettles for shoddy workmanship or laziness. Being deprived of water was also a punishment, forcing thirsty children to drink out of filthy lavatory bowls. At a Workhouse in Huddersfield 10 children slept in a single bed, and one child was made to sleep beside a rotting, diseased corpse of a fellow child inmate.

Other punishments included deprivation of a meal, and humiliation punishments such as shaving women's hair or the use of a stock. Nothing more than a medieval punishment leaving the accused to abuse and rotten fruit, urine and faeces thrown at them by the public as they bent over, locked in the stocks. For reward, there wasn't really any such thing, and the only day given as rest was Christmas. Bathing was considered a luxury and had to be earned; such a treat happened on rare occasions, and when only absolutely necessary.

Knocking on the door of a Workhouse could be interpreted as the modern equivalent of signing on at the Job Centre for unemployment benefit. But what other choice could you possibly have when desperate to earn money and feed a family? Nevertheless, most people managed to steer away from Workhouses due to the incredible rumours living and working in one.

Becoming unemployed threatened being tarred with the same brush as paupers, so any kind of other work would suffice. Even begging, although illegal, was common and could be quite profitable, especially when a young child was used to pray upon naïve pedestrians with a soft nature. To emphasise the need for cash, extremes were sometimes used to open wallets by injuring a child, even blinding them. For a more legitimate way of earning money dockyards were a source of immediate income, although not guaranteed.

London, like today, was the traditional attraction to seek work, as were other docks around the country. Offering similar prospects of manual work, where recruitment methods remained the same: groups of unemployed desperate for work would gather at dock gates hoping to be chosen for a day's paid labour. And pay was exploited by dock owners offering extremely low wages, earning no more than a few pennies for a 12-hour shift. No different to the modern equivalent of a zero-hour contract offering a minimum wage.

During this particular era, moaning about working conditions, wages or even living conditions fell on deaf ears. The working class was deemed nothing more than an expendable tool to exploit and make business owners rich, where any protest meant losing a job. As for legal aid, there wasn't any. Should you belong to one of the rare yet illegal unions, chance of any representation was virtually impossible in fear of reprisals against the union and its members – threatening wage cuts or even job losses. So you kept quiet, put up with poor wages and bad conditions.

You were also expected to work a 6-day week, every week, including Sunday. Monday was accepted as the usual day off because the weekend wasn't adopted as the end of a working week until the late 1800's. As for holidays, forget it. Not even bank holidays, as they too weren't around. Women were also exploited, in particularly by the clothing industry making prison and army uniforms – sewing by hand in poor candle light, where the cost of candles came out of wages being no more than a few shillings per week. Of course, there was still a very lucrative and widespread industry women dominated – prostitution.

Many succumbed to this particular trade had a naïve approach of being on the game for only a few years so to save enough money for education or buy time to search for a more socially acceptable income. Of course, there were many unwanted pregnancies due to ignorance, poor or even non-existent sex education, sexual experimentation and rape, leading to a staggering 20 percent of all pregnancies in the early to mid 1800's.

Although rape was a crime, anyone found guilty was incredibly low, more so due to lack of evidence. Servants were particularly in danger from their employers, seen nothing more than property. Women working for upper class homes, some as young as 12-years old, were subject to sexual harassment and rape regularly. Inevitably there were pregnancies, resulting in dismissal and homelessness. Instant poverty now beckoned, leaving very little option other than begging, the Workhouse, or prostitution to earn a desperate living.

Sooner or later the young mum to be will give birth; an incredibly dangerous situation for a 12-year old homeless servant in the early 19th Century, let alone mature women from the upper classes. Hospitals will help, of course, providing she can pay for treatment. But mum isn't out of the woods just yet. Pain relief was non existent, although chloroform and ether was used in the mid 1800's for those that could afford it. But the church believed pain relief was a sin against god. Religious leaders emphasised this by publicly voicing, if god wished labour painless he would have made it so.

As for the perpetrator, it would be incredibly doubtful his wife, mother or any other family member ever knew about the incident. And should there be any doubt or suspicion of rape, it was simply down to his word against hers, and guess who is believed? Should the servant girl be 12-years old, not even a charge of under-age sex could be enforced. It wasn't until 1885 the age of consent was raised from 12-years to 16-years of age.

Once sucked into prostitution it was extremely difficult to get out. And the lack of medicine, combined with a dangerous lifestyle, disease became rife amongst thousands of prostitutes in London alone. Some hospitals catered for the odd infected woman, but kept away from other patients by admission in a Foul Ward, where further hardship occurred. Most towns had one or two segregated Foul Ward buildings situated on its boundaries to cater for contagious diseases and fallen women. Check your own town history, you will probably discover one, or even two.

Not really sympathetic to their symptoms, doctors carried out quite painful experiments researching sexually transmitted diseases – STD's. Their research for cures, however, remained futile, limited by technology, knowledge and medicine. But if symptoms from

---

particularly diseases, such as syphilis, appeared to subside by taking tablets with a high concentration of mercury, the patient was thrown back onto the street only to continue her trade. But the disease was destined to worsen, and the tablets would cause the patient to eventually hallucinate, go mad, quickly followed by involuntary vomiting and defecation, ending with a certain and painful death.

Doctors of influence became concerned prostitution was getting out of hand and spreading STD's to a more affluent part of society. Whether rich or poor, prostitutes weren't fussy when it came to earning a few ill-gotten shillings or even pennies. STD's have no morals either, so parliament passed a new law to try and protect the upper and middle classes first and foremost, not really caring about the welfare of the prostitute. The Contagious Disease Act was introduced in 1860 allowing the enforcement of examination to any women suspected of selling herself for sex, including wives suspected of having affairs by their husbands.

There were a few wealthy sympathisers from the upper classes that tried to save fallen women by funding charities. Even Charles Dickens attempted to introduce a home where prostitutes would be safe from men, providing, in return, they worked for their bed and board. But the cost of these safe houses and charities soon outran any form of income and simply couldn't cope with the influx of prostitutes. Women who managed to find sanctuary had no choice but return to the streets, where a vicious poverty-stricken cycle continued.

Workhouses also suffered from poor income and ever- increasing bills. Charities found it harder to raise funds as people grew suspicious of inmates being nothing more than too lazy to find real work, whilst the middle and upper classes despised taxes raised by local government to help fund these establishments. The Poor Law Act simply failed its objective, appearing to punish people who were poor through no fault of their own.

Latter part of the 1800's brought with it hope in the form of an end to working class persecution. Or so it was thought. This particular period, and the working class that grew up within it, still lived a hard life not dissimilar to their parents. Putting it simply, if you didn't work you starved. If you became ill, you weren't paid so you starved. And if you were the breadwinner that found yourself out of work due to injury or ill health, you and your family starved. In other words there was no social or unemployment benefit safety net to help towards some kind of survival whilst searching for work.

Before the industrial revolution work was predominantly found on the land where women, men and children worked as labourers. Women in particular were not only earning money from labouring; they often brought in extra cash from weaving, darning, repairing and making clothes as well as running the house. Cooking, cleaning, raising children… the list went on. But within 100 years almost all factories, foundries and mines embraced new steam engine technology that enhanced production at an incredible pace. That meant a huge influx of farm labourers pouring into towns and cities to fill millions of job vacancies, at first only advertised to employ men.

Of course, the industrial revolution at its peak meant that work was plentiful – for the time being. In the meantime the rich certainly became richer, whilst the poor certainly remained poor – on purpose. A controlled workforce meant cheap labour for the cotton mills, foundries, factories and mines. But work was a necessity if you wanted to survive and have some sort of existence.

———

Tradesmen of great skill, such as Masons and Coachbuilders, were in comparison big earners with an average wage of 5 pounds per week. But the scale of wages dramatically dropped towards the casual labourer end of the market, earning only a few shillings. Menial jobs such as selling newspapers, sweeping a path across filthy streets so upper classes didn't get their shoes dirty, clearing faeces off pavements or collecting pots of urine from the poorest of households for the local tannery might earn a few pennies per day.

Not forgetting the humble honest chimney sweep employing a small boy to climb inside a chimney and sweep away soot – without any protective clothes or respirator, of course. All these jobs, and many other similar menial and dirty tasks earned very little, but nonetheless, managed to keep someone alive – just. But if labourers had a certain skill, such as miners contributing towards shift efficiency, earning 30 shillings per week wasn't uncommon. Semi-skilled trades such as taxi and bus drivers could earn around 20 shillings per week. If you could read and write, a clerk earned 5 pounds per week, and a foreman at a dock or factory earned around 3 to 4 pounds per week. Salaried factory managers could earn 1,000 pounds per annum.

Pride, however, sitting along side decades of hand-me-down Victorian values, remained extremely high on the working class priority list, no matter what their trade or social stature. That meant looking after things hard-earned cash bought: clothes, furniture, linen, kitchenware, utensils… basically everything. To be incredibly frugal also included repair when worn – not replace. After all, you couldn't afford to just throw away, only to replace with a new whatever needed replacing, unlike today.

Money was extremely tight no matter how prosperous the economy, so possessions remained priceless. This is why items were over-engineered and made to repair over many lifetimes. This make do and mend attitude certainly reflected the Victorians as being a true recycling generation. If beyond home repair or maintenance a passing repairman, such as the local knife sharpener or tool setter, were always at hand.

On that incredibly rare occasion of an item wearing out they were recycled for other use. Newspapers once read were used as firelighters, wrapping waste or fresh food, wedged behind a pipe in the toilet for wiping bottoms – toilet paper hadn't been invented yet – or sold in bundles for a few pennies to shops and other trades. Worn bed linen was cut up and used to make clothes or rags. Even outgrown clothes were handed down to younger siblings. When old clothes were finally beyond repair, they still didn't go to waste. Local brewers would buy them to use for digging into hop fields, which, apparently, improved the taste of beer. Or sold to rag and bone men, who in turn sold on to paper mills, used in the process of manufacturing paper.

Plastics and polystyrene was a century away from invention so packaging would have been made out of wood shavings, paper, card or clean rags. But most items were sold without wrapping or packaging, as were every day food items. Shoppers simply carried unwrapped items in wicker baskets. Once these were worn out they too were either repaired or used for storing fruit and vegetables.

Milk was delivered by horse and cart in churns, or even dogs and cart, favoured by the poorer milkman in large towns and cities, where a customer's quart jug or pint pot would be filled for a day's use, and not just for drinking. Luxury items too expensive to buy such as butter and cheese, were often home made.

Delivery of milk in churns remained popular well into the 1960's in small towns and rural areas. Inevitably the electric milk float soon monopolised the market, delivering milk in reusable glass pint bottles, where empties were swapped for refilled bottles of gold or silver tops. Amazingly, this environmentally friendly way of supplying milk has almost disappeared in the environmental aware 21st Century.

Victorians tended to return most receptacles made out of glass to shops, factories and chemists for recycling or reused again, including beer bottles. Not unlike the 'pop man' collecting empties and returning beer bottles to the Off Licence. But yet again, strange to think in an eco-friendly 21st Century, this environmentally friendly, low carbon footprint habit has also disappeared.

Metal items worn, broken or no longer used would be returned to the Ironmongers or scrap metal merchant for a few pence. Dustmen collected actual dust, then sold it to specialised manufacturers – and not just from the hearth. Everyday dust swept off windowsills and floors was gathered in home made cloth bags for collection and sold to brick manufactures to use in clay mixtures. Even boot and shoe manufactures used dust between layers of soles as a shock absorber, making the footwear comfortable to walk in.

Household refuse was collected on a regular basis in large towns and cities, but there was never a huge amount compared to modern household waste. Before anything was thrown away wives would remove anything that could be of use. Fruit and vegetable peelings were thrown on a compost heap, and other food scraps fed chickens or rabbits bred for food. Whilst recycling remained a natural chore throughout the Victorian era, as the industrial revolution took hold more and more people headed to new industrialised towns up and down the country in search of work and a better life.

The population of England and Wales was just over 8,000,000 in 1801. Over the next 50-years the population rose to almost 17,000,000. And by 1901 there were over 30,000,000 proving the enticement of steady continuous paid work and promise of a better life was too great to ignore. Putting these huge figures into comparison, over the same period the whole of Europe increased its population by 100,000,000 where Britain sustained a massive 25 percent of this surge alone. But why was this?

Immigration is nothing new, including during the Victorian era. Thanks to the industrial revolution needing a continuous flow of workers, no matter where they came from. But linking businesses needed a huge transport network where Ireland predominately supplied navigation engineers – navies. They were the backbone of Victorian engineering projects for the construction of canals, tunnels and railways. And the reason Irish immigrants were chosen before local labour was simply down to skill, experience and free to travel.

Those that migrated from Ireland had no problem moving with the work, often taking them hundreds of miles between locations. Locals were more settled with working closer to home. And whilst staying either on site or in town, Irish navies did like a drink, where tempers frayed from time to time when drinking amongst locals. Womanising – not caring if they were married or not – upset many husbands. Even prostitutes grew weary of their strange sexual requests. After several months or so navies moved on to terrorise the next town or city as railway construction worked its way across the country, laying an incredible 5,000 miles of track within 40-years, predominately by pick and shovel.

Others continued to migrate across the Irish Sea in search for work, many settling in the North West region, including Liverpool and Manchester. Their strong Irish accents even influenced a twang on the Mersey, where before the Irish invasion Scousers had a more Lancashire accent. The North West, notorious for its damp climate, was perfect for the production of textiles made from cotton. Hundreds of cotton mills expanded across both side of the Pennines, employing thousands of labourers from Ireland.

Birmingham may have been the heart of industrial engineering, but Manchester became the first industrialised city in the world. Nicknamed Cottonopolis by the locals, the population increased 6-fold by 1830. Whilst in the East of the Pennines, population of Bradford grew 4-fold by 1850 where half of which could only be classed as indigenous.

Not dissimilar to English labourers, Irish immigrants originally worked for Landlords and farmers, but the potato famine of 1846 devastated the country. Although a tough root vegetable that can grow in poor soil and cold conditions, the disease destroyed crops across the entire country – including those in Scotland. And it is quite possible American ships brought over the disease, lasting almost 6-years. Over 1,000,000 died due to starvation, forcing a quarter of a nation to leave and find work elsewhere.

Predecessors on my father's side were one of those Irish families forced to find work in another country, settling in Northamptonshire. Oddly, not to work in the hundreds of boot and shoe factories synonymous with the county. During the Victorian era my family were painter and decorators in Ireland. But the famine caused a domino effect across the country where many businesses relied upon income the humble potato created. Painter

———

and decorators were certainly not immune, so my family decided to up sticks and rebuild their trade in England.

Italians, already a steady immigrant for centuries, slowly increased their numbers during the industrial revolution, but many didn't work in factories. Italians were seen as great entertainers, street performers, artists and sculptures. If they weren't playing musical instruments in small travelling bands, local orchestras, or singing in operas, they were painting portraits and sculpturing statues – for a price. And, of course, making ice cream. This new icy cold delicacy became a favourite in the late Victorian period, enjoyed by children and adults alike, bringing with them many fruitful flavours.

Not all Italians had a particular skill or trade. There were those of poor or no education where labouring also became their only income, finding themselves working in hot, sweaty foundries, mines or asphalt manufactures in London. Nevertheless, they rarely succumbed to any resentment due to the overall small number of Italian immigrants didn't encroach on local competition for employment. In the cities, however, it was a different story. Italians were blamed for bringing disease, creating crime waves, even unsociable noise pollution caused by street entertainers playing instruments into the early hours. And Irish immigrants in cities were treated with much worse contempt and ridicule in comparison.

Jews suffered the same intimidating treatment from locals, yet thousands migrated from Russia to escape economic restrictions and ridicule. Settling in the East End of London, at first they were treated with utmost respect and even sympathy for what they endured. But it didn't last. Spitalfields, in the East End, became known as the Jewish Community. They spoke a different language, bared shops and wares with a foreign tongue and even refused to translate into English. It was only a matter of time before unrest developed throughout the indigenous population, seeing Jews as people not to trust.

Walking down an English street, seemingly run by a Jewish community, became an uneasy experience. When addressed many simply shook their heads, not understanding any English and even refused to learn. Others reacted in their own language to the point of antagonising locals. In effect they renounced themselves from society in an attempt to prevent infiltration and adopt English law.

Although immigration was rapid during the industrial revolution, exacerbated by the potato famine in Ireland, the overcrowding in towns and cities was really due to millions of the indigenous population. It wasn't uncommon for a family to have 5 or even 10 children, where it was socially accepted to raise large families complimented by the sign of the times.

Whilst the mid Victorian era showed an improvement with infant mortality than earlier years, poor parents continued to have large families due to obvious factors: lack of contraception being one. Others included an inherited fear that children were more susceptible to die young, coupled with the fact that large families brought in much needed cash once old enough to work. But the Factory Act of 1833 started the demise of child exploitation. Working a 12-hour shift down a coal mine or even 14-hours in a cotton mill wasn't uncommon for children under the age of ten. And should a child die due to an unfortunate accident – crushed by machinery, loss of limbs or illness – there were plenty more cheap children to chose from at the local Workhouse, the street or desperate parents wanting their young ones to bring money into the house. Abuse was also common, including beatings for falling asleep due to exhaustion, where remarkably detailed reports of punishments and disciplines persuaded the government to react and save children from poor treatment.

Liberal thinking rich Philanthropists and politicians grew a conscience over cheap child labour, where factory owners, inevitably, disagreed. As far as they were concerned factory owners allowed children to work so they wouldn't die of starvation and kept them off the streets committing petty crimes – thus out of jail. Nevertheless, the Factory Act of 1833 meant that businesses employing children under the age of 13-years had to provide education.

Of course, this was rarely executed, often leading to the odd lesson before or after a shift, making a working day even longer. To combat this the Ten Hour Act was hastily introduced, where children under 18-years of age couldn't work more than a 10-hour shift, and under 25-year olds were banned from working night shifts. Guess we've gone a little backward since. There was also another factor persuading mid-Victorian families to be large, and that was steady employment. Having an almost secure job meant raising children was easier than ever before, but where do you house these large families?

Every town and city still has Victorian terraced housing lining its main and side streets, now costing a fortune to buy. My first house was a Victorian end-of-terraced built in 1887 commissioned by Timpsons Footwear to house its many boot and shoe workers of Kettering, Northamptonshire. Designed as a 3-bedroom dwelling, the back garden had a brick-built out-house at the rear where a coal bunker was added to one side. And not unlike thousands built at the time, out-houses were a workshop for home-workers employed to work from home, earning extra money to pay rent whilst the husband worked in the factory.

The living room (parlour, as it would have been called) was already knocked through to the back room (living room) creating a long living and dining area. I knocked through the kitchen to expose the downstairs bathroom and outside toilet, which I moved upstairs, converting the third bedroom into a modern bathroom. The kitchen was also modernised, leaving only a 1990's fashionable arch to where the downstairs bathroom once stood.

The outside toilet all terraced houses had, accompanied a tin bath hanging on the wall outside. Amazingly this style of bathing and toiletry requirements were still used until the early 1970's in this style of housing, before it became a little more affordable to bring toilets inside and move bathrooms upstairs to suit a more modern convenience. As a young child I remember my Nan's tin bath hanging on the wall of the outdoor loo of her terraced house, accompanied by an old rusty tin helmet hanging from its nail, last used during the Second World War when the Luftwaffe paid a visit.

During modernisation I came across original features such as old lead water pipes feeding the inside tap and lead gas pipes to light internal wall mounted lamps. There were also decorative black iron hearths in every room, detailed plaster coving around every ceiling, patterned black and terracotta tiled hallway floor and an etched glass panel above the front door, synonymous with mid-range Victorian living.

Northamptonshire employees were lucky to rent housing that were built to last, and with relative mod cons, where boot and shoe factory owners recognised the true value of building houses, if not for a long term investment. But not all Victorian housing was constructed to a good standard.

———

Terraced houses spread rapidly across the entire country, expanding towns and cities to bursting point, desperate to accommodate manufacturing workers, yet creating a massive breeding ground for disease and poverty never experienced before. Kerbsides were lined with horse, dog and human faeces, contents of chamber pots owned by those not so poor to sell to tanneries for a few pence, were just thrown out of a door or window onto pavements.

Private ventures joined forces with building societies to try and keep up with demand, resulting in cutting many corners, restricted construction budgets and build time quotas. Many houses were just thrown together, where ground levels were left without floorboards, leaving only soil, sewer and water pipes simply forgotten and missing lead flashing caused leaks.

Victorian Landlords jumped on the moneymaking bandwagon to exploit an extremely high rental market demand by charging well over rental value for low cost housing – nothing more than a shabby brick shed without mod-cons we take for granted today such as clean running water and a working sewage system. Rooms were also rented to families in small two-up, two-down terraced houses, where 3 or 4 families shared one house. Even cold, dark and damp cellars were rented to large families.

Rooms were usually left to tenants to furnish. But with very little money spare for tables, chairs and beds, husbands tended to make furniture from anything they could lay their hands on, including repairing old and broken furniture upper classes threw away. Beds tended to be nothing more than a mattress left on the floor, made out of frayed linen stuffed with straw and rags. Discarded filthy and damp mattresses were sometimes salvaged but were often infested with fleas and bed bugs, spreading skin diseases such as eczema and scabies.

Head and body lice were also a huge problem, seemingly only curable using mercury tablets – 1800's pharmaceutical wonder drug – crushed into a powder and rubbed into scalps and skin to kill the bugs. It was also taken orally for various ailments, eventually creating obvious mercury poisoning reactions. Although washing clothes a little more often could have helped. Bathing wasn't really an issue for the poor either, as personal hygiene was virtually non-existent. It wasn't uncommon for children to grow into adulthood without ever having a bath. As for deodorant, it wasn't invented until 1888.

Soap was expensive and considered a waste of money, so a quick wash in a bowl of cold water sufficed, as it was feared hot water encouraged disease and viruses to spread through the household. And women used rags as sanitary towels, or nothing at all. Just let everything flow naturally. Toothpaste was actually invented by the Romans, only forgotten when they returned to Rome. After which, charcoal was used in the dark ages. Toothpaste in its form we know today has been around since the late 18th Century, but again, it was regarded a waste of money. So using a toothpick or simply rubbing a rag across ones teeth was the closest Victorian poor got to dental hygiene.

Staying fit, working hard and earning social respect in a Victorian working class society wasn't easy. As for a healthy diet, food, although mainly fresh, was bought on a daily basis due to its poor quality, where the poorest working class could only afford cheap and almost rotten food classed unfit for human consumption today. And trying to keep uncooked meat and vegetables fresh for a few days caused problems, especially during summer months. So pantries and larders sufficed as cool areas to store eggs, bread, milk, and placing meat on a slab of marble to keep cold.

The only option to preserve meat was to either boil, salt or smoke it, which we still enjoy today. Tinned food as we know it wasn't an option as this particular process of conserving food wasn't invented until the turn of the 20th Century, so pickling or soaking food in brine and storing in jars was common. As for eating out, it simply didn't happen, unless you were on your allotment reaping what you sewed as you harvest it. Even the upper class only ate at restaurants occasionally.

Although teashops existed in large towns and cities, the majority never had any because the working class couldn't afford a cuppa served at a shop. As for fast food establishments, again, there wasn't any, other than good old pub grub similar to home cooked food. It wasn't until the 1880's did humble fish and chip shops appear in High Streets, creating the first true fast food outlet in the UK.

Because of vast overpopulation during the entire industrial revolution malnutrition was a major problem for the poorer communities. Death caused by starvation and lack of quality nutritional food were also linked to various illnesses due to the body unable to fight infections as simple as a common cold, bringing down life expectancy to a national average of 40-years. Remarkably, the percentage of children dying under the age of 5-years decreased from 75 percent in the mid 18th Century to around 32 percent by the early decades of the 19th Century.

If possible, growing vegetables and keeping a few chickens was a great way to spread the cost and enjoy fresh, wholesome food to feed a large family. Basic groceries such as milk, bread and dripping were relatively expensive, especially meat and fresh eggs. So keeping poultry and trapping game birds was definitely a cheaper option. As for treats, they were as rare as a 21st Century teenager without a mobile phone. Many 19th Century children didn't expect a meal every day let alone treats, and sweets were only eaten at Christmas, if you were lucky.

More often than not, during the mid 19th Century children lucky enough to go to school left by the age of ten, only to start full time work no matter what Factory Act enforced. Younger children, including those aged 4-years and over that didn't go to school, were still employed by scrupulous factory owners, mines and chimney sweeps, determined to use and abuse the young as cheap labour.

Wages were often given to mum and spent on replacing worn out trousers, shirts, dresses, shoes and boots that were no longer repairable. Even on food, tool repair, and towards paying rent. So very little left for the must have Victorian equivalent of an X-Box game. Hard reality was children rarely had money to buy toys and the latest must-have for themselves; they were too busy working every spare hour for a living. And those that did have a few pennies usually spent it on beer, cider and tobacco, including 10-year olds. Adults ignored children smoking, as there wasn't any recognised health risks. It was simply something everyone did, and tobacco was cheaper than sugary sweets and cakes.

The chances of contracting a disease from drinking water was far greater than drinking beer and cider due to the brewing process, which in turn killed all the bugs. And beer was considerably weaker than today, with an alcohol content of around 2 percent, compared to an average 4 or 5 percent today. So young children were encouraged to drink beer and cider to keep them hydrated. Drinking water from garden wells or kitchen taps was virtually forbidden due to the lack or inefficient water treatment works; often leading to stomach upsets and sometimes death from fatal diseases such as cholera. So children did as they were told and kept well clear of water – even for washing.

Victorian children also understood the meaning of being seen but not heard, and carried out chores around the house after a hard day's work without quarrel or dispute in fear of punishment should they dare say no. And if by chance there were free time, sleep was priority, if only to be fresh for another long hard day. Children, working or not, were also often beaten by parents – usually by an alcoholic father – so running away from home happened quite a lot. Only to join thousands of other homeless children on the streets, either running away from a hostile environment, neglect, abuse or simply orphaned because parents could no longer afford to raise them.

Should a breadwinner die, rest of the family were more often than not thrown onto the streets for non-payment of even only one week's rent, and a jobless mother losing a working husband to ill health rarely received sympathy. With no money for rent or food, many desperate mothers had no choice but knock on the door of a Workhouse or gamble the fate of their children by abandoning them to the mercy of passers-by with hope of someone will at least feed them. Children as young as 3-years old could be found wandering filthy streets, either begging, stealing, and some not that much older turning to prostitution simply to survive.

Public serving jobs were invented by the more entrepreneur-thinking child, earning the odd penny by clearing shop doors of rubbish and excrement left behind by horses and beggars. Collecting cigarette butts for recycling could also earn a halfpenny or two, and collecting urine pots from houses for the local tannery

---

earned enough to buy a simple meal. Hence the old saying 'having a pot to piss in.' In other words, if you didn't even have a pot to piss in, you were, indeed, destitute.

Something had to be done; the poor had had enough and could no longer continue to live and work under such bad conditions, where local authorities, employers and business owners effortlessly cast aside any pleas or demands. Putting it simply, the common worker was denied opinions, rights, better working or living conditions, higher wages or even a pension, just because the upper classes said so.

Towards the end of the Victorian era, with the industrial revolution at its most productive, it was about to suffer something never envisioned, yet became a recurring reality where the common worker has had to endure ever since – an economic downturn. In this particular case a depression lasting from 1873 to 1896 although many industries managed to survive and thrive during this unforeseen decline.

Actual tell-tail signs of this depression started 30-years previous, where the 1840's introduced various laws and reforms, including The Mine Act, making it illegal to employ women and children to work down a mine. Coupled with having to educate child workers under the age of 13-years had quite a profound effect upon production. The Corn Law of 1846 determined an end to tariffs on foreign food imports, and the cholera epidemic of 1848 caused widespread panic for employers and employees alike.

By the 1870's with previous influences already taken their toll, the introduction of amalgamating industrial giants into even larger corporations created a need to streamline businesses by investing in better technological advancement in more efficient industrial automatic machinery. Ever changing to compete with other manufacturers the introduction of advanced machinery meant the need for manual labour and casual machine operatives were no longer required, forcing a large number of workers redundant, and inevitably onto the streets.

Skilled workers were instead urgently needed to operate newly installed advanced machinery, but they lacked experience. To remedy this, engine, turbine and machinery manufacturers grabbed a potentially huge market opportunity by introducing training to use new technology. Although new machinery brought with it a new evolution of skilled employee, training eventually became the norm for employers to offer existing employees, if not to get the most out of their dwindling skilled workforce.

Factories no longer kept gates open for passing casual labour looking for work. Instead they had to keep their gates locked in fear of rioting for not recruiting. Factories that did have casual vacancies were now inundated with applicants, where managers could now be picky with potential offerings of labour. Interviews became common for the most menial of jobs, where in the past applicants were quickly shown what to do then left at the mercy of a foreman.

Other radical factors contributing to the world's first industrial depression was the increasing threat of North American expansion and German imports to an Empire where the sun never sets, coupled with supply overtaking demand. In turn Victorian values showed signs of slipping, where hundreds of thousands of manual labourers – which were also consumers – were thrown on the scrap heap, desperate to find work elsewhere and become consumers once again, keeping other workers in a job…so on and so on.

Although trade unions were around throughout the Victorian era, only a few had the nerve to pressurise some concerned businesses with illegal all-out strikes should employer exploitation worsen. By 1867 and after many decades of growing protests, trade unions, or at least some of them, were legalised by Royal Commission, creating the Trade Union Congress (TUC) providing the congress and its members were favourable to both employer and employee. Yeah, right. Like that was going to happen.

However, within only a few years trade unions gathered momentum throughout the country. By 1871 there were enough unions to join together and fight for national reform, leading to the birth of the Labour Party. Gas Workers and General Union was formed in 1889 after its success reforming working hours. Within a decade the Labour movement dramatically extended its members with the introduction of the National Amalgamated Union of Labour for ship builders from the North East in 1889. Together with the Municipal Employees Association and the National Federation of Women Workers, the four unions came together in 1924 to form the National Union of General and Municipal Workers. Even clerks believed they needed a union and in 1890 joined together to form the Clerk's Union.

Despite the depression workers finally united and beat the system that screwed them into the ground for centuries; proving to the upper classes they could get what they deserve. After all, this generation had something to fight for, and boy, did they deserve it. Nothing was going to stop this impressive movement fighting for workers rights, better wages, working conditions and improving welfare.

However, with the second industrial revolution of the 1870's well under way, and the popularity of unions, the UK continued to suffer an agricultural catastrophe due to cheaper meat imports as well as the incredible loss of labourers amazingly still enticed to drop pitchforks and work in factories. The huge influx of farm labourers moving to towns and cities finally had a profound impact on land and farm owners, where the upper class aristocracy that employed them were forced to sell land, houses, even valuable furniture and paintings to raise much needed cash.

In the meantime another revolution was in the making: votes for women. Protests outside parliament by women had surprisingly been around a long time before Emmerlie Parkhurst and her suffragette movement. The use of petition was a favourite tactic used by the suffragists as far back as 1832 during the Great Reform Act where the vote was expanded to other classes of society, but not for women.

Member of Parliament, Henry Hunt, submitted a petition on behalf of Mary Smith, but of course, nothing came of it. Protests and petitions continued throughout the following decades, and in 1866 Parliament was presented a petition by MP John Stuart Mill, on behalf of the Women's Suffrage Committee, created by Barbara Bodichon. John Stuart proposed that the forthcoming Second Reform Act 1867 be amended to allow women the vote.

Once again it was laughed out of the chamber, but women's movements didn't give up. In fact they presented petitions on a yearly basis with hope that one day Parliament will take the women's movement seriously and include an amendment to allow them to vote. It was a start of a long and difficult journey, and by 1884 the Third Reform Act became law, increasing the right to 58 percent of males allowed to vote, including working class men.

Well, not quite all. Only a certain class of working class, providing they weren't living at home, employed as servants, in the armed forces and aged over 21-years of age. As for women, some high-ranking ladies in society were finally allowed, but the rest still couldn't, even though many were paying taxes into the coffers of the exchequer. However, at least the government was showing signs of agreeing with the masses, but there was still a long way to go.

Chapter Four

Battered, bruised but the fight goes on

The late 1880's brought with it a concerned Queen Victoria for the working classes by successfully campaigning for children to receive compulsory education from the age of 5-years and up to the age of 10-years, and better living conditions for poor families. Housing remained a priority so a huge project was introduced across the UK to rid the slums by building tens-of-thousands of terraced houses on clean streets for those in work.

I emphasise the word 'work' as homeless paupers never received any help, other than from the mercy of Workhouses. And the majority of these new houses for low income workers that were built to stringent regulations even came with clean running water from a single tap in the kitchen, gas for cooking and lighting, later converted to receive electric light – if affordable.

On the flip-side of the coin upper classes with bags of free leisure time continued to entertain themselves with crazes such as collecting Egyptian artefacts, curiosities, exotic plants, the opera house and performing seances. Victorians were obsessed with death, both rich and poor. When a family member died women were forbidden to wear jewellery whilst in mourning, lasting upto 2-years. They also wore a type of coal called jet to reflect their strange demure, and it was customary to wear a lock of hair from the deceased and a dark heavy bonnet with a veil for the first 3-months. After which, only the bonnet was worn for a further 9-months.

All mirrors were covered with sheets in fear of breaking, thus taking another life whilst a body remained in the house. Death portraits were also painted with living family members sitting beside the deceased, later having portrait photographs taken once the camera was invented. They were dressed in their Sunday best and made to look alive by using make-up powder and leaded paint. Guess that didn't really matter considering they were already dead. Sometimes eyelids were glued open to make the deceased look even more alive.

When it came to burial Victorians carried with them a huge fear of being buried alive, so if affordable, coffins had a bell installed. A piece of string was tied to a finger of the body with the other end attached to the bell, fearing if they woke 6-feet under they could trigger an alarm to alert the mourners. But not all Victorian traditions were morbid. Outdoor pursuits became extremely popular including tennis, golf, cricket, shooting and fishing. Women of upper classes had their own pastimes such as attending charity events – if not to catch up with gossip and show off their latest attire – horse riding, skating, playing croquet and even archery.

Working classes also enjoyed their own modern entertainment. Theatres and music halls were built for the masses to enjoy in most towns up and down the country, with shows on a daily basis. Saloons became increasingly popular with having dances, singing and shows including plays, drama and comedy acts. Alcohol was also sold in many saloons, adding gayety and merriment to the event. Museums and libraries were popular with the rich and poor, and remain free today to enter – as long as State owned.

Football was a major pastime for young clubs – players and fans alike. It became so popular amongst the working class employers had no option but give their workforce Saturday morning off so they could watch the match, then return to work as soon as it ended. Sunday morning was for church, although numbers were dwindling, then back to work after service. Monday was the traditional day off because the weekend wasn't yet recognised as the end of a working week. So a stroll through the park in your best cloth, having a picnic or going to the circus created huge excitement for grown-ups, as well as children: daring skill of the knife thrower, trapeze, amusing clowns, not forgetting the exotic and dangerous animals.

It wasn't until towards the end of Queen Victoria's reign did the weekend become adopted as end of a working week. With football so popular, and even the dwindling church service on a Sunday morning, shift patterns were disrupted, so it made sense to scrap Monday as the day off and have two full working days off to prevent disruption and retain shift patterns. Of course, the best time in the week to do this was Saturday and Sunday, which is why we term these days as a weekend – days after a working week. Day trips and even weekend breaks to the seaside became increasingly popular for the working class, and with railways introducing cheaper third class return tickets, a proper get-away meant a proper rest from a busy working week.

Children played many street games – once household chores were done. Playing soldiers, football, marbles and hoop-stick were amongst their favourite for boys. Skipping rope games and pretend tea parties were favourite for girls. Other games for both boys and girls were Cupid's coming (kiss-chase), bulldogs, whip and top (spinning a pointed wooden top using string), blind man wand (trying to whack your friends with a stick whilst blind folded), deer stalker (sneaking up on a mate and grabbing them without hearing or seeing you), and skittles using bottles and pebbles.

With the Second industrial revolution in full swing goods and wares were cheaper to buy due to mass production and technological advancement in automated machinery, so working classes could enjoy the odd treat and spoil their children a little more than usual, if not for the first time. Upper classes enjoyed the finer and more refined pleasures of life. Having a huge wealth usually included a huge appetite for everything produced at home and abroad. Keeping up with the Jones's was born.

Clothes made from exotic fabrics, best silver and chinaware, not forgetting the very latest in gadgets such as gramophones and a box that captured an image, only to magically appear upon a piece of card. What sorcery was this? Of course, it was the camera. Thanks to this marvellous invention a growing craze ensued a more risqué subject – pornography.

With plenty of 'models' queuing at a photographer's door to earn a few easy shillings for this new, yet illicit trade of photography, working and upper class men enjoyed perving over the latest naughty magazines. Sold from under the counter – naturally – it became known as the English vice for gentlemen. And it wasn't long before gentlemen films were made, which were a tad more daring than the 'what the butler saw' cheeky machines found on seaside promenades.

Gambling was always a favourite pastime for the rich and poor, where the working class sometimes gambled an entire weeks wage, and upper classes even wagered one or two of the many properties they owned on a turn of a card. Rat pits and cockfighting was also popular. Again, betting on a potential winner with hard-earned cash desperately needed for the family home. Drinking also continued to be a favourite for the working class – predominately by men – and because the alcohol content was low a concoction known as grog was made by adding rum or whiskey to the beer, making it considerably stronger.

Gender rolls continued to play an important part, no matter what class of Victorian society. Towards the mid-Victorian era it was still illegal for women to play a musical instrument or sing in public, unless accompanied by a band, agent or manager, and the latter era still recognised separate spheres within the household. In a nutshell, the little woman remained chained to the kitchen sink whilst the husband brought in a wage, meeting only at breakfast and an evening meal before retiring to bed totally exhausted.

Victorian men believed women were simply the weaker sex, yet morally stronger, therefore suited to household chores such as cooking, cleaning and raising children so to prepare them for the next sphere generation. And yes, women believed this too. In the meantime husbands worked long hours and denied any interference with running the house, other than display discipline when children – and wife – stepped out of line.

Teenagers were still teenagers, regardless of background or class. Rebelling against ones parents isn't something new, and although not really understood as a Victorian parental headache, it certainly existed. Children from upper class societies were more often than not sent to public schools – usually boarding – from an early age of around 7 or 8-years old, returning home for a short stay between terms. By the time they reached mid-teens their destiny had already been pre-arranged.

Be it doctors, lawyers, factory owners or the political elite, their offspring usually followed suit in one way or another. Joining the army or navy was also popular with military families, quickly finding themselves at Sandhurst officer training school to serve in the armed forces around a vast British Empire. Some were even bequeathed to another family in the form of a forced marriage for capital gain and business interests.

Working class teenagers didn't have the luxury of having a guaranteed prosperous life pre-cast for them, so hard work remained the only vague guarantee, providing work was consistent. Prospects were still bleak and hunger was always on their minds. Chores still had to be done around the house – unlike upper class teenagers – and mending clothes remained a relentless task.

Nevertheless, scholarships were available and apprenticeships were offered to those showing an interest as a tradesman but often unpaid for the first few years; only offering a meagre wage in the last few, which could last several years. So a young apprentice would have to come from a family with a few quid to spare. The master usually had the apprentice live with him, where his board, clothes, food and tools were paid for by his parents. Once qualified some continued to work for his master, others joined companies, whilst some started their own business. And depending upon the trade could earn quite a good living.

Universities were a completely different education system compared to today. Although an established seat of learning for many centuries to the privileged elite, they only enrolled single male students belonging to the Church of England. By the 1800's, however, universities across the country started to open doors to many walks of life, including married men: Durham in 1832, Manchester in 1851 and Birmingham in 1900.Women first studied at Bedford and the Royal Holloway Colleges of London universities in 1878. Oxford and Cambridge remained stubborn regarding female students entering their colleges, but reluctantly had to relax their rules soon after.

Whatever their education, something happens in the developing brain of adolescent children that turns them – how can I put this – into insufferable gits. Smoking and drinking had always been part and parcel of Victorian life for all, including children, so that wouldn't have been an issue. No, it's those typical attributes all teenagers have: an overwhelming need to answer back, be cocky, believing they know better, it's always someone else's fault, moody and disobedient. Oh yes, these particular teenage traits were certainly around in the 1800's.

However, unlike today, teenage tantrums didn't last long within the lower class societies. They didn't have time to revolt – too busy working. Nevertheless, upper class teens had nothing to do other than finish Public school, where discipline was harsh. In between leaving school and their chosen career they never had to lift a finger around the house because servants did all that cooking, cleaning and washing malarkey, so boredom soon set in.

Reading and studying were productive time-filling pastimes, but to let off a little steam rebellion was the only outlet. Staying out later than told added to the excitement, with visiting brothels, getting drunk or walking the streets of a poor area of town whilst showing off wealth was thought to get the adrenaline rushing through veins, although an extremely dangerous game to play.

Upper class graduates, particularly those from industrial new money, started to return home from university without bothering to learn anything. Professors from many subjects recognised that the privileged few belonging to up and coming industrial wealthy families appeared increasingly disinterested in studies and more interested in their social life. Even treated learning as nothing more than a disturbance and a chore to endure. Instead, they preferred to sit around in groups conjuring new ideas and naïve theoretical remedies on how they could solve social and political issues such as Reform Acts, the poor and homelessness. Even accusing pillars of society as nothing more than failures and that they simply didn't have a clue how to run a country.

Young inexperienced heads full of ideology, yet no ambition other than scrounge off mummy and daddy for the rest of their lives, pursued creating social unrest. Spreading university encouraged political belief to the masses whilst waiting for parents to croak it and claim their industrial fed inheritance. The champagne socialist was born.

Other political persuasions nurtured at university included Whigs – later becoming the Liberal party – and the Conservatives, with their right-wing arrogant attitude of the working class, equally spreading political rhetoric around campus. Not forgetting the increasing belief in socialism favoured by the working class – the opposite side of the political spectrum - which grew at an incredible rate throughout the Victorian and Edwardian eras.

With young inquisitive – yet easily influential minds – and thanks to the telegram and later the telephone, printing technology, coupled with education as a whole, reading of political leaflets and newspapers around university campus, as well as the masses, exploded from around 40,000,000 per annum in the 1850's to an incredible 120,000,000 within 20-years, spreading news, and most certainly gossip.

A massive popular revolution engulfed an entire country with this new concept called reading. Once restricted to local gossip, those with only little education could suddenly tap into every story told through newspapers, now obsessed with national and even international gossip. By the 1870's around 70 percent of the population could read and write – to a degree. The working class could now easily grasp headline topics of conversation, discussing its contents and persuasion amongst friends and neighbours.

Editors quickly learnt sensationalism sells newspapers. Journalists were just as eager to change their old and dull methods of providing news to selling drama and excitement en-mass. William Thomas Stead was one such controversial journalist, bringing with him a written word that influenced a reader's opinion. Whether it was government policies, legislation or reform, war or even crime, he reported stories with headings in a manner that created scandal, social division and even riots due to how a story was written. In other words create hot topics and portray his opinion. Something journalists never previously did.

This particular method of story telling brought with it huge attention from both sides of social and political spectrums, such as demonstrations by anti-war movements against the UK declaring war with Russia over the Crimean crises in March 1854. This particular demonstration gained rapid momentum thanks to the newspaper. Further demonstrations continued throughout the following decades, such as the women's suffrage movement campaigning for women's right to vote, all because of the newspaper.

In 1884 Stead nurtured journalism with his pioneering skills to suit his new way of portraying sensationalism by printing a story about General Gordon, who led a British taskforce in Sudan to protect civilians in the besieged city of Khartoum from rebellion forces. Fighting against overwhelming odds, General Gordon

---

and his men became entrapped whilst evacuating its citizens, but managed to get a message to the British government asking for reinforcements. However, the government frowned upon his failure, expecting a swift mission, so ignored his request.

The story was suspiciously leaked, and Stead jumped at the chance to sell the story to the masses, instantly making General Gordon a national hero. Likewise the government were despised by the public for not helping the General, calling parliament cowards and unpatriotic. Eventually the government bowed under public pressure and sent a relief force, but they were too late. In fact, William's headline read 'TOO LATE' in large block capitals, emphasising the reluctant attempt of rescue.

Impact headlines became the new habit to capture a reader's eye, in effect creating a better story rather than just reporting it. Didn't take long for other newspapers to follow this simple yet effective way of selling stories by there millions, and has since been adopted to suit our modern times. Advertisements were also introduced, bringing with them large profits whilst bringing down the cost of newspapers to the public, thus selling more. That meant businesses and services could advertise their wares nationally in one hit to thousands, if not millions of potential sales. Naturally other 'services' were advertised for gentlemen disguised somewhat to hide there true meaning, but recognised by certain customers.

With this brand new concept of sensationalism and advertisements filling newspapers, the Evening News was launched in 1894 and within 2-years the Daily Mail hit the presses, including fashion articles for women. Welcome to the dawn of the second Renaissance. And with it followed a fast growing social recreation – the use, or rather misuse of drugs, in particular opium, taken by the young, old, rich and poor.

Not realising its medical effect upon the human body, it succumbed little disgust, other than knowing the drug was addictive. Its reputation particularly excited the upper classes, resulting in a want for more, if only to emulate upper class heroes such as Charles Dickens and Lord Byron. Drug addiction was rife during the Victorian era, kept quiet behind closed doors of clubs and private homes so not to appear weak in front of the working class.

Another faux pas kept behind closed doors was homosexuality. Not exactly accepted in Victorian society, gay relationships were not uncommon. Males in relationships would do their utmost to keep it under wraps, never showing a hint of affection in public. Even married couples were frowned upon for holding hands. As for kissing in public, this was the height of impropriety.

Straight couples would court first, where the upper class would only accept any approach towards their daughter by means of permission from her family. This included a chaperone – usually a family member – to generally stick around whilst the courting couple drank tea in the parlour, and most certainly never left unaccompanied.

Should the couple find an interest in each other, it would take a few more 'dates' at her home before venturing out. Once again with a chaperone at first, making sure no holding of hands or showing any remote signs of affection were performed in public. If all went well a trust would bond between the couple and her family, and only then could the happy couple be left to date alone.

Working class couples meeting for the first time wasn't so formal, yet there was a code of good conduct to adhere. And a daughter's working class family with even only an ounce of self-respect still insisted upon meeting the gentleman in question before any 'dates' became anywhere near the next step towards a relationship. The gentleman in question would ask the father's permission to take out his daughter, and would have definitely titled him as 'Sir' at first, then maybe, just maybe, Mister later. First name terms only came to any fruition when the courting couple were either engaged or married, and only if given permission by the father.

Victorian homosexuals also courted, but kept extremely quiet, no matter what class they belonged to, be they pauper or Lord. But society didn't, wouldn't and couldn't accept this way of life. It was bad, unnatural and believed it to be a disease of the brain, so meeting a potential partner wasn't easy. Throughout the Victorian era upper class homosexual brothels were formed in the guise of gentlemen's clubs and became popular amongst the gay community, where men went to drink, discuss politics and decide whether or not a potential partner was in fact gay and not a journalist or a undercover detective.

The Criminal Law (Amendment) Act of 1885 was clear in that any form of sex between men was a crime, where any act of gross indecency will be punishable with a maximum 2-years imprisonment with hard labour. This Act was put to the test over the Cleveland Street brothel scandal. Becoming infamous due to the story of upper class members, including Lords and even Prince Albert Victor, eldest son of the Prince of Wales, were part of a huge investigation by Scotland Yard, creating exciting newspaper headlines in 1889.

During court trials, amazingly, Prince Albert Victor was never mentioned in any newspapers, but unfortunately for Lord Euston and Lord Somerset, their names were revealed to the public eye. It was claimed that young telegram delivery boys were enticed to their rooms and paid for sex. Newspapers couldn't get enough of the scandal, and its readers were shocked and totally disgusted with the thought of pillars of society involved in such lewd acts of debauchery.

French newspapers soon caught up with the story and didn't hesitate to mention Prince Albert Victor. Even going one further with accusing him, and other high-ranking Lords, of being part of a paedophile ring. Witch-hunts quickly formed, exacerbating the public hatred of homosexuals, believing all to be paedophiles and demanding their capture to rid them off the streets. Irish poet and playwright, Oscar Wild, also became a news headline when found guilty of gross indecency in 1895.

Although Oscar didn't really hide his homosexuality, as soon as it became public knowledge he was gay and having many partners, society simply couldn't tolerate this filth, and the law finally caught up with his relentless promiscuity, finally sentencing him to the maximum sentence with hard labour. Upon release he travelled to France where he wrote The Ballad of Reading Gaol, reflecting harsh times in the Berkshire prison, only to die a pauper at the age of 46-years in 1900.

Lower classes were not so privileged to have gentlemen clubs so caution was adhered with prevalence when meeting fellow like-minded men. Otherwise, the thought of a street mob catching anyone remotely connected with homosexuality wasn't worth the risk. Incredibly, lesbianism was never mentioned in The Criminal Law (Amendment) Act of 1885 and neither was it a concern for the public. Unaware such behaviour between women actually happened. After all, what a preposterous notion to contemplate.

The same Act remained untouched until 1967 where it was reformed, including decriminalising homosexuality in private. But much of the law remained intact for a further 20-years or so, where it was still illegal for homosexuals to carry out sexual acts in private under the age of 21-years.

Other crimes during the Victorian era were, as you can imagine, common, especially in large, overcrowded towns and cities. Petty crime, such as shop lifting, was usually carried out by children, if only to survive. Pick-pocketing was also common, again, usually by children, where many were forced to work for organised gangs run by an adult not unlike a Fagin character in the 1960's musical, Oliver. Only the real Fagin's weren't singing loveable rogues.

Violent alcohol related crime was rife in most pubs, bars and homes up and down the country, where drinking heavily became a huge habit for many trying to escape a poor existence. Unfortunately, wives and children were easy targets from drunken husbands, only attracting interest from the police when a murder was committed. Thankfully, this didn't happen too often. Nevertheless, the law tended to shy away from wife beating, but to be involved in a pub brawl could easily be sentenced with a few weeks or months in the local gaol, where a punishment of hard labour was often awarded.

Lord Robert Peeler, whom introduced the Metropolitan Police Force in 1885 took crimes, such as murder, a little more seriously. Constables, known as Peeler's after Lord Peeler – later Bobbies, after his Christian name – quickly realised the need for a national Police Force to combat petty, as well as serious crimes, including organised gangs around the city of London.

And dealing with criminals made a significant difference throughout the 1800's where transportation to His Majesty's colonies around the British Empire became commonplace, even for the most pathetic of crimes.

Whether stealing a shroud off a corpse or impersonating an Egyptian, many convicted criminals were banished to suffer a long punishing sentence in the Americas – a favourite destination by the Courts. Thousands found themselves having to work long hours with hard labour in searing heat year after year for plantation owners, farmers and land owners to pay their debt to society. But the American colonies came to an abrupt end in 1776 when King George III decided to let the Americans have their independence from England. And no, they didn't win the war against the British. The King just left them to it because likes of Lord Nelson and Duke of York had a more pressing engagement beating the French further north.

Five years earlier Captain Cook discovered Australia, and this massive Island on the other side of the world became a perfect place to deposit criminals. Transportation to Australia, however, also came to an abrupt end, but not because of war. Disgruntled free citizens that up-sticks and left crowded slums and cities to start a fresh by emigrating to Australia could no longer tolerate thousands of criminals festering their shores. By the 1850's they'd had enough and kicked up a fuss in parliament, which, amazingly in their favour, ended transportation.

The relentless battle for better political reform, better working and living conditions throughout the 1800's seemed to finally pay off. Life was finally looking a little rosier amongst the grime and choking smoke of the industrial revolution. At the beginning of Queen Victoria's reign, from pauper to the working class,

---

survival to live another day remained priority. Leaving little time for anything else, let alone dare to complain or make demands. Towards the end of her reign reform acts began to recognise some of the masses desperate pleas, including a right to vote, and employers finally recognised the importance of better conditions for employees, if not to benefit production and profit.

Working class families, however, still had to work hard, but found themselves healthier than their forefathers, better educated, cash on the hip, and even a little leisure time. For the first time ever, working class society dipped its toe in the ocean of luxury living, creating a huge appetite for it. But their new-found voice was nowhere near loud enough to match the still mighty upper class to hear. So the struggle continued.

Chapter Five

Me, me, look at me

With the death of Queen Victoria on 22nd January 1901, remarkably captured on a motion camera – yes, even in 1901 – the Trade Union movement during later years of the Victorian era gained incredible ground fighting for better working conditions. Now in the Edwardian era King Edward VII reigned, inheriting an unbelievably huge Empire to oversee.

Meanwhile, across the North Sea, King Edward's Nephew, Kaiser Wilhelm II ruled the German Empire, although incredibly smaller than the British. Nonetheless, he wanted to increase his navy to match the vast size of his British counterpart, having ambitions to spread his Empire, as were other European countries, including France, Belgium, the Balkans and Romania. Without realising, the Kaiser almost started the First World War in 1904 when he upset the French by invading their territories in Morocco and Algeria, only to claim they actually belong to him.

Kicked out by the French and licking his wounds, Kaiser Wilhelm decided to look further east at the failing Ottoman Empire, immediately staking a claim it now belonged to him knowing they were financially and militarily weak. Meanwhile, the Austria-Hungary Empire jostled with the Russian Empire over Balkan territories where Russia believed to be protector of the Slavics. But Austrian-Hungary believed to own the Balkan Peninsula. Adding a further ingredient into a boiling pot France was still recognised as a potential enemy to the United

Kingdom thanks to a rocky history. Nevertheless, UK and France were becoming closer with trade and commerce, allowing a strange alliance between the two countries.

In 1907 Russia also joined an alliance with the UK having an already long relationship with France. The Triple Alliance had now been formed; much to the disgust of Kaiser Wilhelm, as he always believed the UK would naturally bond an alliance with Germany. But King Edward VII regarded Kaiser Wilhelm as too arrogant to have any kind of relationship, and the up and coming industrial USA too immature.

The Edwardian era had well and truly begun, reaping rewards from the Victorians, along with new inventions from the industrial revolution and an inherited Empire. But the world had shrunk thanks to ocean liners, motor cars, railways and not forgetting a boom in telephone and telegram networks stretching across seas and land, joining countries and continents with the world first internet, although primitive.

Edwardian innovations grabbed headlines and intrigued scientists with Einstein's Theory of Relativity, atomic and quantum physics, sonar technology and the overwhelming diversity of electricity. Electric light became increasingly popular in shops, factories and homes. Household goods, such as food mixers and vacuum cleaners, became an exciting 'must have' item, making chores a little easier for those that could afford them.

Another huge Edwardian technological jump for mankind was when the Wright brothers made their first powered flight in 1903 covering a distance of no more than the wingspan of a Boeing 747 Jumbo jet – around 120-feet, flying at a height of 20-feet. Powered flight encapsulated the imagination of many enthusiasts, including Frenchman Louis Bleriot. In 1909 he became the first man to fly across the English Channel, sponsored by the Daily Mail and the newly opened Selfridges store in Oxford Street, London: a store unlike any other, even Harrods. Claiming to sell everything that everyone would want to buy, from the latest fashion in clothes, electrical goods, to Ford model T motor cars first introduced in 1908.

George Selfridge wasn't afraid of trying something new to grab customer's curiosity. He invited everyone to visit his store, be they young old, rich or poor, everyone was welcome. As he saw it, a rich person may walk into his store and never spend a penny. Much can be said for someone poor. But the poor shopper will tell everyone they know about their new experience, enticing other poor shoppers to do the same, where at least some will buy his wares suited to their pocket. The rich person, on the other hand, won't tell anyone, because why should they, there're rich.

Gordon also displayed cosmetics in view of everyone as soon as they walked through the door. A practice never seen before as it was considered embarrassing and vulgar. Previously, women quietly shopped for make-up entering through a back door of a salon whilst heavily veiled. But Gordon said that women's beauty must be celebrated with the enhancement of cosmetics. And they did just that by celebrating in droves. No longer was it taboo to buy lipstick thanks to Gordon.

Although Harrods and House of Fraser sold a varied choice of goods, Selfridges introduced a trend by spreading it to all cities and towns, where fashionable clothes and must have items tended to be purchased by upper middle class societies. Poor working class were still spending hard earned cash on much needed repairs and food to survive, where only the lucky few had expendable cash on the rarest occasions. So electrical goods and fashionable clothes were never given a second glance.

Turn of the 20th Century, however, introduced by invention and innovation, brought with it a new middle class – the lower middle – synonymous with established Edwardian careers: shop managers and factory foremen, to clerks and teachers, all submitting a huge important contribution to a new-money economy. And the biggest influence for this spending frenzy was none other than King Edward VII and his fragrant followers.

Unlike Queen Victoria, King Edward VII loved to be seen in public, so being suitably dressed was utmost important, and with it came a new Edwardian fashion. Clothing manufacturers from Europe and the United States quickly caught on with this exciting trend influencing a huge market. The upper classes couldn't get enough of the latest range in suits, gloves, shoes, coats, dresses, handbags, hats and purses. The new lower middle classes wanted the same, and they were not left disappointed. Cheaper lines soon entered shops to exploit a huge potential lower class market.

Majority of the masses, however, remained working class, where lifestyle didn't mean anything to them; good sturdy old-fashioned Victorian clothing was still the in-thing, and wages reflected this. Upper middle classes were salaried anything up to £1,500 per year, where the lower middle earned around £400. Poorer working class remained incredibly low at an average of £20 per year.

Adding further anguish and frustration, King Edward enjoyed large expensive meals, accompanied by cigars, where a certain brand took his name. His huge appetite continued a new fashionable theme: Art Nouveau became the rage, with French style clothing,

—

82

furniture and home decorative design. Houses were now lighter and airier than Victorian homes with less clutter. Pastels and light floral wallpaper replaced heavy leaf greens and contrast purples.

Keeping up with the Jones's increased its pretentious popularity, and some of the poor considered themselves belonging to a higher society inspired by better living, which was in reality nothing more than unaffordable snobbery. But with human nature as it is, the latest discovery of compulsion became impossible to ignore, and being one-up on the neighbour became almost impossible to resist. One third of the lower classes attempted to emulate their peers, only to find themselves living above their means. But the lavish Edwardian lifestyle was too good to miss, thanks to a flamboyant King.

Rolls-Royce opened their first car manufacturing production line in 1904 and Herbert Austin completed his factory in 1905 so it was inevitable roads will no longer be able to handle the influx of growing internal combustion engine vehicles, as well as the humble horse and cart. One answer was to upgrade road networks, and yet another national housing investment, similar to the later Victorian era. Otherwise factories and businesses would simply cease production due to workforces either dying prematurely from poverty and disease or emigrating to America, Australia and other British Empire countries to escape overcrowding.

Although further construction of terraced houses continued to supply working class family homes near factories and foundries, a different kind of housing development took hold never seen before. Due to an influx of upper middle classes working in towns and cities, they took an interest in living outside of town away

---

from the hustle and bustle of dirty crowded streets and into peaceful suburbs. The commuter was born.

Houses were built with internal bathrooms; no longer was there a need to bathe in front of the fire in a tin bath that took an age to fill with a bucket from the stand alone kitchen tap. Houses were also bigger than average Victorian dwellings, with lower ceilings, airy rooms and proper kitchens comprising of cupboards and storage units. Housing estates emerged on the edge of town comprising of Avenues, Crescents and cul-de-sacs, with new styles of houses appearing including detached and semi-detached.

All looked bright and easy in a new, clean living and prosperous Edwardian era. Brilliant, life looked fantastic for all. The huge sacrifice their forefathers fought and suffered, including employment and human rights, had surely finally paid off. Well, no, not really. For the working class, poorly furnished crowded homes, little food and hard work remained the same day-to-day chore as it had always been.

1901 census revealed a total population of the UK to be 38,000,000. Almost double the census carried out in 1851. Inevitably premature deaths once again soared due to huge overcrowding, causing a widespread increase in diseases such as typhoid and dysentery becoming an epidemic due to poor sanitation, poverty and overcrowded streets. Central government, however, eventually provided much needed cash for local authorities to build social housing, sanitation and road improvements.

Poorer working class welfare continued to be ignored. As far as the upper classes were concerned the working class had had enough improvements and luxury. They simply didn't deserve any more. But factory workers, dockers and transport unions disagreed, having to still endure a very evident Victorian harsh treatment, with poor wages, bad conditions and long working hours their main concern.

King Edward's government also had an issue with a sudden rise in support of Labour Party candidates from working class societies. A year before Queen Victoria died a Labour Representation Committee was formed to promote candidates for Parliamentary seats where a separate Labour group would sit within the House of Commons masking its true socialist nature. From Parliament a voice for the common worker could now be heard for the first time in such honourable political surroundings.

Unions and liberal thinking Members of Parliament attempted to pursue better employment conditions, higher wages and shorter hours, but the government favoured to retain the status quo, until Liberal, Herbert Henry Asquith, successfully made life a little easier. When the Liberals came into office under Prime Minister Henry Campbell-Bannerman in 1905 Herbert Asquith became the Chancellor of the Exchequer. In the 1908 General election Asquith became Prime Minister, where he was eager to pass his Reforms and Parliament Act reducing the power of the Conservative- led House of Lords.

After three attempts and another two General elections, in 1910 he finally managed to pass his Act. The first election was held due to the House of Lords turning down his proposal for the 'People's Budget,' even though the House of Commons came to agreement after fierce debate from the Conservatives. His second success, with a smaller majority, continued to allow plans passing his Parliament Act.

David Lloyd George, Chancellor to Asquith, introduced a Welfare State. Not quite like today's Welfare system, nevertheless, it was a start – called the

---

National Insurance Act of 1911 – adding regulation on working hours including a minimum wage for a few low paid trades enforced by the 1909 Trade Boards Act. Politicians, factory owners and the upper classes had no choice but agree – through gritted teeth – with the reform.

For the working masses the 'People's Budget' was too little too late. By 1908 the country was in the midst of a recession amongst industrial giants, where unemployment rose to around 8 percent. By 1911 unemployment actually fell to around 3 percent – still considerably high in real terms – where the unions continued to put across their grievances. But employers, once again, and believing to be in an even stronger position, simply ignored concerns.

Despite opposition from factory owners and alike, unions successfully organised themselves and by 1914 trade union membership doubled since 1900 reaching an unprecedented 4,000,000. Inevitably strikes begun to spread across varied industries, later known as the Great Unrest. In 1909 an estimated 180,000 union members walked out on strike. By 1911 the walkouts increased to over 850,000 and in 1912 reached its peak to over 1,000,000 workers walking out in support of brother members. From dockers to ship builders, railway workers to road transport drivers, even police and fireman, all downed tools in support of increased wages, better conditions and shorter hours.

From the start of industrial unrest in 1908 there were 389 strikes. Towards the height of industrial action in 1913 an unprecedented 1,459 strikes were recorded. During this period King Edward died in 1910 seeing only 9-years of reign. The crowning of King George V inherited a confused population in the midst of industrial action with the era continuing to be known as Edwardian, at least by the stubborn upper classes refusing to let it go.

But the poorer masses couldn't care less, having more pressing concerns.

Although the majority believed in their Royal family, a rise in militancy catapulted local disputes towards national concern with the railway and coal miners strikes of 1911 – 1912. Their obvious grievance was apparent, but others included large union organisations not recognised by their employers. And whilst middle and upper classes enjoyed higher wages and better conditions, the poorer working class wages actually fell.

The Seamen Union in Liverpool grew to 70,000 members by 1910 and was quickly recognised as the epicentre of joining other unions in recognition of solidarity. One year later demonstrations were organised in support of the seamen, including a newly formed Transport Workers Federation (TWF) later amalgamating with other transport unions, increasing its members by thousands.

Other unions, such as the National Union of Ship's Stewards, Cooks, Butchers and Bakers, were joined by the National Sailors and Fireman's Union (NSFU) and 4,000 dockers belonging to the National Union of Dock Labourers (NUDL) as well as non-members, walked out in support by refusing to load and unload ships. Boiler scalers and coal heavers joined the demonstrations, now growing to more than 10,000 in one day.

Railway workers totalling 15,000 also downed tools, encompassing many other railway depots and sidings. Gathered in Liverpool City centre they picketed the railway station, gaining huge support from the working class public. Upper classes were disgusted and complained to authorities for not being able to travel. It was only a matter of time before public disturbances occurred between pickets, supporters and non-striking police, inevitably resulting in riots.

Local authorities brought in further police and soldiers armed with live ammunition to quell the violence. Influx of force exacerbated the problem with more and more supporters and sympathisers, including dockers and other transport union members pouring into the city in support of striking railway workers. 100,000 supporters rallied to hear speeches from union leaders at St. George's Plateau, highlighting that the rail strike was spreading to other towns and cities around the country. Suddenly, towards the end of the demonstration, police started to attack demonstrators and innocent bystanders with considerable force to clear an incredibly large crowd.

Strikers and sympathisers retaliated throwing broken pavement slabs, curb stones, cobbles, and whatever else they could find in an attempt to keep the police at a distance. But the police prevailed, eventually managing to disperse the crowd into nearby streets where further scuffles broke out. Supporters even climbed onto rooftops to throw slates and tiles at the police and soldiers caught in the crossfire below.

Emergency talks between railway union leaders and employers commenced, where a deal was hastily put together in an attempt to bring peace back to the city and return strikers to work. Union leaders knew they had the upper hand, offering a bitter pill for the employers to swallow: give in to demands for higher wages and shorter hours. And for the first time in union history, with such great strength and show of solidarity, a clear and hard message was sent to the government and employers alike that the working class had to be accepted as a large player in society. Not simply cast aside and treated as insignificant members.

Thanks to a liberal minded Prime Minister who actually listened, remarkably the rest of the Edwardian era stood for employment rights and opportunity. There wasn't a national depression as such, although poverty was most definitely rife. But prosperity, as a nation, was good with a GDP unrivalled by Europe and the USA combined. Trade across the world experienced an all-time high, including foreign investments reaching not only all four corners of the British Empire, but also South America and the USA – especially with the construction of railways.

Religion continued to take a bit of a blow, where the masses found themselves too busy for the church or converted to other beliefs. Anglican Church was no longer the daddy of Christianity in the UK. Atheism grew amongst the working class, in particular the younger generation, and the Islamic faith started to gain interest. Catholics and Jews were also no longer barred from political roles. Sunday found itself distant from its original cause, instead becoming a day of contemplating a new humdrum, monotonous dreary working week.

Visiting art galleries, museums and parks – weather permitting – were very much a necessity before starting a new week for the upper classes. Lower working classes, although ventured in such activities, tended to either spend the day preparing for the working week ahead or – mainly men – drunk themselves to the point of unconsciousness as part of their preparation.

Teenagers from all classes were still brought up with Victorian values: respect elders and either follow in their father's footsteps with businesses and trades or find a job to bring money into the house. Most left school at the age of 13 or 14-years of age and knew they had to find work. But the Edwardian era also brought fresh desires for opened minded young adults to move away from family businesses and venture forth to start a new life in different cities and even countries.

Adventure for young adults became the forefront of importance, be they rich or poor, thanks to new modern transport taking them anywhere – almost – around the world. Young women, encouraged by the suffragette movement, dared to live alone, enrolled in colleges or created new businesses of their own. But this remarkable modern time of industrial disputes, prosperity, improvement of employment rights and a strong GDP came to an abrupt end on 4th August 1914. Nevertheless, seeds were sewn for a massive cultural change, but placed on the back burner, at least for a while.

Chapter Six

Keep the home fires burning

Threat of war in Europe had been simmering for years, reaching boiling point when Archduke Franz Ferdinand was assassinated on 28th June 1914. After which, it took only a month for Europe to wake from the thought of war to actual absolute all out conflict. The UK having a huge Empire had in comparison to Germany a small army. Although professional, it was poorly equipped with only 450,000 men at its disposal and a further 260,000 in reserve. Overall, Germany had 2,000,000 men, including reserves. The Royal Navy, however, was Britain's strongest attribute to deter Germany invading UK shores and her Empire.

Protests were inevitable, where socialist movements alongside Marxists, anarchists, Irish nationalists and women's groups marched in London against any possibility of war starting. Protests in Germany, France, Italy, Russia and even the USA also rallied in support of stopping any escalation of war in Europe. Remarkably the German socialist movement (SPD) changed its mind on 4th August 1914 in support of its government, as did the French Socialist Party (CGT) when war was declared. After which, unions in both countries accepted that socialists should now support their country in time of war.

Other socialist groups in countries such as Luxemburg, Canada and Sweden opposed any European war, where Sweden remained neutral – although had some sympathy towards Germany – and women protestors outnumbered any unions and socialist movements on all anti-war marches. In the USA the Women's Peace Party marched with other groups, including Jeannette Rankin, the first elected women into Congress, where she voted 'no' for America to enter the war in Europe. However, the British suffrage movement generally supported the war, if only to attract confidence from the government to support their campaign for women's right to vote.

After re-election of Woodrow Wilson in 1916 it was inevitable America would soon enter the war when Germany carried out attacks on civilian shipping in the North Atlantic using battleships and wolf-pack submarines. When the Lusitania cruise liner was torpedoed and sunk, killing many Americans, the public were furious over the loss of innocent American lives. President Wilson was also a tad annoyed and could no longer tolerate German aggression, finally declaring war on Germany 6th April 1917.

With only 175,000 soldiers at his disposal prior to declaring war, a staggering 3,800,000 were conscripted soon after. But anti-war temperament remained high in the USA, even protesting conscription to fight a European war that had nothing to do with US citizens, where an incredible 300,000 men – one-in-twelve – refused call-out notices. Back in Blighty, with a war only 22-miles away, patriotism remained incredibly strong. And with the thought of having an adventure in the guise of war – coupled with actually getting paid for it – appealed to millions of young men scrambling to enlistment centres.

Lord Kitchener stirred up excitement by raising numbers of volunteers with the introduction of Pals Battalions: local battalions made up of men that worked and lived together in the same area. A proportion of which took the King's shilling if only as an opportunity to bring them out of poverty. So there was no need to introduce conscription, not until January 1916 for men aged between 18 to 41-years and up to 56-years in some cases by 1918 due to the onslaught on the battlefields.

Two days after the declaration of war parliament sanctioned an increase in army strength of over half a million men aged between 19 and 30-years. By late August, Liverpool alone enlisted enough men to form 4 battalions within 3-weeks, where the war office only expected the possibility of only one could be raised. And by September 750,000 men had volunteered throughout the country, adding to the 710,000 full time and reserve soldiers already serving.

Younger teenagers also wanted a piece of the action, but many were shown the door, only to return once they reached 18-years of age. But patriotism remained high within the younger generation too, where an incredible 250,000 under eighteen's managed to slip the net and don a uniform by lying about their age upon enlisting. Some of which were only 13-years old. And yes, many died on the battlefield.

Everyone in the UK was either part of or knew someone who contributed to the war effort. Every city, town, village and hamlet suffered incredible losses due to the conflict. From the very start soldiers marched to Northern France believing they were invincible. That naïve notion was soon forgotten when reality unleashed what war can do to flesh when facing, bombs, bullets, mortars and shrapnel.

Such was the outrageous loss Pals Battalions had to be abolished due to almost all of the men that volunteered in any given location, district or village, were simply wiped out by German machineguns and artillery. By 1916 casualties were mounting in there tens of thousands,

---

and it was only going to get much, much worse. July 1st saw the first day of the Battle of the Somme. The objective was to capture German positions and push them back south to Foucaucourt.

The whistles blew at 7.28am after a huge artillery barrage lasting a week came to an abrupt halt, signalling the detonation of enormous mines previously dug under enemy positions. The explosions were so loud they could be heard as far away as London. Even the Prime Minister sitting in his cabinet office heard a distant faint rumble. Soldiers waiting to go over the top were told that the enemy will be either dead or so badly shaken they could simply walk towards the Germans without fear of being shot. Officers even supplied footballs to encourage men to kick them around whilst marching towards enemy trenches.

As they walked into no-mans land they faced not a dead or bewildered enemy, but an almost intact one, battened down in deep concrete bunkers, waiting out the bombardment so they could fight back. And boy, they did just that. What happened next was nothing more than shear carnage. Within the first hour alone around 20,000 men were cut down dead or wounded by bombs, shells, mortars and machinegun fire.

The Germans, disgusted by the atrocity laying before them, actually called a temporary truce so the allies could retrieve casualties. Once recovered, in what can only be described as surreal, the carnage resumed. Unbelievably, despite the onslaught, British generals continued to order thousand after thousand of soldiers over the top. By the end of the first day around 57,000 casualties lay in the mud. Total killed and wounded on the first day amounted to more than the first 2-years of the war put together.

Two of my Great Uncles on my father's side volunteered for this remarkable and exciting adventure. Great Uncle Charles served with 1st Battalion, Northants Regiment, and was in Northern France at the start of the war. Aged only 24-years, he was killed by machinegun fire attacking a German trench on 17th September 1914 at La Ferte-Sous-Jouarre, where his grave at the local memorial stands proud next to his comrades in arms who also fell on that terrifying day. Charles' younger brother, Cyril, with his entire platoon from 7th Battalion Northants Regiment, was wiped out by machinegun fire as they attacked a German position defending Theipval railway station.

The plan was to take the station intact so to bring forward supplies and ammunition; hence the reason not to bombard it with artillery fire and make the station unusable. Thanks to a tour guide I stood in the exact position of that German machinegun post. Amongst the wild bushes and long grass I held out my arms to represent the arc of fire where Cyril and his platoon fell only 50-metres ahead. An impression of peace and tranquillity filled that moment as birds sang high above on that clear April afternoon in 2002. On 18th August 1916 bombs and bullets, not to mention sweat, screams, blood and fear would have been Cyril's last impression. He was only 22-years old.

Eventually the station was taken, but at a huge cost. The largest British Memorial where 75,000 plaques cover every column, one of which is my Great Uncle Cyril, stands proud near Theipval, emphasising the incredible loss of British soldiers at just one of many battles during the First World War. Each plaque represents those cut to pieces or blown up, where only parts of their bodies could be identified. The rest of their bits were left in blood soaked putrid mud, either tangled around body parts belonging to someone else or simply destroyed beyond recognition.

When guns fell silent on the eleventh hour, 11th November 1918 millions of young men on both sides of the trenches didn't cheer. They stood in amazement to an unbelievable and almost forgotten sound of silence, broken only by bird song previously unheard throughout the entire war. 9,000,000 soldiers died on those battlefields, 6,000,000 were missing, presumed dead, and a further 23,000,000 were wounded. Including civilians, an unbelievable casualty loss was a staggering 40,000,000 – almost the entire population of the UK in 1914. Marching to war they were certainly young. The average age was only 19-years old. Those lucky enough to survive definitely returned home as men.

The huge sacrifice of so many created a huge labour shortage across Europe, let alone the UK. Unbelievably businesses presumed it would be a breeze employing veterans eager to return to some sort of normality. But no, far from it. Many soldiers witnessed and experienced terrible horrors never seen before. Some wounded in battle found themselves back at the front line once recovered from wounds, only to face yet more muck and bullets. Not to mention witness once again friends blown up in front of their eyes and having to hear constant screaming from soldiers cut to pieces by machineguns in no-man's land.

Such atrocities left many with terrible flashbacks that lasted a lifetime, suffering with, what was known as, shellshock – since labelled PTSD (Post Traumatic Stress Disorder). During the battle of the Somme, not a few hundred, or a few thousand, but tens of thousands were listed as shellshock victims. When the war ended there were over 250,000 men – one-in-twenty – that returned home with PTSD. And it is believed the actual figures are much, much higher. Everyone mobilised knew someone with similar symptoms.

Incredibly 306 soldiers were shot by firing squad for supposedly deserting or found guilty of associated cowardice. However, this wasn't the case. If an understanding of PTSD were around in 1914 their lives would have been spared and offered treatment instead. But government recognition of shellshock was ignorantly and arrogantly ignored, to the point of actually banning any description of the alleged condition ever being mentioned verbally or in print. And generals believed it was nothing more than a soldier displaying weakness.

Now home, totally disoriented, aimlessly wandering in all directions and prone to sudden outbursts of violent tempers, thousands turned to crime, either due to PTSD or simply because they found it impossible returning to civvy street, yet needed money to survive. But what they all had in common was the refusal to work under the same terrible conditions they endured before the war. They had suffered enough, and were no longer going to accept employer exploitation. When the First World War started, any employment rights under negotiation were postponed or even totally forgotten about whilst the country concentrated on winning the war. But grievances were not forgotten, so the pursuance of better conditions prevailed in Ernst.

Employers wanting to put the war behind them and pick up from where they left off, or start a fresh with new industrial and engineering innovations, could no longer get away with mistreating employees as they once did during the Victorian or early Edwardian era. Veterans returning to civilian jobs did so with demands: higher wages, better conditions, even pensions, to name but a few. In other words, they were no longer afraid of anything – especially employers. Trade unions became popular once again, and grew extremely fast, to the extent of persuading the odd factory owner surrendering to union demands.

This incredibly important generation picked up the batten from a courageous mini revolution their forefathers endured to succeed, and with a little determination gained considerable momentum by the beginning of the 20th Century. These new revolutionists determined to accomplish what their forefathers started later became known as The Lost Generation 1883 to 1900. The term Lost, popularised by Ernest Hemingway, reflected those returning home disillusioned with society and unable to settle down. This amazing generation is also known as Generation of 1914 due to the fact they were of age to join the army. In France they are known as Génération au Feu – the Generation of Flames. Says it all, really.

To experience a war that ripped apart an entire continent politically, financially, physically and emotionally, any optimism left behind from the latter Victorian era was now dead and buried. The extent of casualties left nations dangerously close to never recovering. In the UK so many died it left only an estimated amount of marriageable aged women coined as the surplus two million. Nationalism became a dirty word; disgusted by how it was perceived as the reason behind the Great War and the unconscious waste of life it split. Governments across Europe never wanted a return to the atrocities they'd experienced so a more favourable pacifist approach ensued the world encouraged by the creation of the infamous League of Nations.

Millions across the world believed the war to end all wars ended Capitalism and Imperialism, highlighted by the revolution in Russia October 1917. Socialism became the flavour of the masses, in particularly Russia,

France and Central Europe, wishing to put an end to corruption and any threat of future wars. Socialist movements across the UK and Europe spread like wildfire, and with it an increasing popular belief that together we can live in perfect harmony.

Generals and other officers returning home from the trenches knew there would be some kind of backlash within industrial relations. The Revolutionist seed first sewn by the late Victorians had finally sprouted, where, for the first time, upper class society felt their lifestyle was threatened by the lower classes. What followed was unprecedented for the UK: countless industrial strike after strike after strike, and much worse than the disputes before the war. Veterans returning home from the trenches were under the impression that if grouped together, as they were now used to, their demands would be granted. In most cases, however, that wasn't to be.

By 1919 a social unrest spread throughout towns and cities once again, due to an unseen turnaround of cheap employment to counter-act the disputes. This cheap labour suddenly swamped the country in the guise of immigrants. Sound familiar? Only these immigrants travelled from all four corners of the vast British Empire that fought alongside British soldiers to protect the freedom of their mother country. Riots spilled into the streets protesting against colonial economic immigrants taking their jobs in ports at London, Liverpool, Southampton, and many others around the country, agreeing to wages considerably lower than their British counterpart.

During this uneasy time even the police went on strike against a Police Act that banned all officers from joining a trade union, in particularly the newly formed National Union of Police and Prison Officers. Whilst all this malarkey was going on the UK and mainland Europe, still suffering with open sores from the war, carried yet another catastrophe – the influenza pandemic.

It was believed to have started in Spain, hence the name given at the time – Spanish flu. But further investigation indicates it actually started in France near Etaples during the last year of the war, where a huge military hospital tendered to thousands of sick, wounded and dying soldiers in one small area. Sanitary discipline was extremely poor due to lack of medicines, technology and the incredible numbers of patients, so disease was inevitable and spread quickly throughout the camp in one form or another. One particular disease took prominence – the flu virus.

British, French, Belgian, German, even American and Canadian soldiers became infected. And although not realising at the time, many took this incredibly infectious virus home with them to spread across their own country. It killed more than the entire casualties of the war, and world wide it is estimated to have wiped out an astonishing 50,000,000 people.

Despite the war and flu pandemic, between 1918 and 1920 the UK economy steadily recovered, regardless of the many industrial disputes around the country. Employment prospects were slowly getting better, providing a wage cut was accepted, but money was there to be earned. By the end of 1920 predictions of a boom was quashed by a sudden slump in the economy with unemployment growing sharply to almost 10 percent of the working age population; continuing through the decade and into the late 1930's. The land fit for heroes turned out to be a land fit only for desperation.

Funding the Great War finally caught up with the UK economy from being the world's largest overseas investor to one of the world's largest debtors. Not only troops took a pounding. Material loss took a hit with almost half of all merchant shipping sunk by German U-boats. Meanwhile, the working class, although slightly better off than the early Edwardian era, became a new generation of have and the have not. Hundreds of thousands of veterans continued to wonder aimlessly in a world of their own, still confused over what happened and questioning why their country deserted them. And Women also felt their social position was ignored, until this lot came along.

In 1903 Emmeline Pankhurst, and with a few friends, didn't think women's rights had gone far enough. Continuously ignored, even laughed at, the only way women could grab attention was with a more hard approach. Peaceful means were definitely non-productive. With that in mind Emmeline created the Women's Social and Political Union (WSPU) using a strong and direct motto 'Deeds not words'. Sort of straight to the point. But it was short-lived, ending its movement by 1918.

During those 15-years the suffragettes certainly sent a few ripples through society, government and even royal circles. Causing disruption was one of their main tactics, which in itself created huge publicity and popularity amongst women spreading the word. In 1908 a group of suffragettes attempted to storm the Houses of Parliament, where 60,000 people gathered to watch or even join in the protest for their right to vote. The government remained steadfast, so protests became increasingly radical, which included damaging property, violence and vandalism, resulting in imprisonment for a few of the hardcore. But protests didn't end there. Whilst serving sentence women would go on hunger strike, determined to send a message to parliament that they were serious about their right to vote.

Emily Davison, an outrageously serious activist, was arrested 10 times, serving 2 short sentences in 1909: one for attempting to enter a room where the Chancellor of the Exchequer was delivering a speech, the other for hurling rocks in a public place that may cause damage or injury. Whilst in prison Emily went on hunger strike, so her sentence was cut short with hope not to cause a flap with an ever-increasing sympathetic public.

Upon release Emily soon found herself banged up yet again for throwing stones at the chauffeur driven Chancellor of the Exchequer. Whilst serving her third sentence in Strangeways prison Emily protested with another hunger strike – 7 times in total – but this time her sentence wasn't cut short. Instead she was brutally force-fed on 49 occasions. But Emily wasn't about to give up and barricaded herself in her cell. In response she was subjected to a hose down with cold water, almost drowning during the ordeal. Emily took her case of brutality to court and, remarkably, rewarded 40 shillings compensation.

Emily's time in prison certainly didn't dampen her struggle for women's rights. If anything it was exacerbated. Undeterred, she was about to execute an incredible protest witnessed by thousands, including King George V and Queen Mary, at the 1913 Epsom Derby. The King's horse, Anmer, was running in the race, and it was his horse Emily targeted, easily recognised by the jersey of the jockey wearing the King's colours.

The horses raced around the track as Emily jostled into position by forcing her way through spectators towards the barrier. As the horses thundered towards her she saw the King's horse fast approaching and stood in front of it brandishing a suffragette flag. But it was too late for the jockey to avoid Emily, hitting her at full gallop, throwing the jockey into the air whilst the horse ploughed straight through Emily. Remarkably the jockey survived with a few broken ribs. Emily was taken to hospital but died a few days later of her injuries.

The protest didn't really go to plan. The overall effect of the tragedy was interpreted to have been carried out by someone with a mentally unstable nature. Supporters of the suffragettes renounced the movement's cause, only to be more concerned about the horse. Print media, although reporting the incident, directed a somewhat larger interest with what was happening in Europe, so the entire event became nothing more than tomorrow's chip wrapping paper.

When the inevitable war started, 6,000,000 men marched to France, leaving 2,000,000 women to take over their civilian jobs, including farming, mining, milling, and working in foundries. Traditionally, employers regarded women less worthy than men. And although carrying out the same duties, if not better in many cases, were paid less than their male counterpart. Towards the end of the war, however, employers realised women could carry out similar tasks as good as men, and were respected for their industrial output, changing all perceptions of the role women play in British society today.

Reflecting the importance of women's huge contribution to the war effort, and popularity growth of the women's movement supported by a handful of MP's, the Representation of the People Act was passed: allowing women over the age of 30-years of age to vote – providing they met a property qualification, of course. It also allowed all civilian men over the age of 21-years and all men serving their country could now vote from the age of 19-years.

Arriving into the roaring twenties with women finally getting the vote and the poor in general were still fighting for better working conditions, for the upper classes it was nothing but a huge party. Seemingly still celebrating the end of the war, whilst the new lower upper class continued to expand their segregation from the poorer working class, new leisure inventions hit the shelves of fashionable stores and shops such as electrical gramophone record players and wireless sets.

New dance steps accompanied new fashions, especially for women. Faster music styles equally favoured new dance routines such as the Charleston and the Shimmy. Jazz clubs infiltrated British society on all levels where dance halls became a huge attraction to young men and women. Upper class women started to play golf, as well as roller-skate and cycling, which became extremely popular for all classes. And women even had their own special cycling skirt so not to flash any under-garments – heaven forbid.

Long brown hair was considered to be the style for early 1920's women, only to change to short hair by the mid 1920's. Even nipple piercing grew popular. Photography became increasingly popular too, as the humble box camera evolved into something a little more compact and easier for the novice to use. And home-movie cameras were great fun filming the family outings – providing you could afford one. Wireless sets were sold in there millions by the 1930's but only affordable to the middle and upper class societies.

Across the pond Hollywood spread its tinsel town wings and flew to Blighty, instantly producing vast profits from a new leisure pass-time – going to the cinema, or the 'pictures' as it was termed – and still is today. For a few pennies the working class could escape stressful, dull and tedious lives for an hour or two and watch their favourite stars on the big silver screen, although no soundtrack as yet. An organ player at the front of the cinema played music in accordance with the silent films genre and scenes. To grab some understanding of what was happening subtitled breaks in the film popped up from time to time to explain situations and give character dialog. Movies with sound – or talkies – weren't introduced until the early 1930's.

Actors from silent films became huge international stars, including Charlie Chaplain. A master in his art of suggestive behaviour, he became a genius at acting comical scenes. Without the need of screen break dialog he could simply explain any situation with clever mannerisms and certain facial expressions. His audience laughed until it hurt, as fans do today. Other silent film actors, such as Harold Lloyd and Buster Keaton also attracted huge audiences.

When talking movies arrived they also attracted large audiences, as well as glamour and fashion. Women desired the same clothes, make-up and hairstyles as leading lady actors, such as Greta Garbo. And thanks to Clark Gable the pencil-thin moustache became the choice of facial hair design for men.

With film came a huge market to exploit. And with power of the wireless and a sudden expansion of magazines, fashion could now exploit airwaves as well as the print media. Large billboards started to appear with huge advertisements for the latest fashionable clothing, accessories, shoes and make-up. Even lower class men started to gain an interest in their appearance, with Clark Gable haircuts and moustaches, new suits and shiny shoes instead of flat caps and hobnailed boots.

But throughout the 1920's and into the early 1930's social division remained noticeable, particularly within large industrial towns and cities. And with the sudden economical downturn, ship builders, steel and coal, predominately from the north of England, Scotland and

Wales, was hit the hardest. Overall output had fallen by an incredible 25 percent since 1918 where flip side of the coin showed middle England wasn't hit so hard; relying more so on services, imports and retail, generating a growing economy within a dwindling national economy.

The downturn hit crises point when Chancellor of the Exchequer, Winston Churchill, restored the Pound Sterling to the Gold Standard in 1925, immediately increasing a surge in interest rates and creating a much stronger currency against others including the American Dollar at $4.86 to the Pound. Heavy industrial exports became more expensive, including coal, steel and ship building.

Tens of thousands of workers had to endure wage cuts once again in an attempt to off-set the strong pound, much to the contempt of union members. Up until the mid 1920,s unemployment remained a steady 1,000,000 but the latest industrial unrest created a huge surge in job losses, where a total unemployed reached 3,000,000. And unemployment benefit was, at best, incredibly small to non-existent.

Although the 1920 Unemployment Insurance Act extended benefit for all workers that earned a maximum annual income of £250 the Act introduced a Seeking Work Test the following year. A test where each claimant had to prove they were seeking work – not unlike today. A difficult task considering work was non-existent in many industrialised areas, making millions of families impoverished. And with the government tax revenue decreasing by the day there was no money left in the pot to help. At the height of the now depression demand for British made products fell by half.

Rubbing salt into many working class wounds 1926 brought with it coal mines locking out over 1,000,000 miners due to a dispute over reparations in the form of free German coal depressing local industry. Further strikes ensued, with other unions persuading its members to go on strike in solidarity of the miners. Dock workers, gas, steel and power station workers, tradesmen, railway workers and many others, all hit hard by the strong pound, downed tools and kick-started the General Strike, initiated by the TUC. By the end of the first day an amazing 2,000,000 workers were out on picket lines.

Situation of the economy was heading towards disaster; something had to be done to turn around the strike and get the masses back to work, having a worse effect than the unrest between 1908 to 1914. Talks took place between union leaders, company bosses and business owners whilst the strike continued to cause havoc. The printing industry unions called members to walk out, and the commercial haulage industry created a massive food shortage by preventing deliveries. Further riots and fights between police and strikers made the miners strike of 1984/85 look like a picnic.

The government appealed for calm over the radio, but fell on deaf ears. The army had to be called out to quell civil unrest, restore order and protect drivers that would work to drive buses and trains delivering much needed food and goods to shops. Nine long days later the TUC called off the strike after secret talks with coal mine owners, leaving meetings without any gain. In fact miners returned to work having to endure longer shifts with less pay.

The government embarrassed by how the General Strike occurred, immediately held a debate in the House of Commons. Within only one year parliament passed the Trades Disputes Act banning mass solidarity strikes and picketing. Workers hadn't gained anything, and remarkably subjected to the same conditions suffered before the war.

Chapter Seven

OMG! Like so depressed right now

Arrival of the 1930's brought with it a mixture of societies with very different social attitude from the Interbellum, Greatest and Silent generations that followed. The Interbellum Generation (1901 to 1913) gave birth to those that were too young at the time to fight in the First World War. Their understanding of what it was like, by definition, differed from those that actually fought. However, they understood the belief of good morals, discipline, family values, hard work, growing and working through difficult times with the previous Lost Generation. Much can be said for The Greatest Generation (1910 to 1924) and The Silent Generation (1925 to 1945).

Between the wars lasted only 21-years before nations across the world disagreed once again. The Greatest Generation are so called for reaching call-up age when the Second World War started September 3rd 1939. To be fair, many from previous generations also fought, as did those from the Silent Generation old enough to join up towards the end of the war. Overall, thirty nations fought in the First World War, and there was about to be another, involving all but 2 of the 7 continents (no bugger lived there - Arctic and Antarctic) and on a considerably larger scale.

Whilst the UK was suffering from hastily drawn government reforms and industrial action, across the pond was having huge problems, even though America, on the whole, was doing quite well before the Second

World War. Factories were buzzing, order books full and employment was plentiful. But leading up to the roaring twenties proved to be a difficult path to walk. The decade of 1920's started with a nation divided by economic and political differences. Again, not much different to today.

Men returning home from the Great War did so with a similar disposition as the Brits: having no fear, demanding better conditions in the workplace, and so on. Businesses, just like in the UK, disagreed, so in 1919 industrial disputes swamped a nation for higher wages and better working conditions. More and more union members walked out of factories in solidarity – a naughty word in the US; perceived to be nothing more than Bolshevik anarchists.

The population became angered by shortages because of disputes but frightened of the strikers aggressive attitude, thought as venting frustration after fighting in the Great War. But the severe shortage of food and other essential products turned those in support of the strikes into a mass scorn. It wasn't until 1921 did the strikes end, inevitably with fruitless achievement of any reward.

To make matters worse a law was about to pass through Congress that would add the final ingredient to divide a country not seen since the Civil war – the Volstead Act: 18th Amendment that prohibited the sale, manufacture and distribution of intoxicating liquor. Even possession of anything that can produce or designed to manufacture alcohol was now illegal, resulting in fines and even a custodial sentence if caught.

Although passed in October 1919 it didn't go into effect until January 1920. But do you think anyone took notice of this odd law? The Temperance movement certainly did; they were proud of their achievements. As they saw it, the country would be cured of all crimes such as murder, social unrest and debauchery. They also believed that drunks would become better husbands and the economy would benefit by ending thousands of lost working hours due to alcohol related illnesses.

There were, however, a few fundamental loopholes in the Amendment: it failed to mention that drinking alcohol was no longer allowed. People knew this and took favourable notice. In doing so purchased stacks, cases and crates of all kinds of booze – initially panic buying – to store in any receptacle available before stocks ran out. And because of this loophole a sinister group of entrepreneurs appeared from the shadows: a bunch of dodgy characters that exploited the ban and flouted the law to obtain alcohol – gangsters.

Due to an incredible high demand gangsters exploited the need for a glass of a favourite tipple by smuggling alcoholic beverages from Canada and the Caribbean or brewed their own concoctions in hidden locations. Secret bars started to open to selected members-only establishments disguised as clubs where members could socialise and, of course, drink. Huge profits were made from over-priced liquor, but the demand remained high.

To try and counter-act the illegal consumption government officials employed agents to raid bars, dens and drinking pits to dismantle manufacturing establishments. But bribes taken by agents was rife due to poor salaries, so turning a blind eye became profitable for the agent and gangsters alike, allowing them to continue their unlawful trade. Another loophole was a tad more legal and an embarrassment to the Temperance movement, quickly exploited by the masses: become sick and in need of a doctor.

An oversight in the Act naively allowed alcohol consumption if prescribed by a senior medical practitioner. This particular loophole was a massive blow to the Temperance movement and tried to get the Amendment updated. But their efforts were futile, quashed by leading medical surgeons and doctors partial to the odd glass of wine, emphasising the use of alcohol in medical practice. The Temperance movement was never popular and started to lose grip with society.

The anti-prohibition movement gained strength right from the start of the Act, growing larger as the decade headed towards the 1930's. But with prohibition coming to an end the Stock Market Crash in 1929 kick-started the Great Depression. The government was desperate to create more jobs and bring an end to it. Making alcohol legal again would create a huge amount of work, thus jobs, and also raise much needed tax revenue, was one recommendation. By 1933 the government was in a corner and under huge pressure from campaigners and more importantly, voters.

On 5th December the 21st Amendment was passed, repealing the 18th Amendment and made the sale, manufacture and distribution of alcohol legal once again. This fundamental political decision was the first time an Amendment was repealed in American history. But as one door opens another one shuts – as my old boss used to say. And in this case he was right. Alcohol may now be legal once again, and came about due to a gigantic market crash, but there is a whiff of irony. After all, what will many do when depressed?

A modern equivalent to the depression would be termed as an economic downturn. But what the world suffered in 2008 supposedly ending by 2018 was nothing compared to what happened in the 1930's. Nevertheless, similar to recent downturns, the symptoms that created it were uncanny: cocky stock brokers and over-confident bankers. But there was also another major ingredient that caused the crash and that was a drought that decimated Southern States – breadbasket of the USA.

Overgrazing and dry hot winds lifted seeds from poor soil that baked in the sun. Dust storms destroyed everything, creating the infamous Dust Bowl. Farmers found themselves in a catch-twenty-two situation: they needed loans from the bank for seeds and machinery to grow crops, only to repay loans when crops were harvested and sold to market. But the drought meant crops weren't growing and loans remained unpaid. So banks foreclosed on small farms, leaving the farmer and his family penniless and homeless.

Now unemployed many travelled west in search for work. Some managed to find agricultural work, albeit temporary or seasonal, only to be despised by locals. The sudden influx of farmers offering their labour were thought of as being nothing more than cheap immigrants, even though they were from the same country. During prohibition, on the whole, the USA was enjoying a time of relative prosperity, according to the upper class. But their ignorance was about to take an enormous blow.

When the stock market discovered cracks in the boom, by late 1929 it was too late. Shares plummeted to a hopeless level of ever recovering, and became incredibly cheap to buy, but no one had any money to buy them. The stock market created a way to make an absurd amount of money, and many did. But the stock market also has no morals or conscience, and with the enormous losses came a huge cost with redundancies and bankruptcy.

For common folk the crash soon entered their lives with hard-hitting consequences. Banks that invested customer's hard earned money lost the lot, forcing sudden closure of all accounts. And the few remaining banks still open, customers withdrew all of their money, causing further problems for the economy and commerce. Shops and retail outlets found themselves without shoppers as people stopped buying. The downturn in consumer confidence had a ripple effect upon shop workers, where employees had to take wage cuts to keep their jobs or face redundancy. Many shops even closed without paying any owed wages or severance pay at all.

Businesses could no longer arrange loans, withdraw their own money or lost huge amounts on the stock market. Companies were forced to close due to cash-flow issues and industry came to an almost grinding halt. Redundancies spread like wildfire, with no compensation packages and empty pension pots. Unemployment across the nation grew at an alarming rate, reaching a staggering quarter of the nation's workforce.

Millions of people joined countless farm labourers searching for work across the vast country with hope of making a new and better life. Most travelled by foot or jumped onto railway cattle wagons heading to other towns and cities. On the rare occasion finding a vacancy thousands applied. By 1932 an unbelievable three-quarters of the population were now living in poverty, and unemployment grew to one-third of the working age population.

Faced with these incredible figures, remarkably the upper classes remained arrogantly unsympathetic; ignoring the fact that they were part of the reason as to why there was so much poverty in the first place. Upper classes even opposed the government stepping in to feed the millions of starving families and the homeless. Industrialists renounced unions and refused negotiations of any kind. In fact, those remaining in business exploited the depression by cutting wages further still, but at their peril. What followed was a national protest brought onto the streets of America.

The upper classes, hell-bent on protecting income and wealth from slipping through their fingers, used powers of persuasion within political circles to respond with, as they saw it, justified violence. Police were ordered to bring order – by all means necessary. And whilst a hunger protest marched in the streets of Detroit, police opened fire upon thousands of protesters, where 4 demonstrators were killed and many injured.

Shantytowns appeared around towns and cities known as Hoovervilles – named after the President, Herbert Hoover – made out of anything at hand: discarded wood, cardboard, bits of tin sheeting, even newspapers. Cars no longer affordable to maintain were converted to be pulled by horses – nick-named Hoover wagons – and newspapers became known as Hoover blankets. Walking around with trouser pockets pulled inside out became known as a Hoover flag – a protest of poverty and an insult to the President.

In 1932 a General election was held, where Herbert Hoover was beaten with a huge majority by Franklin D. Roosevelt. New optimism emerged from the election with a nation's trust that Roosevelt could deliver a solution to the depression. First, he declared that all banks must close, only to open once they stabilised. He then created the New Deal where programs were set up to help the economy and put people back into work.

The National Recovery Act was passed in 1933 where workers had the right to organise unions, but unwelcomed by nervous employers. Without hesitation workers queued to join their appropriate union, much to the annoyance of employers, where inevitable violence ensued. It would be a further 8-years before the Great Depression actually ended, and that was due to Japan attacking Pearl Harbour in Hawaii, drawing the USA out of the world's largest depression into the world's largest War.

The incredible growth of industry that quickly followed resulted in almost full employment across the country. Farmers were subsidised to produce plenty of grain and meat for the war effort, whilst factories churned out armaments such as shells, tanks and aeroplanes. Millions of men were drafted into the armed forces – earning more than their British counterpart – and women, like those in the UK during the First and Second World War, worked on the land and in factories.

The USA, although in a war, was relatively untouched by air raids or threat of invasion – unlike the UK. So production of the war machine could carry on 24/7 unhindered. And during the war years the economy grew stronger, as did wages. But what did all this carry-on in the US have to do with the UK and the rest of the world, I hear you ask? Well, as the old saying goes: when America sneezes the rest of the world catches a cold. A saying still relevant in the 21st Century let alone the 1930's. And the UK caught one hell of a cold.

The economy remained virtually unchanged during the 1920's and even showed signs of becoming a boom era in Blighty. Unlike America relying on credit to sustain the economy – hence the Great Depression – the UK had already suffered a long economic stagnation but didn't rely on credit, only trade. Nonetheless, due to the Great Depression, global trade fell by almost half, and industrial output in the UK fell by a third, causing the economy to take a rapid nosedive in the early 1930's.

Europe was also struggling after the First World War, in particularly Germany. It was basically skint; unable to repay its outrageous bill to the allies and suffering a catastrophic depression. Maybe not the world's largest, but certainly the world's worst. German banks inevitably failed, ironically having a damaging effect upon the UK. The Sterling currency was overvalued and became under pressure to keep Stirling's value in the gold standard, creating further ripples at the London Exchange.

The economy couldn't take any more blows from a threatened pound. Interest rates were already at 8 percent and the Bank of England didn't want to increase it in fear of steering the economy into deeper waters. By leaving the gold standard devalued the strong Stirling, where past government budgets failed, but offered relief cutting interest rates. Nevertheless, the Chancellor of the Exchequer, Lord Snowden, continued to make further cuts to unemployment benefits and public sector wages.

On the global stage, devaluing a strong pound against the US dollar helped with trade exports the UK relied upon. By 1935 industry made a slow recovery, eventually reducing unemployment and stimulated growth in house building and a re-armament initiative, giving a much needed boost to the economy. Within a few years the re-armament initiative became a greater concern as Europe, inevitably, headed to all-out war.

Meanwhile, in 1922 Liberal Prime Minister, David Lloyd George, had no alternative but resign, creating an era of uncertainty for the British political elite. The Conservative Party grew concerned of the increasing popularity of the Labour Party, in particular the far left and its political persuasion controlling the government during uncertain years between 1922 to 1924. By 1925 however, the Conservative Party was back in control, quashing any Marxist revolution slowly climbing towards leading the government.

Within a few years workers had their say by means of the ballot box once again, and the Conservatives lost the 1929 General election – just – resulting in a hung parliament with a Labour Party coalition. Celebrations by the working classes, however, were short-lived. By the time New Year festivities became a memory, short days and long cold nights reflected the state of the British economy. The governing coalition disagreed with each other on how to react to an impending economic slump, and the nation was also divided.

Labour wanted radical change by spending huge amounts of tax payers money on reform yet cut public expenditure to pay for it, whilst the Conservatives advocated restraint. And as the political parties battled it out in the chamber, rest of the country carried on regardless, living in hope that the government will eventually find a solution to the economic crises. But no, nothing. Unemployment, once again, grew at an alarming rate; heading towards a staggering 3,500,000 where many of those working were part time as full time work was incredibly scares.

Popularity for the coalition collapsed and it wasn't long before no confidence spread across the nation. Large industrial businesses, including ship builders and coal mines in northern counties, suffered the hardest with closure after closure, making almost three-quarters of the working population finding themselves unemployed, creating further poverty and deprivation. The masses had had enough; the Labour Party failed and the nation cried out for another General election, resulting with a new National Government controlled by the Conservatives with a majority vote.

Remarkably, lessons were learnt from the past, ending austerity, replaced with investment. Within a few years the economy excelled and actually produced a surplus of £3 million in old money. Although starting a little shaky the remaining few years of the decade embraced a new prosperous era in commerce, industry and new initiatives securing a bright future. The car industry created new and exciting models, house building and construction enjoyed a boom, and employment was good.

The UK had ridden the storm and come out the other end smelling of roses. However, whilst the US and UK enjoyed the fruits of their labour and a well-deserved life, the economy in Germany was a very different story. Poverty was at critical point with starvation and disease running wild throughout towns and cities. Hundreds of thousands remained displaced and homeless due to a country unable to recover from austerity caused by allied reparations and a huge war bill to pay.

At the Paris Peace Conference Germany officially surrendered to Britain, France and Italy on 28th June 1919 where Germany was forced to admit all responsibilities for starting the war by signing the Treaty of Versailles. Germany also had to agree to pay for the war by handing over £6.5 billion in old money (132 billion German gold Marks), creating a huge print of money. Inevitably inflation soared to the point of becoming one-trillionth of its original value. Economic reparations on coal and iron reserves were stripping Germany's resources bare, and its army was reduced to next to nothing. Germany even had to surrender its entire naval fleet, including submarines, to the British.

The Treaty also enforced Germany from producing any military hardware such as ships, tanks, armoured vehicles, artillery even aeroplanes. Although gliders and rocket development was strangely allowed. German territories were carved up and occupied by Belgium, Denmark, France, Czechoslovakia and Poland. Separation from East Prussia was a major blow, and the British occupied Germany's overseas territories.

Whilst Germany, with its resources and territories stripped and redistributed to various allied countries, a young Austrian became very annoyed about the whole affair. He noticed a prosperous UK and an increase in development for the rest of Europe, but Germany was forced to live in abject poverty. He didn't agree with this one bit, so decided to do something about it. His name was Adolf Hitler. Here's a little more about him.

Dropping out of school in 1905 he moved to Vienna 2-years later after his mother died, finding work as a casual labourer to fund his passion of painting. He applied to join the Academy of Fine Arts, but was rejected – twice. With no hope of getting into the academy and no job he was desperate for money, to the point of – how can I put this – rent himself to obliging gentlemen of that particular nature. At one meeting he was arrested for committing a lude act. Thrown out of jail and onto the streets he was forced to sleep in homeless shelters, where he nurtured his hatred of Jews, blaming their belief on his and Germany's downfall.

Early summer of 1914 saw the assassination of Franz Ferdinand, the Archduke of Austria-Hungary, on 28th June, where Austria-Hungary immediately declared war on Serbia. Within a couple of months Germany, sympathiser to Austrian-Hungary, declared war on France for declaring war on Austria-Hungary declaring war on Serbia. Believe me, it got incredibly more complicated. Hitler saw this fracas as the perfect opportunity to end his destitution by joining the German army, although technically still an Austrian citizen.

Finding himself in the trenches he fought in many battles; later wounded during the Battle of the Somme. At one point he fell injured in a mud-sodden shell crater as a British soldier charged towards him, bayonet fixed to finish him off, but stopped in his tracks as a young Adolf

Hitler screamed in pain, begging the young Tommy to spare his life. Being a compassionate British soldier, as of course he would have been, unlike the vile hun, saw pity and carried on past with his advancement. Hitler was later rescued by German soldiers and recovered from his wounds, only to receive the Iron Cross and the Black Wound Badge for bravery.

After Germany lost the war Hitler felt betrayed by the German government and bitter towards its surrender to the allies. He refused to believe Germany should be held accountable for starting the war and despised the signing of the Treaty of Versailles, claiming it was degrading for those that fought for the Fatherland.

For a while Hitler remained in the military employed within intelligence to keep an eye on the ever-increasing popularity of the German Workers Party and their activities, disliked by a liberal thinking government. But rather than believing they were a threat to national security, he in fact admired their nationalistic views, including anti-Marxist and anti-Semitic attitude. Whilst fuming over Germany's surrender, Hitler resigned from intelligence, only to join the German Workers Party (DAP) where the movement later changed its identity as the Nationalsozialistische Deutsche Arbeiterpartei (NSDAP) – abbreviated to the Nazi Party.

Hitler's rise through party ranks reflected his mesmerising speeches in halls around the country. He called upon locals to rise up against, how he saw it, a soft government allowing socialism to take over the country and Jews keeping hold of German wealth whilst millions starved. Gaining immense popular support his confidence, along with his ego grew.

During a speech by the Bavarian Prime Minister in one of Munich's many beer halls, Hitler, along with a small number of his loyal followers, stormed in, cast aside the Prime Minister and declared that the national revolution had begun, led by a new government – the Nazi Party. A scuffle broke out resulting in terrible injuries, including deaths. Hitler was immediately arrested, found guilty of High Treason and sentenced to 9-months imprisonment. Yes, only 9-months for High Treason.

Prison made Hitler determined to climb the political ladder and become Chancellor – leader of Germany. During his incarceration he plotted a fiendish plan to rise to the top, and even wrote a dreadful book titled Mein Kampf: autobiography about his political ideology and how he would govern the Fatherland. Nothing could stop him, and was prepared to kill anyone that got in his way. Loyal activists – the Brown Shirts – spread fear and violence wherever they went, causing havoc throughout an otherwise peaceful society, turning law-abiding liberal citizens to hate Communists, homosexuals and Jews.

Germany was desperate for change. The masses would accept anything on offer to pull them out of the worst economic crises in history and restore order. Hitler promised this, but first had to dispose of the remaining old hierarchy by scare-mongering with threats of death. His tactics worked, and quickly found his way to the top, demanding a General election immediately, only to win by a landslide. Hitler's notorious aggressive plan to cleanse Germany of its enemies could now begin unhindered.

The rise of Hitler's government and threat of placing Europe into another war did not go unnoticed, but not an awful lot was done to prevent an illegal increase of his armed forces, re-assemble armament factories or an airforce. By the time Britain and France woke up to what was happening it was too late. In 1937 Prime Minister Stanley Baldwin resigned after failing to recognise the threat, leaving Neville Chamberlain to run the country. Chamberlain flew to Berlin in an attempt to appease Hitler from any aggression towards France and the rest of Europe, even though he had already invaded Czechoslovakia, reclaiming, as he believed, German territory.

When Chamberlain returned to the UK waving his piece of paper claiming he made an agreement with Heir Hitler to behave himself, Hitler invaded Poland. Consequently, Britain declared war on Germany – again – 3rd September 1939 after Hitler refused to withdraw his troops. What followed was the darkest 6-years human kind has ever experienced. Incredibly, worse than the First World War.

Chapter Eight

Pack up your old kit bag

From the declaration of war to May 1940 all at home seemed peaceful, dubbed the phoney or false war. But on the soil of mainland Europe French, Belgian and the BEF (British Expeditionary Force) fought against a determined foe as it took country after country using a new kind of terror tactic: Blitzkrieg – lightening war. By co-ordinating a massive force of air power, artillery, tanks and infantry never seen before, the whole of Western Europe was under Nazi rule within 9-months.

Shores of southern England was next on Hitler's shopping list, but the English Channel, radar, Royal Navy and the Royal Air Force were a huge obstacle to overcome before absolute control of Europe could be achieved. The BEF however, were in a critical situation, where German troops had squeezed British and French soldiers into a small area around the port of Dunkirk. Now in a desperate position it was only a matter of time before most, if not all allied soldiers, were either captured or, as many were, executed on the spot.

Operation Dynamo was hastily thrown together to bring as many soldiers as possible back to jolly old England. The RAF offered what they could to protect troops and deny the Luftwaffe air supremacy that would have otherwise wrecked the operation, but only a few fighters were available due to other commitments. Not only the Royal Navy, but also hundreds of civilian vessels sailed towards the dangerous French coast to rescue stranded soldiers. Returning again and again, the little ships, as they became known, ignored constant shelling, machinegun fire and the Luftwaffe closing in fast.

Under tremendous odds it was thought that around 40,000 troops could be saved. It was actually 338,000 British, French and Belgian soldiers rescued. Prime Minister, Winston Churchill, gave a speech aired to a bewildered country to praise the operation, Her Majesty's Armed Forces and a resilient civilian population:

I have, myself, full confidence that if all do their duty, if nothing is neglected, and if the best arrangements are made, as they are being made, we shall prove ourselves once again able to defend our Island home, to ride out the storm of war, and to outlive the menace of tyranny, if necessary for years, if necessary alone. At any rate, that is what we are going to try to do. That is the resolve of His Majesty's Government-every man of them. That is the will of Parliament and the nation. The British Empire and the French Republic, linked together in their cause and in their need, will defend to the death their native soil, aiding each other like good comrades to the utmost of their strength. Even though large tracts of Europe and many old and famous States have fallen or may fall into the grip of the Gestapo and all the odious apparatus of Nazi rule, we shall not flag or fail. We shall go on to the end, we shall fight in France, we shall fight on the seas and oceans, we shall fight with growing confidence and growing strength in the air, we shall defend our Island, whatever the cost may be, we shall fight on the beaches, we shall fight on the landing grounds, we shall fight in the fields and in the streets, we shall fight in the hills; we shall never surrender, and even if, which I do not for a moment believe, this Island or a large part of it were subjugated and starving, then our Empire beyond the

Unbelievably, and knowing what the country faced if lost
to Nazi Germany, 8,000 anti-war activists marched to the
Houses of Parliament and protested against Britain
entering the war, even though the UK faced total
annihilation from an evil regime. Communist movements
were amongst the demonstrators demanding an end to the
involvement, but strangely withdrew their comments
when Germany invaded the Soviet Union 3-years later.

The British Union of Fascists, led by Oswald
Mosely, opposed the war believing that another conflict
with Germany wasn't in Britain's interest and even
demanded the government should negotiate peace. In the
US Henry Ford, a Nazi sympathiser, refused to
manufacture much needed military hardware and
aeroplanes for the British prior an impending German
invasion. Only to change his mind when America was
drawn into the war when Japan attacked the US Pacific
Fleet at Pearl Harbour 7th December 1941 and could
make a few bucks out of it.

Meanwhile, reality witnessed what the Luftwaffe
can do with a relentless bombing campaign of English
airfields, towns and cities. It lasted from May until
October 1940 not before killing 40,000 civilians and
destroying a million buildings. But the British masses
refused to be beaten. Whilst the RAF fought for survival,
the civilian population stood fast against the enemy with
a strong belief that they will never surrender. But with
Nazi Germany occupying Europe, Britain stood alone,
and did so for the following 2-years to fight a mighty
organised and professional power.

Death toll of World War Two, including civilians, was staggering. Unbelievably worse than the First World War, with a mind-blowing 70,000,000. That's roughly the entire population of the UK [2020] wiped out in only 6-years. Millions more were either injured or displaced with nowhere to go due to entire towns and cities across Europe wiped off the map. France, Holland, Belgium, Denmark, Britain, Russia, and all of Eastern Europe took a huge battering. As did German cities such as Hanover, Berlin, Dresden and Hamburg.

Civilians had no choice but evacuate homes, leaving most, if not all of their possessions behind, or stay put and risk being shelled or bombed. The London Blitz bore witness to countless bombing raids, day and night, as did Nazi occupied Europe, with air raids causing mayhem and carnage across an entire continent. Remarkably, out of all this death and destruction, civilians did their utmost to carry on regardless. Shops that weren't blown to bits remained open, proudly displaying hastily painted bits of cardboard saying 'open as usual'.

Food was grown in every spare patch of soil available, even window boxes grew vegetables, as everything in every day life became scares due to rationing. The make do and mend attitude remained steadfast, so not to waste valuable resources and materials such as aluminium, steel, coal, cotton, silk, wood, and definitely food, became second nature. Even fuels for vehicles were produced out of coal by heating it to extract gas. But the UK still had to import a vast amount of goods from around the world, including half of its meat consumption to feed the country. Fruit, sugar, cereals and cheese were also imported.

With the UK under constant aerial attack the Atlantic blockade of German U-boats sunk many vessels trying to reach Britain with much needed supplies and food from its Empire and sympathetic countries not yet in the war, such as the USA. The idea of the blockade was to defeat Britain by restricting its war machine of materials and starve it into submission, as tried in 1917.

Rationing during the First World War was nowhere near as drastic 22-years later. And although reluctant at first, the government had no choice but restrict the purchase of some foodstuffs such as meat, cereals and sugar towards the end of 1939. Other restrictions quickly followed, and fines were enforced for wasting food by feeding pigeons or wild and stray animals. Rationing included the maximum consumption of 2 courses in restaurants during lunch and 3 courses in the evening. Bread was also rationed towards later years of the war due to a shortage of wheat, and butter.

Resources continued to run low and drastic situations create drastic measures as the country found itself in a much worse state than first thought. So the government had no choice but expand rationing with the introduction of petrol coupons. And in January 1941 food items such as bacon and ham were rationed at 4oz per week, butter at only 2oz per week and sugar at a pitiful 8oz per week were the first to be implemented upon the nation. Cheese quickly followed at 2oz per week, milk at only 3 pints per week, and just one egg. Tea was sold loose, as teabags hadn't been invented yet, with a meagre ration of 2oz per week.

Ration books were supplied with coupons to every registered household where a shop would stamp or mark off the weekly rationed item. Even children had ration books. Additional food and other goods were allowed to those with certain jobs regarded important to the war effort: miners, members of the armed forces and land workers – namely the women's land army. However, greengrocers would hold back fruit for children and pregnant women at one extra item per week, and the surrender of meat rations was compulsory for vegetarians.

By 1942 almost all foods were now rationed, apart from vegetables thanks to the Dig for Freedom campaign encouraging everyone to plant vegetables in every possible free space. Clothing also became rationed, including silk, as this particular material was needed for producing parachutes. And the purchase of a coat, suit or dress with matching top, was limited with a clothing coupon allowing one purchase per year.

The Ministry of Food publicised various ways of preserving food and recipes to save on waste. And if lucky enough to live near or in the countryside, game was ready available as it wasn't restricted, so pigeon and rabbit pie become particularly popular. When the war ended in Europe on 8th May 1945 rationing certainly didn't, only to continue on a sliding scale until 1958.

During rationing, falling bombs and Atlantic convoys constantly attacked by U-boats, everyone had to get used to restrictions: Keep calm and carry on. Meanwhile, hundreds of thousands of families were receiving telegrams from the war office stating that their sons, husbands and fathers were either killed or missing presumed dead. 386,000 British soldiers died, leaving families back home totally devastated, but they had to carry on with the vital war effort whilst smothering personal emotions by keeping busy – the stiff upper lip mentality. In total, world-wide military casualties are estimated to be around 25,000,000 including 5,000,000 prisoners of war.

Civilians suffered the most, and considerably more so than the First World War. The UK totalled around 400,000 casualties due to Luftwaffe bombing campaigns.

In Germany around 17,000,000 died, including those executed refusing to accept, comply or deemed unworthy of Nazi policies: political prisoners, homosexuals, disabled, mentally unstable and terminally sick. Not forgetting 6,000,000 Jews and 5,000,000 Communists. In the Soviet Union there were around 27,000,000 casualties, ¼ of the entire population killed or injured by disease, famine, bombs or bullets.

This generation certainly had enough to contend with. Moaning or complaining about it was pointless, as was, to a certain degree, shrouding oneself with bouts of depression. Yes, many were depressed – and who could blame them – but to express feelings of depression in public was simply a sign of weakness. In private, however, for some, the enormous cost was too much to bear and suicides were inevitable. But this incredibly strong attitude became a state of mind. Living with it day in day out, year in year out, created a stubborn and astute discipline towards daily life. In effect, these symptoms can be interpreted as suffering with PTSD.

Nevertheless, for the first time in modern history 4 generations cast aside social, political and moral differences to work together and fight a common enemy to protect their precious and vulnerable freedom. Many of which remembered the last time it came under threat and the importance of what freedom means. Such was the common bond during those war years, old fashion values and discipline continued decades after, determined never to return to those darker years by rebuilding a battered country and a safer future for generations to come. To live in peace and harmony, rather than poverty, threat of invasion and occupation of an evil dictatorship. So what in all that is holy went catastrophically wrong?

Chapter Nine

Baby Boomers: Sex, sex, and even more sex!

What followed after the war – and there really isn't any other way of putting this – was loads of sex. You see, the thing is about millions of soldiers returning home after years of separation is that they were greeted by wives and girlfriends. And when such a meeting takes place a deluge of lustful, guilt free, hot, passionate – although probably quite quick – sex follows. And the thing is about sex – your basic unprotected sex – babies are produced. And because there were millions of sex-starved randy sailors, soldiers and airmen returning home it caused a deluge of births around the world never seen before or since, kick starting the Baby Boom Generation, which my mum is a proud member.

Baby Boom Generation started in 1945 ending in 1964. And like the generation before, their parental values or at the very least, similarities, survived well into the latter part of the 20th Century. But the Millennial generation will have you believe that the Baby Boomers were from a black and white era, utterly racist, anti-social disciplinarians, and struggled to make ends meet. In fact, Baby Boomers were the first generation to experience a rapidly changing world of commerce, culture, technology, fashion, music, leisure, entertainment, racial equality and not forgetting a shed-load of demonstrations.

Just after the First World War Edwardian's were first to change an old rope and tackle, horse and cart, steam driven world, into a sleek modern petrol driven and electric world. Flip-side of the coin, both world wars brought an abrupt end to extravagance and a taste of easy care-free living, replaced with a bland and boring existence, coupled with bouts of excitement, fear, anxiety, frustration and a prolonged exposure to just survive. Baby Boomers didn't want to just survive, quickly realising they could experience that sweet taste of extravagance denied to their parents during those war years, having no choice but sacrifice pleasures of grandeur whilst rebuilding a future for their children.

Young single working class Baby Boomers enjoyed expendable income, spending it on make-up, fashion, music, even motorbikes and cars. Family homes bought kitchen and electrical appliances, and the ultimate extravagance, a television set, where television made a rapid return to the airwaves after its brief suspension during the war years.

After World War Two Britain experienced yet another radical social change, but there was a subtle difference. Technology was now churning out invention after invention, and many were produced for the leisure and entertainment industry, particularly targeting young adults with cash on the hip to burn. Record players, amongst other must have items, were sold in there millions, kick starting another growth industry – music – in particular, rock and roll. What hadn't changed was class division, in particularly the north and south divide - rich in the south, poor everywhere else.

The BBC – radio and television – continued to use presenters, journalists and reporters that spoke a certain vocabulary with perfect Noel Coward pronunciation and tone, reflecting their pompous upper class university education. And almost certainly to give an impression that they were better educated than their captive audience. This condescending attitude lasted way into the early 1990's, after which commoners from that awful working class slowly took over prime presenters and newsreader positions.

The tantalising treats that spread before Baby Boomers, however, tended to be out of reach for most. Instead, that make do and mend attitude from the war remained strong amongst the masses, lasting well into the 1980's. Rationing for some items remained until 1958 where petrol rationing didn't end until 1950, so at least cars could run, should they be affordable. Families even retained their wartime 'dig for freedom' discipline by growing as much as they could to sustain a healthy diet well into the 1970's. But with rationing slowly creeping to an end, food shopping still remained more important than the purchase of labour-saving devices and leisure goods.

Shopkeepers still wore aprons, smocks and hats, serving wares and food behind counters with a smile. Shoppers, mostly women, walked into the butchers with sawdust on the floor and greengrocers with sacks of sprouts, carrots, parsnips and potatoes greeting them in the doorway. Food was also displayed loose in open cardboard boxes, and not a single plastic container or bag insight. Instead, food was purchased and wrapped or parcelled in yesterday's newspaper and placed in the shopper's wicker basket by the shopkeeper.

Women often did the shopping as they were in charge of buying food, receiving the traditional housekeeping money from the husband. They also tended to leave full or part time work once married to concentrate on a family. This was still an era where women knew their place and grew up believing husbands went to work whilst the wife looked after the house and children. But that doesn't exclude women from earning their own money before marriage, and they were certainly more independent and vocal thanks to the war.

Teens often left school at 15-years old to earn money and bring a few quid into the house in a way of board for mum, just as previous generations did. And leaving school at such a young age led to a passage of adulthood, and a duty of paying your own way was part of it. In doing so school leavers quickly learnt the value of pounds, shillings and pence. But going out and meeting friends also became normal practice for 1950's teenagers growing into the baby boom era, increasing the need for events and group interests where young adults could gather.

As for getting presumed lifts from parents to events, meet friends in town or just too and from work, forget it. Nine times out of ten parents didn't own a car, and if they did, all teens made their own arrangements to travel anywhere, or just walked. Even children from as early as 6-years old found their own way to school. Often walked, but some lucky elder children cycled and others caught a bus – on their own. After all, being independent was one of those disciplines handed down from previous generations, and such skills certainly came into fruition when they grew into adulthood.

For the growing teenager, by the mid-1950's men's fashion reflected film actors or clothes from the Edwardian era that gave birth to the unique Teddy boys. Slightly different to the Edwardian clothing, Teddy boys wore long jackets and white socks – on the whole – with ankle length tight and narrow trousers or turn-up jeans. Crisp white shirts accompanied by a thin tie, and footwear known as beetle crushers – uppers of suede and usually blue – with a thick black cushioned sole, or black narrow leather winkle picker bootlets – ankle high shoes that narrowed to an almost point. And with their Tony Curtis haircuts – known as a DA (Ducks Arse) young gents strutted their stuff around the pubs and dance halls.

It is thought that the idea of the typical Teddy Boy attire was influenced by Saville Row Tailors wishing to bring back an Edwardian style clothing, where it claimed some success with the young as it tied in perfectly with the increasing popularity of rock and roll music. When Bill Haley and the Comets hit the music scene, the Teddy Boy was born. Rock Around the Clock hit picture houses with a storm, influencing the Teddy Boy image to dance and even riot in the aisles. Rumours soon spread throughout the Teddy Boy jungle telegraph and rioting became their chosen image. But their carefree, double-hard bastard attitude soon came to an abrupt halt: National Service.

During the First World War conscription was introduced in 1916 after the tragic consequence of the Pals Battalions. When the Second World War started conscription was re-introduced almost immediately, known as Military Service. After the war conscription continued, becoming known as National Service in 1948, lasting until 1960 with the last soldiers demobilised in 1963.

From the ages of 18 to 30-years all men were eligible to complete at least 2-years National Service either in the Army, Navy or Airforce. But up and coming teenagers of the 1950's were enjoying their rebellious years. As far as they were concerned conscription ended with their fathers, not them. The war was over, and the thought of another one was far from their minds.

National Service was certainly resented by the latter birth years of the Silent Generation, to the point of believing it disrupted their freedom and lifestyle. Hating the thought of being bullied by a drill sergeant and the military experience that lay before them, there was a legitimate way to dodge the Kings Shilling in the guise of university exemption courses. These particular degrees created a huge surge of applicants willing to put pen to paper and vigorously demonstrate their human rights, but too scared to don a uniform and protect freedom and liberty they enjoyed to exploit.

As you can imagine there must have been an influx of 18-year olds proudly enlisting for sociology courses. However, once over the initial shock, thankfully most conscripted soldiers learnt a great deal serving their King, later Queen and Country. In doing so military training became so interwoven into their lives it improved their very existence, providing discipline and moral standards that past generations were proud of. Some of which carried on as regular full time soldiers and made the Armed Services a chosen career, completing a full 22-years service, rewarded with a modest pension.

Demobilisation day meant the issue of a demob suit and due pay. This was spent on beer, records and fashionable civvy clothes, where many, still in their early twenties, returned to being Teddy Boys. If you were frugal with your money, and saved throughout National Service, rather than spend it on beer and loose women – yes, many did – motorbikes and cars were a must purchase to show off in front of mates, and of course, girls.

One of many American imports was dating. Yes, dating has been around for centuries, but the term dating in the 1950's meant going out on dates with one or more suitors before going steady. Previous to this new Americanism, European and British men, as did older American generations, courted. An outdated concept that is sometimes repeated in conversation between older generations overheard by a bemused youngster wondering what on earth they're talking about.

Old-fashioned courting was updated somewhat by the 1920's: a boy seeing a girl, maybe at a dance or party, where eyes would meet through a crowd. The boy would then show his interest by introducing himself, or through a friend, where hopefully conversation will forego any awkward silence. By the 1950's meeting girls had a fresh approach and girls liked the idea because they could hang around in groups with friends whilst being eye-balled by boys at dance halls, coffee shops and pubs. It also offered freedom from prying parental eyes and a chance to meet numerous potential partners whilst having fun. And this new dating experience fitted well with post-war fashion and the influence of a carefree rock and roll lifestyle.

With a new car – driving licence often issued during National Service – flash clothes and a flashier 1950's hairstyle, young men were on the prowl. And with dance halls, coffee shops and picture houses spreading across the nation offering the perfect first date experience, there was no stopping them. Even taking a girl to a record shop was considered to be a good venue for a first date. Here you could actually play records before you bought them, and of course, smoke cigarettes in the shop.

Chat-up lines for young men were, and still are, a difficult and somewhat clumsy obstacle to overcome. Some had no problem, whilst others found them to be an impossible task. Cheesy lines today were new in the 1950's and depending upon the girl, flicking a coin in front of a potential girlfriend and saying 'phone your mum because you'll be late going home tonight,' actually worked. It was always down to the boy to make the first move. And boys always paid for the date – always.

Sex, as far as girls were concerned, was off the menu. This was still an era of virginity and preservation for that special moment only when married. So heavy petting was all a boy could get – maybe – be it in the dance hall, back of a car, at home on the settee or on the back row seat at the cinema. But that was it, thank you very much. However, passions obviously ran high from time to time, and the inevitable happened. Afterwards young ladies would often feel dirty, cheated and even suicidal. That most precious moment for any young woman had been stolen. Boys, on the other hand, felt no different, back then or today.

Attitude to sex was very much thought of the same way as previous generations. They were still curious and had urges, but stemmed by parental discipline and morals passed down from mother to daughter. Sex education at school, and most definitely at home, remained incredibly rare or unheard of. Pregnancies out of wedlock were inevitable and treated with contempt, to the point of renouncing the un-wed mother from society altogether.

Many parents threw daughters out onto the street, if only to stem gossip and uphold a moral position in society. The remaining options were to keep the pregnancy secret or abort the child. But abortions were illegal, leaving unregistered practices to perform dangerous procedures with a threat of serious infection, continuous bleeding, and sometimes death. These particular unfortunate women were the unlucky ones. For others, chivalry amongst some men remained a moral obligation.

If fortunate not to have been hung-drawn and quartered by a raging father, asking permission to wed his pregnant daughter, or sometimes forced, was a silver lining for both parents, if only to save face and social acceptance. Even better when marched down the aisle early enough not to notice a bride with a bump that would otherwise stir gossip and innuendo.

Taking all into consideration divorce was rare in the 1950's compared to today. Whether forced to marry or not, when a marriage faced difficulties – child related,

<hr>

lack of money, unemployment or poverty – couples generally stuck together through thick and thin and simply rode the various storms that lay ahead. These values were passed down by their parents and parents before, keeping some Victorian values alive. Even standing by a violent husband, no matter what.

Newly weds, from whatever background, worked at a new life together with hope of emulating their parent's success. Traditions, morals and habits followed suit, where husbands came home from work with a meal waiting for them on the kitchen table. Those with a growing family would sit around the table talking about their day whilst they eat. Recreation would be pub time for dad to sink a few jars, leaving mum at home to bathe the kids before bedtime.

Paid leave entitlement was now law for employees so family holidays were saved for by means of putting aside a few shillings each week. The more affluent would take their once a year trip to Butlins or Pontins holiday resorts sprouting all around the coast. Others strapped for cash would try and get away for long weekends to the seaside. Camping and caravan holidays grew in popularity where campsites took advantage of the trend by offering onsite shops, bars, and shower facilities for a more relaxed stay to entice bookings.

War-torn Europe and the UK's economy were on the up. Work was plentiful and life was good, but such a healthy economy came at a price by creating the most populated industrialised country in the world. Pollution became a huge problem; unseen since the Victorian era, with an abundant of coal powered stations producing electricity for homes as well as industrial outlets. This incredibly dirty fuel created the infamous smog of London in 1952 lasting 5-days, where 4,000 died and thousands more suffered from asphyxiated illnesses.

Heart disease and lung cancer inevitably increased living in or near populated industrial areas. Other towns and cities suffered similar problems, in particularly the north such as Manchester, Liverpool, Barnsley, Sheffield and Newcastle. Birmingham in the West and Corby in the East Midlands also suffered. As did Cardiff and Port Talbot in South Wales and Glasgow in Scotland. Waterways were also polluted from coal powered electricity stations, with underground and open-cast mines scarring the countryside to feed a vast appetite of coal and iron.

Remarkably, on the whole, health of the masses remained good, partly due to lack of processed foods and fat during the war, but also from recently introduced National Health Service Act of 1946 that came into effect on 5th July 1948. At first dental care was included, but due to cost the government U-turned by putting in place charges for some treatment. Nevertheless, rich, poor, young or old, the NHS was there to assist when needed. Antibiotics were administered for free, along with vaccinations, eradicating diseases such as tuberculosis and eventually polio. Life expectancy suddenly expanded at a rate never seen before.

With virtually no unemployment, and businesses with full order books, employees were never happier. Britain remained the world leader in ship building, steel production, car manufacturing and textiles. Oil and chemical refineries churned out millions of gallons of fuel to haul the many trucks thundering up and down the highways, science continued with its breakthroughs and discoveries of chemical compounds and pharmasuticles.

The British aeronautic industry was also at its best during the 1950's. Frank Whittle's jet engine had improved immensely since inventing it in 1937 and was now powering the first intercontinental airliner – the

Comet – as well as a huge airforce. Record breaking speeds and performance were constantly beaten with British innovative improvements, including the RAF English Electric Lightening. Although top speed remains classified, it is documented to have flown over twice the speed of sound whilst in a vertical climb.

To sustain a massive industrial output the UK produced for Europe and the rest of the world, a shortage of labour was created. The 1951 census proved this problem with the population figure of 50,000,000 where half were of employment age. But demand for labour soon exceeded the working population to keep up with aggressive industrial production. Only three percent of the population was foreign-born; majority of which were Irish, closely followed by 160,000 Poles, Jews and Germans escaping Nazi persecution during the war.

Immigration became a huge concern for rebuilding the nation after the Second World War and feed its ferocious appetite for labour. Many German and Italian Prisoners of War decided to remain in the UK rather than return to their native country for many reasons. Most had worked as agricultural labourers and some had met English sweethearts, whilst others felt they would have a better life staying in Blighty in fear of persecution from their homeland.

But it wasn't enough to feed a hungry appetite for British made products. Britain was already head of multi-racial reform with the 1948 British Nationality Act advocating unrestricted entry to Commonwealth members, so in 1951 an influx of Jamaicans arrived on the shores of Britain to help rebuild the nation, but still only totalled around 140,000.

Chapter Ten

Nuclear family: what is it good for?

The 1950's witnessed a minority – yet vocal – group from Scotland wishing their independence, to the point of disgracefully removing The Stone of Destiny from Westminster Abbey. Even Welsh groups campaigned for a self-governing parliament but gained little interest throughout the country. The more populated south was too involved with English industry, where the rural north didn't have enough support to sustain a national majority. And industrial disputes throughout the UK were almost unknown during the 1950's whilst the economy grew at a staggering rate. Unemployment was low, with half of men and a quarter of women in the workplace belonging to a trade union.

Although there were still many unpaid bills from the war Britain remained an important world power, investing in a huge defence budget. The Royal Navy and RAF were comparable in size to the USA. With the ending of the Second World War the UK remained a militarised country, even with a non-military sympathetic Labour government spending almost 7 percent of GDP on defence. The rest of Europe during the 1950's was a delicate place to be with the carving or forcefully amalgamating countries during the early years of the Cold War.

USSR (Union of the Soviet Socialist Republic) forcibly annexed East Germany, Poland, Hungary, former Yugoslavia, Albania, Bulgaria, Latvia, Moldova, Estonia, Lithuania, Romania, Georgia, Ukraine, Crimea, former

Czechoslovakia, Kazakhstan, Kyrgyztan, Tajikistan, Turkmenistan, Uzbekistan, Azerbaijan, Armenia and Belarus – whether citizens wanted it or not – creating the Warsaw Pact. This Communist Alliance ruled by Moscow was the equivalent deterrent for any invasion by NATO (North Atlantic Treaty Organisation) which included the UK as well as France, Denmark, Canada, Belgium, West Germany, Netherlands, Greece, Iceland, Norway, Italy, Luxembourg, Spain and Portugal, with the USA spearheading the Treaty.

In later years Japan and South Korea joined an affiliation of the Washington Treaty – NATO, as they were not situated in the North Atlantic but feared a Soviet nuclear attack. As did Australia, but being situated in the South Pacific ANZUS (Australian, New Zealand and United States Security) Treaty was put together in 1951 should them pesky Soviets attempt to attack capitalist allies further south. Once again 2 vast opposing armies were created, only this time on a far greater scale than the First and Second World War combined, and with far greater firepower – including nuclear weapons.

For the UK nuclear power was just around the corner, and with it came the nuclear defence programme. USA already had their own nuclear arsenal, and the UK was part of USA defence strategy in Western Europe, but wanted a home grown system to protect her shores. Due to a young and naïve socialist BBC television and a gossip-fuelled print media, they quickly spread panic and fear, and for the first time it had nothing to do with losing jobs, low wages or poverty, as it were for past generations.

On this occasion, mainly supported by the university ilk with misguided socialist views and nothing better to do with their huge amount of spare time, took this new fear as gospel and set about conducting demonstrations for world peace and injecting the masses with their perspective of stock piling nuclear weapons. This new fear was titled MAD (Mutually Assured Destruction). In other words, both sides guarantee to press the red button should one side decide first.

On Good Friday 1958 a small group of young academics, post-graduates and religious leaders gathered in Trafalgar Square to march in protest against the escalating arms race. The word soon spread amongst universities, raising further interest with far-left activist groups seeking any excuse to cause mayhem with their ill-educated political rhetoric, nuclear or otherwise. Interest from other students joined the protest, making up the majority of draft-dodgers, and within 4-days 10,000 demonstrators walked 60 miles to the atomic weapon establishment at Alder Marston to express their concerns. Campaign for Nuclear Disarmament (CND) was born.

The movement quickly gathered pace, spreading unsolicited fear amongst the masses that World War Three was just around the corner and about to wipe us all from the surface of the earth. They were hell-bent on stopping the nuclear arms race, yet totally oblivious as to why we had it. They'd already been used twice in anger, proving their worth by shortening the Second World War by at least one year and saving hundreds of thousands of lives – military and civilian alike.

However, they were now stock-piled in the West due to those pesky untrustworthy Soviets stockpiling theirs, who showed continued aggression by invading surrounding country after country. They simply could not be trusted; that's why the West had them. Nuclear weapons were now here for a very long time and nothing was going to stop bigger and more powerful weapons being designed and tested just because a bunch of campaigners didn't like them. But there was a genuine concern World War Three was about to explode in a giant fireball.

April 1961 certainly was a test amongst tests for world leaders. Cuban officials feared the USA would invade their country when Communist believer, Fidel Castro, forced his way to power. A joint US military and CIA (Central Intelligence Agency) operation was put together to topple Castro and his Communist government, but failed miserably; infamously known as the Bay of Pigs invasion.

Undeterred, the US continued to believe Castro gave the Soviets permission to build nuclear missile bases on Cuban soil. On 14th October 1962 a CIA U2 spy aeroplane flew incredibly high over Cuba to see if there was any truth behind the rumour. The reel of film confirmed that the Soviets were indeed building bases on Cuban soil to stockpile missiles with the capability of launching a nuclear strike on the USA reaching targets far north as Washington DC and California.

President Kennedy's hard talks with Soviet leader, Krushchev, at a meeting in Vienna, said he could destroy the USSR many times over should he continue building nuclear missile sites in Cuba. Krushchev replied, is no difference. All I need is to destroy you only once. When the talks between the two super-powers turned sour US strategic air command went on alert to DEFCON 2 just one away from total war. On 22nd October a huge US naval blockade enveloped the entire coast of Cuba, creating the most dangerous and tense times in human history.

By 27th October UK Forces were on full alert. Whilst the majority of the country carried on regardless the RAF set about heading towards their highest state of readiness – Ready State 02. A total of 150 Vulcan bombers, crewed, fuelled, armed with nuclear bombs and engines ticking over, stood ready on runways waiting for the order to take off within literally minutes and fly east – Ready State 1.5 – Scramble. After which, Ready State 0.1 would mean nuclear war had been waged.

The RAF was tasked to be the first of many NATO strikes and hit targets within the Baltics and west Soviet Union. The Americans would fly in afterwards with huge B52 bombers to hit targets further east as they had the range. All targets were pre-determined, strategically placed so the B52s could fly between blasts and drop nuclear bombs on inner cities and military sites.

On the first wave, should Vulcan bombers survive anti-aircraft fire, surface-to-air missiles and manage to dodge interceptors, they could then head home, but to what? The Soviets would have executed the exact same assured destruction with their nuclear arsenal, so there would be nothing to come home to. The UK as well as France, Germany, Italy, Belgium, Holland, Denmark, in fact the whole of Western Europe would have been obliterated.

Thankfully, at the very last minute, Krushchev, under incredible pressure from the West and his own political and military leaders, ordered his ships to turn around and head back to the Soviet Union. The crises had been averted and the world was finally at peace. Baby Boomers managed to ride through the storm of the Cuban Crises and return to blue skies, or at least for a while, believing their protests paid off. The threat of nuclear war had withered away and the world was on a high. Surely there couldn't be anything else to moan about? The only protests left were, in comparison, pointless. Well, that's not entirely true. Baby Boomers still wanted to make their mark on society.

CND continued to organise marches against nuclear weapons and even nuclear power, fearing both military and civilian use will cause catastrophic destruction. They also marched alongside those against all wars, including the escalating tensions in Vietnam, fearing a war between the North and South will be no different to the previous Korean war in 1953 or the Egyptian Crises over the Suez Canal in 1956.

President Kennedy increased numbers of military advisors in Vietnam with hope to avoid any US involvement using military confrontation. But as the pressure increased between North and South Vietnam, war was inevitable. But his charismatic liberal-minded leadership came to an abrupt end one fateful afternoon 22nd November 1963. Crowds gathered alongside the streets of Dallas as his cavalcade drove slowly down Main Street. Turning into Dealey Plaza his open top car passed the Texas School Book Depository.

Gunshots ripped through the air and screams quickly followed as the crowds dived for any cover they could find, not knowing where the gunshots came from or where they were aimed. But then it came obvious as President Kennedy sat slumped over his wife sitting on the back seat of his open top car, hit in the neck and head. Within only a few short hours Lee Harvey Oswald, an employee of the Book Depository, and former US Marine, was arrested and charged with President Kennedy's assassination.

Within 2-days Oswald was due to be transferred from a police cell to the County jail, where the whole episode was aired over many television channels. A man in the awaiting crowd suddenly appeared holding a pistol and shot Oswald at point blank range, dying of his wound a few hours later in hospital. And within 2-years after Kennedy's assassination the war in Vietnam was inevitable, dividing opinions in the USA, in particular with the young.

From only the previous decade US, including Australian and UK troops, were in Korea fighting the Soviet-backed North Korean and Chinese armies, where most of the US veterans supported their brothers fighting in Vietnam but didn't necessarily support the war. Thousands protested with many marches and demonstrations, predominately populated by draft-dodging students refusing to answer their call. Others even fled to Canada to avoid conscription.

Although UK Forces were not involved in the Vietnam war, mainly because the government couldn't afford to send any, bands such as the Beatles – in particularly John Lennon – appeared on the Ed Sullivan show during their tour in the USA and voiced their protest against the war. In doing so US media brought the conflict to the attention of Beatles fans in the UK emphasised by one of their songs, Give Peace a Chance, targeting the cruelty of war – innocent victims and waste of human life.

British youth started to rebel against the war, gathering in huge numbers to protest and demand an end to all hostilities, challenging the British government to march with them in protest, even though the UK wasn't involved. This act of defiance was something new and the government, as well as other authoritative organisations, didn't know how to react. The youth in such large numbers marching against a war the country wasn't involved with was simply alien and never seen before.

With the first born Baby Boomers now in their late teens and early twenties, finally free from conscription, lived their freedom given by their fathers to do what they wanted. And views on current affairs were completely different to conscripted teens only a few years before. Britain in the 1960's was entering into a new era of expression. Young people began to stand up for personal rights and individuality, rather than a concern for the majority whilst surviving a war. Whether it was politics, the economy, foreign conflicts, social affairs, even racism, youth now had the loudest voice. For good or bad, it was here to stay.

Recreational drugs were also synonymous with the times. Woodstock festival being a sixties icon for hippies, music, weird dancing, expression, sex and drugs. Be it a band member or film actor, high profile celebrities were publicly known to take some sort of hallucinogenic drug such as LSD influencing naïve followers and fans to do the same. The effects of these drugs were also apparent in psychedelic art and films. The Beatles film Yellow Submarine, combining psychedelic pictures and music, illustrates this kind of animation suspiciously close to having a trip on LSD.

Feminism became an influential ideology with an increase in various employment opportunities now available to women, allowing them to move away from being housewives and become more independent. The Women's Liberty movement was in its infancy when 850 women at the Ford plant in Dagenham went on strike for equal pay. Although their grievance wasn't met entirely, such action and media publicity gave way to the Equal Pay Act of 1970. Women were even making a mark within high-ranking government positions, such as Barbara Castle in 1968 becoming the first woman appointed First Secretary of State.

Sixties women were also making their mark in fashion, such as the famous miniskirt, very much an icon of the era. The world leading UK boot and shoe industry in Northamptonshire created outlandish footwear, including thigh-length plastic boots and winkle-pickers to suit psychedelic prints and vibrant colours used on dresses, coats and frocks. Television, radio, print media and magazine advertisements increased ten-fold, and programmes started to discuss views on modern art, culture, music and fashion.

The 1960's became a world apart from previous decades, and also drastically changed how people spent their leisure time thanks to technological innovation of the transistor. Colour television, although available but incredibly expensive, began to appear in homes. But the transistor radio, small in size and easy to carry around, was a must have purchase for teenagers. Whether carried by hand, stuffed in a pocket or tied to bicycle handlebars, favourite music could now be played anywhere.

Of course, the stuffy British Broadcasting Company aired music the oldies only liked, so the only remaining station teenagers could tune into was Radio Luxembourg. But they often played only half a track or cut it short for some advertisement, frustrating the hell out of young listeners. However, pirate radio soon came to the rescue, emerging in the form of Radio Caroline, transmitting pop music – playing the entire track – from a ship off the Coast of Felixstowe, exploiting legal broadcasting loopholes to give huge enjoyment to a growing youth culture. Even records from America never heard before created interest in bands such as The Beach Boys.

Aired for the first time on 28th March 1964 it launched many successful careers. The first DJ (Disc Jockey) to broadcast was Chris Moore, quickly followed by Tony Blackburn, John Peel, Dave Lee Travis, Johnnie Walker and Tommy Vance, where many eventually worked for the BBC and commercial national radio stations. And playing sixties music joined a marriage between youth expression, love and peace in the guise of flower power.

The hippy peace movement was gaining pace amongst students, in particular free love, as it was

---

termed, thanks to a new contraception hitting the market – commonly known as the pill – readily available from the NHS to all women by 1967. It provided opportunity to broaden horizons on relationships before marriage, arguably preventing unwanted pregnancies. But there was one small problem. It didn't.

By the mid to late 1960's birth rates had peaked amongst women as a whole, and almost half of teenage brides marrying for the first time were pregnant whilst walking down the aisle. A quarter of which were teenagers. There was also an increase amongst under sixteen's falling pregnant, and inevitably abortion numbers spiralled considerably compared to the 1950's. Sex education inevitably remained rare, so free love certainly came at a price.

1960's witnessed radical change within the youth movement. Music had shunned away from traditional rock and roll, including the Teddy Boy image, entering into a new age of psychedelic expressionism. Rock and roll, although not totally replaced, was pushed to one side somewhat to make way for new style pop and rock bands such as The Who, The Rolling Stones, Marvin Gaye and Manfred Mann. Pop music was almost monopolised by the Mersey sound with Gerry and the Pacemakers, Cilla Black and The Beatles, shaping new trends and music wavelengths still influencing bands today.

Beatlemania became synonymous with young teenage fans, in particularly young girls, screaming and shouting in large groups, many crying and some even fainting at the sight of their favourite band member. Never before had the older British generation witnessed such emotional outbursts in public, left completely dumbfounded and disgusted by their behaviour. Showing emotions, let alone in public, was completely unacceptable. But this wasn't the first time young fans behaved in a manic way.

As far back as 1841 fans of composer, Franz Liszt, behaved in a manner unbeknown to a Victorian society, accused of having some sort of mental hysteria. Poet, Heinrich Heine, described the strange behaviour as Lisztomania, hence the term Beatlemania. In the USA Elvis created a huge storm with his fans, where teenage girls screamed and behaved in an inappropriate manner unaccustomed to 1950's society. As they did at Bill Haley and the Comets concerts, Cliff Richard and the Shadows, Marty Wilde, The Everly Brothers, and many other fifties icons, although nowhere near as bad as Beatlemania.

By 1964 the Beatles were huge, influencing social change and capturing the hearts of millions around the world. When they first toured the US they appeared on the Ed Sullivan Show, reaching around 73,000,000 viewers. And when radio WWDC in Washington DC played for the first time, I want to hold your hand, listeners couldn't get enough of it, demanding the station play it over and over. The single soon spread to other radio stations around the country, where youngsters wanted to buy it, but record shops didn't have any.

Making it big in the US was a massive achievement for a Brit band, but John Lennon almost destroyed it all when he upset a huge religious following by saying they were more famous than Jesus. Large crowds gathered to publicly burn Beatles records, saying they were the Anti-Christ. The Klu Klux Klan grouped outside concerts chanting their hatred of the band. They even received death threats through the post.

Putting aside god-fearing folk, touring the world for over 4-years with almost 1,500 appearances increased their fame in many countries, to the point of creating a new wave of pop and youth culture. First appearing with bob haircuts and dressed in smart suits, fashion for men quickly followed in their footsteps. By 1965 they'd already made 2 films, the first being A Hard Day's Night, and the second, Help, increased their popularity even further, filling concert halls to bursting. Fans continued to grow with them, but music taste changed to a more mature discipline, such as the following of Bob Dylan.

By 1966 The Beatles were forced to stop touring because it became too dangerous due to frenzied fans appearing from anywhere to everywhere they went, pushing and shoving to get a piece of the band – literally. And as the hippy era took a strong hold on youth culture, the Beatles gained a more mature audience by producing some incredible yet strange music whilst hidden behind studio doors.

In effect they went a tad weird with their next album, Sergeant Pepper's Lonely Heart Club Band. With it emerged a strange looking Beatles – long hair, as well as long coats, bright psychedelic coloured bell-bottomed trousers and even louder large collard shirts. A total contrast to what they first looked like only 4-years previous. But their new look attracted a completely new following.

Late sixties youth was now dominated by music, influenced by global change and political awareness. The Vietnam War, by far the biggest influence, gave music a catalyst to portray what its musicians believed to be right and wrong, in turn enveloped a youth culture believing the same. And with television shrinking the world further still, young opinions became impossible to miss, engulfing a more sober voice from elder generations for the first time in history.

Gone were the days sitting around a wireless listening to popular shows such as the brilliant Goon

Show and The Navy Lark. Effectual to university students such as John Cleese and Michael Palin, who later joined other students to create Monty Python that dominated sixties satire and weird comedic television. And with this new national form of popular media of the 20th Century, art, culture, pop music, children's shows, current affairs and soap operas quickly followed. Coronation Street first aired in 1960 depicting life in a typical northern street. Still popular today [2020] as it was back then, becoming the longest running British soap opera.

Variety shows were always a favourite since the Victorian era, but could now be brought to you through your 3-channel (one spare) television set without having to leave the comfort of your own living room. Acts such as Morecome and Wise, became a national treasure, later having their own shows, as did many comedy double acts. But by far the biggest television crowd puller happened during the Space Race between USA and the USSR.

On 12th April 1961 Yuri Gagarin arguably became the first man in space and carried out a single orbit of the earth before returning safely. I say arguably because there is sufficient evidence to prove that another cosmonaut, Vladimir Ilyushin, was actually the first man to orbit the earth 2-days earlier, but crash-landed in China and was feared dead on impact. But he was found by locals and brought back to health, becoming a distinguished guest of China before returning home. The Soviets immediately ordered a cover-up, only later discovering he actually survived.

NASA (North Atlantic Space Authority) quickly followed suit and sent the first American, John Glenn, into space on 20th February 1962 orbiting the earth 3-times before returning safely. US President, John F

Kennedy, then promised the free world to place a man on the moon by the end of the decade. And on 20th July 1969 Neil Armstrong and Buzz Aldrin not only achieved the impossible by becoming the first men on the moon, but also returned home safely to tell the world about their incredible journey.

This event was, by far, the greatest possible achievement the world had ever seen. And personally, at the tender age of 3-years old, was one of my first ever memories. Woken up in the early hours by mum, she was determined I watched this momentous occasion on our black and white television set. The world, excluding me because I was so tired, held its breath as the countdown begun. Four days later I was woken yet again to watch the Eagle land on the moon.

Back in Blighty the 1960s continued to experience a very low rate of unemployment of just over 2 percent due to the post-war boom. And the last of the conscripted soldiers, sailors and airmen returning home were promised employment by the government once demobilised. Technology and manufacturing continued to rise, securing the government pledge with a confidence to create jobs for all.

Others not so fortunate to be wrapped in peace and love, the sixties was a difficult decade. Yes, the economy was good, but life was still hard for some with little support from the State. By 1966 – one year into Generation X – poverty was increasing, particularly for the younger generation trying to make a living in a cruel world. Desperate to leave home and continue the trend of finding a place of their own, there was one small problem: what can you do when fallen on hard times?

Social security was available but nowhere near in the capacity of today in the form of additional unemployment benefits and government credits. The dole, as it was known, was a minimal benefit reflecting the times that being between jobs was only a short-term inconvenience. On the whole, it was possible to leave a job in the morning only to walk into another by the afternoon, so job security wasn't an issue. Employment rights, however, were. Especially sick pay.

Very few businesses included sick pay; mainly offered to high-ranking managers, so going sick meant no money. There was also a government wage freeze, yet unscrupulous landlords exploited high demand for housing and raised rent when they liked, to how much they liked, if only to feed a lavish lifestyle. And there was no law or regulation regarding rent and minimum accommodation requirements. Should anyone become unemployed through sickness or accident, employers wouldn't think twice to let them go, and landlords quickly kicked out tenants if they fell behind on rent.

There was no adequate social security safety net to fall upon, no rent allowance, no council tax paid (known as rates) and electricity was usually supplied through coin-fed metres fed with a shilling (5 pence) and vastly overpriced for the amount of allocated clockwork time per coin. Raiding the metre, be it gas or electric, wasn't uncommon. My dad did it a lot. But when that had all gone there was nothing else to feed a family.

Welfare State was an unfair State. And those caught within its grasp were pushed around from pillar to post without a care. Always someone else's problem. No one wanted to help or offer support, and the outcome would inevitably become homeless. And families with infants or school-age children falling foul of the system could easily find their children in care without consultation or counselling. Just simply taken away from parents and single mothers.

———

By the mid-1960's 200,000 extra families in London alone needed immediate housing and an additional 60,000 single people were living in rented accommodation without sinks or cookers. Out of 6 Central London Boroughs one-in-ten houses were overcrowded. And families with 2 children requiring social housing at the rate of which they were built would effectively be on the housing waiting list for 350-years before any offer of accommodation. And it wasn't just London with a shortage. Birmingham had over 30,000 on their waiting lists, Leeds over 13,000 and Liverpool had around 9,000.

The 1960s may have started in black and white and in fear of cataclysmic destruction from a devastating nuclear war, but the decade was determined to end in colour and optimism. For many, yes, the sixties did offer a brighter future, and some couldn't remember it, apparently. Student movements also found its voice – albeit very loud, naïve and clumsy – but a concerned youth was determined to make its mark in the world, even though they were young and still learning about the grown-up world.

Manufacturing remained high, as did employment. And with high employment came high spending, and with spending came low inflation. With low inflation came low interest rates, and a surge to buy a house rather than rent. Mortgage applications went crazy, as did HP (Hire Purchase) and credit for those must have expensive items: cars, twin-tub washing machines, television sets and furniture. For those who were single, sports cars, motorbikes, record players and holidays became increasingly popular. Times were good, but hard work remained top of the menu to retain a fruitful living. For others, it was about survival, no different to those living 100-years since.

Chapter Eleven

Growing up in Generation X

I was born 6th June 1966 on a very hot Spring day, where father's waited outside the delivery room smoking a shed-load of cigarettes whilst mum did all the work. Qualifying into the new Generation X my first few years were obviously a complete blur. Generation X started in 1965 ending in 1979. And with the dawn of spacemen landing on the moon, NASA continued to develop more and more gadgets fit for military purposes.

For the civilian market computers were becoming increasingly common, but only in the workplace, providing the business was a huge company such as car manufactures or communication businesses. For others, which was most of us, they were seen only in sci-fi films, with flashing lights spinning massive plastic spools of magnetic tape. It wasn't until the late 1970's did computers warrant any use in mainstream business, particularly companies owned by larger conglomerates abroad that required information from overseas using cables lying on ocean beds to swap information.

My school, for instance, didn't have a computer at all until 1983, and only used by administration staff. It took a further 2-years before student computers were introduced to any curriculum, and they were nothing more than VDU's (Visual Display Units) linked to a mainframe with less memory than a 1990's mobile telephone.

Colour television was around in the late sixties, but was incredibly expensive, costing about £300 or almost

4-months wages in 1967 [£3,000 in 2020]. Becoming a necessity, and thanks to better wages, freezers and fridge units grew popular, replacing pantries and marble slabs. Many could now freeze food and keep it for weeks, even months, rather than buying the same food types on a daily basis. Buying larger quantities cut costs and the making of pies and such like could be frozen for later use instead of eating within a day or two.

Pantries were fast becoming redundant, quickly utilised for storage with items such as vacuum cleaners, ironing boards and the good old-faithful clotheshorse. By 1974 millions across the nation now owned a fridge or freezer, or both. Microwaves, although popular in the US, took a while to catch on in the UK during the early 1970's, mainly due to cost but also cooking habits.

Mum traditionally did all the cooking, and her culinary skills were past down from mother to daughter. So a microwave was nothing more than an alien invader in the kitchen, and there was very little literature or cookery books that promoted microwave-based meals. There were also concerns about safety, and it was rumoured that dangerous levels of radiation could escape from microwave ovens, giving the household radiation sickness and cause children to grow 2 heads.

Food blenders, however, were a must for mum. No more chopping, grating, slicing, mulching, pulping or mixing by hand. A new electronic machine did the lot with one touch of a button. Mums loved this labour saving device and spent hours creating and developing new skills with this remarkable invention for a modern 1970's home.

The continental quilt also became a huge must have for mums. Up until the mid 1970's households tended to use sheets and blankets on beds, as used during my mum's childhood. But to change from blankets to a quilt, we became part of the elite. A family of distinction and even wealth. Well, according to mum, anyway.

Believe it or not, up until the early 1970's tea was predominately sold loose. Then came along this marvellous invention – by the Americans, of all nations – the humble teabag. In 1930 tea company, Tetley, tried and failed introducing the tea bag to Britain, only to have another shot in the 1950's, but failed yet again to enthral British confidence. Remarkably, it was first used during the 1920's in the US, taking almost 50-years to catch on in the UK.

Other 1970's gadgets hit the High Street, and not just labour saving. Recreational and lazy devices became a new in-home fashion, where the market for such items grew in demand. Society started to enjoy these new inventions and would go to extremes to buy them with ever increasing available credit. Some were outrageously overpriced, but manufactures had done their homework knowing the masses wanted them, regardless of cost.

Electronic games, such as the Atari game consul, were the new Christmas present must have. The first games were simple to say the least. But we were amazed with moving a green cursor up and down the side of a television screen and hitting a dot to the other side where another cursor hit it back. We had discovered digital television tennis. And the remarkable thing was, the machine could play slow or fast, with one or two players, and it could change the game to something completely different – squash. Truly a remarkable high-tech game that had surely reached the pinnacle of home entertainment where nothing could possibly supersede.

Other must have items such as music centres became as popular as televisions. And to have a stack system, complete with detachable amplifier, radio, turntable and a double cassette player, you were known as a serious music enthusiast. As was your personal record collection – we all had them.

Light Emitting Diode (LED), a semiconductor that glows when a small voltage of electricity is passed through it, was the essence of modern technology. To see and experience a gadget that displayed LED's was a moment to behold. LED digital watches suddenly became a threat to analogue pieces, and to own an LED calculator you must have been a professor of mathematics, or an accountant. But what they were really used for was making words: 8008135 (BOOBIES) being one. Know any others?

The Teasmade: The most useless piece of 1970's household tat. A machine with a built-in clock and alarm sitting on the bedside cabinet that woke you up with a fresh brew of hot tea. Sounds great. But it wasn't. The machine boiled, gurgled, fizzed and farted, waking you much earlier than the alarm and had you sat up waiting for the tea to be made. And the cost for all this inconvenience was around £30 to £40 – a week's wages.

Another useless fad was the Soda Stream. The fizzy drink it produced tasted disgusting. But in its day us kids crowded around the kitchen door of a mate's house who's mum had just brought this brilliant fizzy drink making machine. One by one we'd watch in amazement as the machine squelched and bubbled to make our exciting fizzy drink, only to pull faces, cringe or even throw-up after tasting it.

The fondue set. Not worth mentioning, other than a seventies fad in a ridiculous attempt to capture a Swiss-style pretentious moment blending cheeses, and then making a party out of it. Thankfully these fondue parties faded out towards the late 1970's when adults were finally brought to their senses.

Furniture took a dramatic change. The 1960's fashioned spindly legged and brightly coloured plastic chairs, tables and cabinets. By the 1970's they became thicker and chunkier, and made from real wood – usually teak and later pine. Bright and bold colours were replaced with boring light browns, oatmeal, beige and magnolia – a complete transition from sixties fashion and taste.

Some household wares weren't always bought. Some, such as standing ashtrays, were a gift from Green Shield. Yes, Green Shield Stamps, given by grocers and shop- keepers as a reward for custom, depending upon what was bought deciding how many stamps were awarded. Even petrol stations offered them to encourage fuel sales. Once stuck in a book it was only a matter of time – and expense – before a useless piece of junk ended up in the cabinet, back of a cupboard or in the loft.

For children of my age 1970's toys were just as much a fad as gadgets were for grown-ups, the space-hopper being one particular icon. A large orange balloon-like creature with horns to grab and a black-lined face printed on its front. We bounced around for hours on it, up and down the street, in the park and around the house. Eventually getting bored, only to play football with it instead.

On those rare occasions when we didn't play outside, games like snakes and ladders, Kerplunk and Lego were our toy of indoor choice, along with Buckaroo, Mousetrap and of course, Subbuteo – a very popular football game of the time. Tiny players with feet glued into half a sphere, we'd flick Kevin Keegan, Emlin Hughes and John Toshack around that cloth pitch chasing a massive (to them) football for hours. Only to lose Kevin under the settee, discovered years later when he blocked the vacuum cleaner nozzle.

If your parents could afford it Scalextric was a must (really for dad). With loads of plastic race track that clicked together, usually covering the entire living room carpet, electric model racing cars whizzed around on straight sections, through chicanes, around sharp hairpin bends, only to spin off at great speed and crash into the skirting board. But it didn't matter. You just started again, entertaining young – and old – imaginations for hours, pretending to be James Hunt, Niki Lauda or Nelson Piquet. Having a Hornby train set was also great fun, especially when constructing a 00 gauge track layout on a piece of 8X4 sheet of half inch chipboard.

For the playground YoYo's became a fad, as did Slime Muck – a jelly-like substance that oozed through fingers, which us boys loved. Not forgetting Klackers, played with by boys and girls, but boys were a tad more dangerously aggressive, thus accident prone with this game. Two brightly coloured solid acrylic golf ball sized smooth spheres joined together by a length of string.

The object of the game was to 'klack' the balls together by holding the centre of the string then moving your hand up and down to bash the balls together in their most lower position. With confidence, or stupidity, you then built up speed to bash the lower and now upper position, keeping up the momentum. With me so far? Girls used precision and patients to achieve this. Boys, well, didn't have precision or patients, only used luck and pain. In doing so there were many bruised knuckles and fingers to achieve the ultimate goal – 'klack' the balls together as hard and fast as possible.

What all the above seventies household inventions, gadgets, leisure and labour saving devices have in common was there tendency to either end up at the back of cupboards or in the loft after only used a few times. These same useless wares, along with fridges, freezers, televisions and music centres, after a determined life cycle of repairs, through lack of interest or due to better and more advanced models hitting the market, eventually they ended up as landfill or in scrap yards. Welcome to the birth of the throw-away society.

Car purchase and mortgage applications continued an upward trend now the masses had more expendable cash. On average a 3-bed semi-detached house set you back anything between £3,000 to £8,000, depending upon where you lived in the country. A brand new small family car cost around £500 to £700, again, depending upon which particular kind of badge took your fancy. And yes, it was extremely important – to us kids, as well as dads.

Should your dad be lucky enough to earn a salary of £3,000 he contributed a staggering 41 percent income tax against it, not including National Insurance and most likely a pension. To get around this extortionate amount of tax employers could lower salaries for managers and representatives to just under £3,000 with an offer of a company car that wasn't taxed. Brilliant. A new car, and with it a new status symbol was born.

I remember my dad coming home in a white 1.6 litre Ford Cortina GXL with a black vinyl roof. And other dad's on our street suddenly appeared with new company cars. It was now time to compare cars and trim with the badge of honour list. A basic entry never even touched the sides. As far as us kids were concerned they were nothing special, but the 'L' badge started the ball rolling with ridicule and laughter. As trim became increasingly exiting, badges became more important – GL, GXL, GT and then the cherry on the top, an E badge. But no dads in our street had one of them.

Having extras was equally important: sun roof, head restraints, fog lamps, twin headlamps, go-faster stripes, rev counter and other added dials, all mattered as much as the capacity of the engine. 1.3 litre engines weren't worth mentioning, but to have a 2.0 litre, that was like being a King. As for owning a V6 and even a V8 you had to kneel before the Emperor that owned it.

I cannot emphasise enough how important this was to us kids – and dads – in the 1970's. The same can be said for our bicycles. All kids had a bike, and we cherished them. The Raleigh Chopper was the ultimate to have, and, of course, only the well-off parents bought their son one. For boys, mind you, never for girls. The long saddle big enough to go two-up was only designed to carry one person, and had a warning strapped on the back of the seat saying, not suitable to carry a pillion passenger. The manufacturer might as well left the warning off, as it was never adhered to. And why would it be? A seat big enough to carry two will inevitably carry a mate on the back.

Bikes were our world. We'd polish them – preferably with a mate who's dad had a garage or driver way – pinch mum's washing-up liquid to wash them, then some of dad's car polish, along with what we thought were rags, but were actually mum's best teat towels. Chains were regularly oiled with dad's 3-in-1 kept for hinges and garden tools, and we also repaired our own punctures. Again, using mum's best cutlery to lever off tyres, and dad's best bucket to submerge inner tubes looking for bubbles. When found, we'd use our very own repair kit to fix the puncture.

We also carried out other repairs and improvements, such as changing handlebars to the favoured cow-horn design, fit our own lights and replace worn cotter pins, pedals, gears, chains and sprockets. And all this was learnt by the time we were 11-years old. First taught by dad, then left alone to think through and solve our inevitable breakdowns. If too complicated – and usually expensive – dad was called to help, but only on rare occasions, and hopefully agree to pay for the repair – after a box around the ears for damaging the bike in the first place. But that's how we learnt about simple mechanics and repairs. With this knowledge we went on to repair our own mopeds, motorbikes and cars.

Going to school in the 1970's was growing up in an era of confusion. Fresh faced post-graduate university students were slowly incorporating socialist teaching methods whilst old school teachers had their backs turned. Although they still had the upper hand, eventually they'd all retire, leaving the door wide open for left-wing anti-establishment teachers to indoctrinate vulnerable young 1970's children with biased views on politics and social issues.

In the meantime mature teachers strictly enforced old school practices whilst still suffering with PTSD caused by fighting in the Second World War. Barking discipline at us was normal as far as they were concerned, and canes, wooden rulers and blackboard rubbers were weapons of choice to inflict corporal punishment. And yes, I fell victim on a few occasions. Three times, actually: twice by cane – caught smoking and fighting, and once for talking in class – ruler across an open palmed hand.

Not forgetting the infamous blackboard rubber thrown at me. And it was a 50/50 chance on how you would suffer. Felt side – used to rub chalk from the blackboard – covered you and your blazer in chalk dust. The wooden end left you almost free of chalk dust, but bloody hurt when full flight was suddenly halted by connecting with your head.

Reciting times-table was a lesson I never enjoyed. Having to learn parrot fashion, it was only a matter of time I was asked to stand up in class and continue where the last poor sod ended, praying it would be the two, five or ten-times table. Of course it never was. Always seven or nine. I would then have to carry on: three nines are twenty-seven, four nines are thirty-nine…and so on. Get one wrong and expect a launched blackboard rubber heading your way. Yep, brace yourself, here it comes!

To remedy memory loss, a quick learning method was encouraged – the ready reckoner: a table of numbers to facilitate simple calculations. Simply a piece of square card large enough to write the 12-times table on a grid and small enough to place inside your blazer breast pocket, used to great effect, sort of. Problem was, playing outside with your mates after school was far more important than memorising tables.

Come rain, shine, wind, snow, drizzle or fog, weather conditions never stopped play. Raining – put a coat on, sunny – T-shirts and shorts, snowing – coat and gloves, if remembered. Drizzle – didn't matter. And all weather conditions invited different games to play. Fog was great to play hide and seek, which could last for hours. Raining: find a discarded receptacle of some kind to fill with rain water and drench each other – although already drenched by rain due to forgetting to wear a coat. In fact, whatever the weather, games often ended playing war. And it was always British verses Germans or cowboys verses Indians – depending upon the last film watched on television.

We all had cap guns: die-cast cowboy six-shooters, Winchester rifles, and the rich kid – as there was always one in your gang that seemed to have every toy – had a Lee-Enfield .303 rifle, complete with bolt action and plastic bullets. Although they never fired, just made a loud bang from caps. If caught short and didn't know we were playing war, we made guns and rifles out of sticks and small branches, mimicking the sound of a gun firing.

Cowboys and Indians: used guns – again – for cowboys. As for those dicked to play Indians, we made bows from a strong yet flexible long stick and mum's best wool. Arrows were made out of the strongest and straightest sticks, fashioned to a point at one end and making slits at the other using our pen knives – yes, we all had a pen knife, usually given as a present from our parents. And not once did we ever think of stabbing each other. They were used as designed – making bows and arrows. The slits made at the base were then fletched using discarded feathers to make it spin and stable in flight. And yes, they most definitely hurt when hit.

Splits was also a popular game: using an open pen knife we threw it at the ground towards an opponent standing a few yards away, hoping it stuck in the ground – blade down. In doing so your opponent would then pull it out and place a foot on where it landed, then throw it back for you to do the same. The idea was to make your opponent do the splits to reach the knife sticking in the ground, eventually falling over to gain maximum points. If you make a miss throw – doesn't stick in the ground – you lose a point to your opponent and have to start again.

Jumping off swings and slides was a great game to play. The idea here was to either swing as high as you can then launch yourself off the seat at the swings highest point and land as far away as possible – furthest away wins. Downside was the odd broken bone and twisted ankle. Using a slide was similar, only you had to stand up whilst sliding to the bottom in socks only, then launch yourself off the end as far as you can.

Combining both games using a football – naming it swing or slide volleyball – here you kick the ball – or punch it if standing on the slide steps – from someone on the ground throwing it at you. As soon as you made contact – whether punching it or not – meant jumping off the swing, or sliding down the slide, then run a lap around the frame before either jumping back on your swing or to the bottom of the slide steps. If hit by the ball thrower before getting back to base, you joined the thrower, so on and so on, leaving one to become the winner.

Throwing stones at each other was also a popular past time. Problem was injuries sustained were often head related, with cuts, bumps and bruises. When this game ended with usually a kid bowing out due to his war wound leaking blood from all angles, and quite possibly losing consciousness, bicycle games were hastily deployed. The most daring of these was to ride up and down the middle of a street using no hands with eyes tightly shut. The idea was to ride as far as possible before – inevitably – crashing into a parked car, or abruptly halted by an approaching vehicle frantically beeping a horn. Furthest to travel uninterrupted won the game.

Many more games were invented to keep us occupied during daylight hours, only going home when night time approached and the street lamps sparked up. We were always out; after school, all weekend, come spring, summer, autumn or winter. Being outside was our playground, our source of fun. Only on that rare occasion when illness crept behind us were we almost forced to stay indoors. But as soon as the slightest improvement of health was detected, back outside we went.

Summer holidays were brilliant. Up and dressed with the lark, we grabbed a bottle of pop and a packet of crisps from mum as we left the house. Never to return until dusk – or when told by dad. To a 9-year old, playing all of our games and inventing others meant all daylight hours were precious. But summer, although our best time to play, was tarnished by the long days. You see, when dad whistled – always stayed within whistling distance –

it was time to go home, even though the sun still shined at eight o'clock.

Next morning, however, straight up and out again, repeating the previous day's events, which was paramount to our childhood. That's what we did – played out all the time. And as we grew older we'd venture further afield – down other streets and into town, discovering a disused factory or bombed out building from the war, left to decay and fall down. These incredible playgrounds kept us entertained for weeks, and just in time for the summer holidays. One in particular springs to mind: the summer of 1976.

From April to September the summer just got hotter and hotter. To us kids it was no different to any other summer, and even if it did rain there's always coats. But to adults it was a complete nightmare. At first, in the early months of spring, the long warm days were enjoyed with barbecues, pub gardens, parks and the seaside. But by June, and with temperatures continuing to rise, the situation became a tad harder for them grown-ups.

The summer of 1975 was hot and with very little rainfall. The dry spell continued throughout autumn and well into the winter months. By spring 1976 only a very little rainfall hit a few regions, and by late April temperatures begun to rise with little hope of rain. When April turned into May, then into June, temperatures rarely sunk below 30 degrees Centigrade. Towards the end of June temperatures increased to just over 35 degrees, creating the worst drought to hit the British Isles in living memory. Rivers became dry and reservoirs were running dangerously low. Some even revealed roads, houses and churches, where small villages and Hamlets once stood.

The situation became so bad parliament passed the Drought Act of 1976 as the summer continued to bake the nation. A hose pipe ban was introduced and main water supplies disrupted with the use of standpipes and monitored by only turning them on a few times per day. Mum's queued in the streets to fill as many buckets of water they could carry back to the house.

Bathing was out of the question, which pleased us lads, and you could only wash when extremely dirty before using any of the precious liquid. However, on the odd occasion, we stood naked in the kitchen, stripped ready for a hospital-type sponge bath, waiting for mum to warm large pans of hot water on the stove. Toilet flushing was also discouraged, where government guidelines insisted, if it's yellow let it mellow, if it's brown flush it down. So the remaining water in the cistern was used only for number two's.

The lack of rain certainly caused problems with water authorities trying to keep the nation supplied, but they also had to take some of the blame. Water leaks were happening up and down the country in there thousands. Main water pipes were constantly bursting under a street somewhere, with millions of litres literally running down the drains. Many of these pipes dated back to the Victorian era, where cast iron pipes had simply perished and collapsed, causing a huge headache for the under-funded, nationally owned water companies to replace them with modern plastic pipes.

Having to contend with rationed water was one headache, the heat being another, but hot weather also brought an invasion of ladybirds: an estimated 24,000,000,000 of them, swarming in huge numbers across the entire country. And they were evil little blighters. With their favourite source of food – the aphid – rapidly depleting, humans became a frustrating target to munch on, biting whenever and wherever they pleased. Wasps were also a pain, and became more aggressive as their same food supply of aphid disappeared. But life went on best it could, and dodging ladybird bites or wasp stings became the norm when venturing outside.

Eating out wasn't nowhere near as common as it is today, mainly due to the fact there wasn't anywhere near as much choice. Restaurants were few and far between for the masses to afford, and fast food restaurants were even rarer. Wimpy was really our only choice outside London. And there was no 'drive-thru' either, it closed by 5 O'clock, and never opened on a Sunday. You also had to wait an age whilst your burger was prepared.

There were a few pizza parlours and fried chicken franchises dotted around, but again, only in large towns and cities. For everyone else takeaway food was only available from the humble fish and chip shop or local Chinese establishments, and you had to physically go to the shop and order it. Although some places accepted phone orders, there was no delivery service. So as a child, if you lived outside London, eating at home was the only real option.

Meal times meant all family members sat around a dinner table, with elbows off, and didn't eat lazily. In other words, kept your trap shut whilst chewing and didn't make any lip slapping or slurping noises. And you couldn't leave the table until everything was cleared off your plate. A tradition past down from generation to generation where food was scares in the Victorian era to rationing during the Second World War. It simply had to be appreciated, no matter what was served, and all of it eaten.

By the seventies food rationing was no longer an issue as food was generally in abundance. Nevertheless, times had shifted towards recognising famine in Cambodia, where millions of people were dying of hunger. So leaving food on your plate was regarded as an insult to those that were starving – weirdly.

Turning 11-years old meant we had to stay strong and face the onslaught that lay ahead – becoming a first-year pupil at Secondary school. Needless to say, being picked on and teased was a duty to endure, so we tensed up ready to receive whatever could be thrown at us. And we didn't care. We'd already toughened up playing outside, as did the older pupils. They knew it, we knew it. It was just a passage of many passages we had to face.

Playtime was now superseded by a more grown up terminology – break time. And there they were, second-year pupils hanging around in small gangs ready to pounce on any first-years that either stood alone or looked petrified. And like a pack of hyenas they attacked, sometimes caught by a patrolling break time teacher – usually holding a cup of tea in one hand and smoking a fag in the other. But they didn't care; they knew the score.

One by one victims fell foul to toilet dunking – head down the toilet whilst flushing. And these were cold, dirty Edwardian outbuildings with no roof and cracked porcelain urine stained latrines that had never been cleaned since they were installed. Brick built toilet cubicles – or traps as we called them – had old rotten wooden doors that never locked and a bare slated roof full of holes. The cistern was above the toilet bowl connected by a long cast iron pipe. Flushing was by yanking the chain attached to a lever on the side of the cistern.

More often than not it was the second-years that did the teasing and played pranks. Sometimes third-years, but very rarely fourth and fifth-year pupils. Much could be said for Grammar schools, not just Secondary Modern. My old Secondary school has seen many changes since I first walked through those Edwardian gates back in September 1977. In 1978 we moved to a brand new school with modern centrally heated indoor toilets, and girls were introduced – to a boys school? However, being the last of the boys, we were kept very much distant from the new modern education era below, including our old school ethics and discipline.

It was strange to see boys and girls running around between lessons, laughing and joking as they waited outside classrooms to go into their next lesson. For us from the older era we had to remain walking and silent, marching almost to our next lesson and stand in columns of two in total silence. Of course, we were always well behaved. Okay, we were good, sometimes, maybe.

Corporal punishment was banned, but not for us. Oh no, we were the last of the old school practices, and our teachers knew it. So awarded with the cane, ruler, blackboard rubber or other punishments remained high on post-war teacher's sadistic minds, but fundamentally undesired by the lower year modern teaching methods. Detention was their worst punishment. Oh, we dreamt of just detention – it didn't sting. However, we were also dicked for that too: part of the package after being caned, smacked with a ruler or a blackboard rubber. Less painful punishments were dished out for memory loss in the guise of making you do PE (Physical Education) barefoot in underpants should you forget your kit. You only ever did this once. After all, what 11 or 12-year old boy ever have clean underwear.

Putting large cities to one side, many towns were predominately white in the 1970's. In fact 99.9 percent of pupils from my school were white. The only ethnic child was Aduk Loi, a refugee from the Vietnamese war. The only black, Indian or Asian person we ever saw was on television. Even our corner shop owners were all white, usually incredibly obese, stunk to high-heaven of decaying body odour, old and grumpy. So it was inevitable we grew up with traditions from past generations that didn't know how to respond, react or understand those from a different country, let alone race, religion, colour or culture.

To us, black folk were from Africa, Indians were from India and Aduk Loi was a pain in the arse. Racism was also a word rarely used outside of cities and large towns because it barely registered as an issue. And living in a predominately white town in the East Midlands we never came across racial slurs or expressed any kind of racial hatred. After all, why would we? There was no need to.

Using slang to describe or identify an individual was nothing more than a simple way to do just that, no matter where they came from. French were frogs, Germans were Krauts, Russians were Ivans, Americans were Yanks, Norfolk was full of carrot crunchers, Northerners were flatcaps and Londoners were all Cockneys. Nothing more than nicknames to describe a genre or region of people in a given area or country. No Different to Anglo-Saxon European whites described as a limey, honky, ang mo, cracker, farang, peckerwood, gammon, hick, gubba, gweilo, haole, medigan or mangia cake, ofay, trailer trash or white trash, whitey…, yep, the list goes on.

Cultural differences were also ignored, but not at fault of my school. After all, why be concerned with other cultures when they didn't bother us. Even politics was ignored. That was for adults only. The nearest we came to discussing politics was the teaching of Communism by our new fresh from university socialist teachers and the threat of Soviet nuclear missiles pointing at us by older generation teachers.

My school was a typical Church of England comprehensive, where all of my teachers were white males and most were authoritative old school disciplinarians, leaving a small minority of young university post-graduates socialists, only to introduce women teachers years later. The older teachers had either served in the Second World War or did National Service, so you can imagine their teaching methods. The remaining 3 fresh faced university teachers that had no military background whatsoever definitely shined through with their slack modern teaching methods.

We thought we could chew them up and spit them out. But no, they were almost as bad as the others; dishing out punishment left, right and centre. One of them, our new physics teacher, was the cruellest when it came to punishing unruly pupils. Not one for corporal punishment, nonetheless, his method of execution was far worse – the power of embarrassment, as one kid in my class discovered to his peril. And out of all potential victims it had to be the class bully.

Okay, not really a bully, or how we perceived bullies to be in the 1980's. Nevertheless, Andy 'prick' Thorne was a boy that loved fighting, smoking, causing trouble and skived off school now and again to hang around town with other dumb wits of his ilk. Unfortunately – for him – his insubordinate attitude was about to become the butt of all jokes for pupils and teachers alike, lasting the rest of his school years.

Our new university trained physics teacher instantly became a test subject – no different to any other new teacher – to see how far we could push and find chinks in his socialist armour. Standing silently in single file we awaited the approach of Mr C. Heavy cowboy boot footsteps could be heard approaching, instantly breaking the silence as we stood almost to attention waiting for him to open the classroom door.

'Enter!' Mr C said in a low meaningful voice, standing in front of the queue. A man no older than his early thirties, with long dark shoulder-length wavy hair that belonged in the 1970's, as did his clothes: black cowboy boots, green corduroy trousers and a tweed jacket with the preverbal brown leather elbow patches.

We walked into the classroom, stood behind our desks and waited for the order to sit, as we always did for any teacher.

'Take a seat ladies,' he boomed.

Being called 'ladies' wasn't anything new. Most of our teachers called us that. It was something they just did. Never bothered or offended us, or caused any physiological issues requiring a session in a crying room or months of therapy. As far as we were concerned it was a term given to let us know they were in charge.

We sat down, opened our textbooks, and waited in silence as Mr C formally introduced himself by writing his name on the blackboard. Straight away the fooling around started whilst his back was turned, with one lad simulating a loud fart by repeatedly squashing the palm of one hand with his other arm under a sweaty armpit, followed by sniggering from the rest of us.

'Settle down,' Mr C calmly said as he finished writing his name. 'Right,' he snapped, clapping his chalky hands together, 'my name is spelt and pronounced as it is on the blackboard. But you will always address me as Sir whilst in class, only to use my surname for introduction, got it?' Mumbling followed. 'Got it?' he said deliberately slowly.

'Yes, sir,' we replied in unison, equally as slow.

Damn, he was no different to any other old-fashioned school teacher. All of us had woefully misjudged him. Well, not quite all. Andy Thorne decided to take it one step further by mimicking everything he said, lasting for, oh, around 2.3 seconds.

'You boy!' Mr C shouted, pointing at Andy, 'got a problem you want to share with the ladies?' Andy kept quiet. 'I said, do you want to share something with the class? Answer me!'

'No need to shout, sir, I'm not deaf.'

You could almost see Mr C's face turn red. We coward low onto our desk lids, slowly turning to face Andy and see what he was going to do next.

'Ah, I see. Because I'm the new teacher, you all want to test me, do you?'

We all shook our heads denying his question. One of us had already received a whack of the cane from the deputy-head that morning, and I was next for getting caught smoking during lunch break, so there was no way we wanted to get in any more trouble.

'Stand up, boy. What do we call you?' Mr C asked. Andy instinctively stood up and placed his hands behind his back, as we all did when told to stand. 'Well?'

'Well what, sir,' Andy replied with a smug grin, looking around the class for amused approval.

'Your name, boy, your name. What is it?' Mr C bellowed.

'Andy, sir.'

Mr C sighed as we quietly sniggered. He knew Mr C wanted his surname but little did we know he already knew it. Also his date of birth, academic grades – being a tad low – which class clowns were expected to be disobedient and cause trouble, including Andy.

'Place your hands on your head, Thorne.' Andy's smug grin suddenly turned into a worried concern, unaware Mr C knew it. 'Are you hard of hearing, Thorne? Hands on head!'

Andy, now unsure of the situation, flinched at Mr C's booming voice and instantly did as he was told.

Mr. C walked towards the front of his desk and placed a bunch of keys on one corner, slowly pushing them over the edge. 'Pick them up, Thorne.'

'What?'

'I said pick them up!'

Andy walked slowly towards the keys and picked them up.

'Stand up straight! Did I tell you to put your arms down?'

'But – '

'Silence!'

We had all now lost the ability to snigger. We'd never witnessed or experienced anything like this before. Shouty teachers, yes, but not quite like this.

'Place the keys onto the floor, stand up straight with your hands on your head, then pick up the keys and hand them to me, got it!'

Andy did as he was told, only for Mr. C to throw them at the back of the class, narrowly missing Gary 'hooker' Fisher's head.

'Pick em up, Thorne.' Andy turned to see where the keys landed, then looked at Mr C, not really sure what to do. 'Pick them up!' Andy did as he was told and started to walk back towards Mr C. 'Stand still! Did I tell you to bring them back?'

'No, but –'

'Silence! Did I tell you to speak?' Andy was now totally confused. 'Come here.'

Andy hesitated. 'I said come here! You do understand English, don't you?' He didn't answer, just in case he shouldn't have. 'I asked you a question!'

'bbbut – '

'bbbut? Is that your answer, bbbut? Are you thick as well as got a stutter, Thorne? Andy didn't answer. 'Thorne! You can here me, can't you?' Andy quickly nodded, fearing a sharp response if he verbally answered. 'Hand me my keys, Thorne!'

He gave Mr C his keys, only to throw them once again at the back of the class, repeating this act over and over, eventually making Andy sob uncontrollably. But Mr C didn't stop because of a few tears. He continued to throw the keys for Andy to retrieve right up to the end of the half-hour lesson. But his punishment wasn't over just yet. As we gingerly left the classroom without learning anything physics-like, Andy was given lines: I am a cry baby and must not test new teachers, repeated 50 times on the blackboard. Once finished he was given a lecture by Mr C.

As always after a huge stripping off by teachers, there were no screaming blue murder, no public enquiry, and most definitely no blubbering to mum and telling her what teacher did to us, if only in fear of further punishment from our parents. And there was most certainly no crying, unless your name was Andy 'prick' Thorne. That was icing on the cake for those that watched his performance in front of the class. Thanks for that, Andy. And there was no naughty corner, evicted from class or made to sit on your own. What would that prove? No, just good old-fashioned punishments, endured because we no doubt deserved it.

We never knew what Mr C said to Andy as he refused to snitch, but he never misbehaved in any other lesson again. And although the butt of many jokes during lunch and break time, remarkably, his grades improved. So did Mr C know his grades would improve by employing such a punishment, or was it a fluke? Andy could have easily skived off school more than he did before, but even his truancy became a lesser reoccurrence. And Mr C went on to become one of our best and most respected teachers in our year, let alone the entire school. So being strict paid off, didn't it?

Religion was also strict, by which I mean in its actual teaching from the bible, at least for us remaining old-school pupils. No other religion was discussed or recognised other than the Church of England. So our upbringing on such a precarious and volatile subject was smothered with a blanket of old-school belief. They were right and all other religions were wrong. No discussion, no debate, just do as you're told because we know best.

Other lessons for our year were metalwork including basic engineering – stripping and re-building a moped, then riding it around the playground to prove we could repair faults. Woodwork, building technology including bricklaying, chemistry (where one lesson was how to make gunpowder), as well as the usual sciences and the 3 'R's. However, for the years below, the new curriculum sacked mopeds, metal work and building technology, only to be replaced with girlie cooking, needlecraft and material handling – combining woodwork and metalwork with other materials.

As for bullying, I don't really remember any, other than head dunking down toilets, name-calling or throwing eggs and fireworks at each other, but that was it, and expected. We just grew thick skin, broad shoulders and put up with it. After all, it was nothing more than pubescent teasing, wasn't it? We dished out as much as we took, without fear, persecution or prejudice.

Fighting happened almost every day, and I too had the odd scrap. Most of us had at least one during our 5 glorious Secondary school years. Smoking certainly happened amongst a small group, and I was one of them. As for drugs – the closest we came to seeing or taking drugs was when someone smuggled in half a bottle of scotch or the odd can of lager. And any weapons smuggled into school were attached to our wrists and ankles. In other words, a punch-up was just that, with the odd boot.

Stereotypes were nothing different, then or now. The typical school squat refusing to muck in with the rest and just wanted to learn; the wanna be squat that always had his top shirt button fastened, wearing his tie and carried a briefcase; the fat lad – always one, and yes, we took the piss; the thick kids unable to learn a bloody thing; the fleabag that always stunk to high heaven. The rest of us, we all had some kind of tick or flaw, and we all took the piss out it, be we short, tall, fat, thin, blonde or ginger.

No one got hurt, no one scarred for life. After all, this was the early eighties; that was the way and part of growing up. There was definitely no need for a crying room to express emotions or group hugs from concerned friends either. I mean, could you imagine if we had such a thing back in the seventies and eighties? The humiliation would have been unbearable.

For those expressing a lean towards homosexuality – there wasn't anyone. Well yes, I know that couldn't possibly be true according to statistics of today, but you would have never guessed, and for good reason. Being gay in the 1980's, as well as previous decades, was something to definitely ridicule and take the piss. And that is because being in a gay relationship under the age of 21-years old or show affection in public was still illegal. And because the law said it was illegal it was okay to poke fun.

We grew up in an era that emulated our forefathers attitude towards homosexuality, and certain television personalities reflected public opinion in the guise of making it funny and even crass by acting the part. Actors and entertainers, such as Franky Howard, John Inman and Larry Grason, made careers out of acting camp with homosexual innuendoes and risky references, knowing it pulled the crowds and made an audience laugh.

Chapter Twelve

Adults of Generation X

In most households television was only switched on for children an hour after school or Saturday morning. Any other time adults were in charge, and that meant having to get up, walk across the living room and switch over one of the 3 available channels on enormous and stiff buttons or dial, as remote controls were yet to catch on in the UK.

Programmes gripped the nation with soap operas such as Coronation Street and politics shows proved ever popular for the working classes. To escape the rigours of a hard working week comedy shows became a favourite must watch, The Comedians being one. Stars such as Bernard Manning, Les Dawson and Frank Carson had audiences crying with laughter telling mother-in-law jokes and taking the piss out of the Irish, Welsh and Scots.

Situation comedies, such as Fawlty Towers, Are You Being Served and Porridge, were in the big league, capturing millions of viewers every week. As was The Good Life, Steptoe and Son, Dad's Army, Citizen Smith, and shows such as Morcombe and Wise and The Two Ronnies. Love Thy Neighbour, Til Death Do Us Part, and It ain't Half Hot Mum, were also loved by the masses, but are now banned from the airwaves for there 'so called' (BBC terminology) racial undertones.

Largely misunderstood by a social media-seduced, bubble-wrapped cotton wool society, reason for the ban was due to a complete Millennial meltdown and understanding of 1970's/1980's comedy content and what the characters actually portrayed. Putting it simply, a white guy, such as the character Alf Garnet in Til Death Do Us Part, constantly made a fool out of himself with outrageous comments about everything and anything.

Actor, Warren Mitchell, who played Alf Garnet, was a stereotypical homophobic, anti-socialist, racist pensioner, raised in an era of simplicity, unhindered by foreign intervention, culture or influence. Incredibly opinionated about politics, social issues, Americans, Germans, the French, Jews, in fact anyone that didn't agree with his perceived generation. Although he raised some hilarious comments on how he thought the country should be governed, he made a complete and utter fool out of himself, not unlike Millennial liberalism.

Stand up comedians of yesteryear are also branded with the same Millennial attitude, accusing 1970's and 1980's comics as being homophobic, racists and sexist, since banned from modern UK television. Bernard Manning and Les Dawson to name but two. Frank Carson's Irish gags are now dubbed racist, yet he too was Irish. Dave Alan, also a brilliant Irish comedian, but re-runs of his gags are now branded racist, sexist and xenophobic in a confused Millennial world. Even Mother-in-law jokes now banned for being, well, mother-in-law-ist? Since, gags about polar bears, dolphins, squirrels, in fact anything regarded fluffy and cute, all dismissed and frowned upon in fear of hurting someone's feelings.

Pensioners, the disabled, stupid people, small, tall, fat and thin, women, lesbians, homosexuals, trans-gender, transvestite, Pakistani, Indian, French and German jokes, all sneered at. Black jokes, poking fun out of the Chinese, Japanese, even the Welsh, all banned. Bikini-clad women chased by a randy milkman, now classed as sexist, but received as nothing more than innocent fun back in the day.

Smoking remained extremely common, where a typical brand of cigarettes would cost around 20-new pence for a pack of twenty. Drinking was still popular amongst all societies, particularly for the masses, where men and women used the local pub, working men's or social club for entertainment. A pint of beer in 1970 was also around 20-new pence. A loaf of sliced white bread was around 8 or 9-new pence. However, the average national weekly wage was in the region of £30.

I mention the term 'new pence' because grown-ups in the early 1970's entered a decade of confusion over currency and the demise of Pound Shillings and Pence after the introduction of decimalisation in 1971. There was also fuel and food shortages, horrific inflation, industrial disputes not seen since 1926, and yet further political rhetoric over something rather important called the European Economic Countries (EEC) issue.

You have to go back to 1815 and the defeat of Napoleon to find the true beginning of free trade between European nations. And in 1823 the Reciprocity of Duties Act was agreed in parliament to allow free trade with Prussia, allowing free entry of ships into each other's Ports. But it didn't last due to existing Navigation Laws protecting import of Corn and British ships around the world. However, over the following decades Europe amazingly became increasingly united.

By the late 1920's France was still torn to shreds due to the First World War and the UK suffered a decline in world supremacy, industrial action and the great depression. The government needed to act in any means necessary to bring coin into the Chancellors coffers. In doing so free trade ceased with immediate effect on all foreign goods reaching the country so to kick-start the economy. And by 1932 the Duties Act created a 10 percent tariff on all imports, except countries belonging to the British Empire that allowed tariff free imports for the Mother Land.

After the Second World War Winston Churchill was desperate for a United Europe to quell any possible future war between its nations, join forces against possible Soviet threat, and restore free trade across European countries. By 1957 the Treaty of Rome created the first stage of the EEC to establish free trade. The UK concerned with the USA arranging their own trade agreement with Europe and other Empire countries, applied to join the fledgling EEC in 1961. But there was a problem – France vetoed the UK. Or rather French President, Charles De Gaulle, vetoed the application.

Prime Minister, Harold MacMillan, and other Cabinet members, had meetings with De Gaulle and his government officials, where MacMillan was accused of wanting to join in fear of losing out on trade agreements with other European countries and thrown into political isolation. Discussions became almost impossible with Europe's two major countries misunderstanding each other and what they wanted. MacMillan tried to explain in his broken French what the UK expects, but De Gaulle's response may have been misinterpreted as saying 'no' to the UK but could have been saying no to something completely different.

Nevertheless, De Gaulle not only said 'non' once, but twice, when the second application in 1967 was submitted. It wasn't until De Gaulle resigned after losing a referendum on reform, where Georges Pompidou won the election to become Prime Minister, and Ted Heath became UK's Prime Minister, that talks between 2 leaders whom liked each other could finally take place. And Ted Heath was determined to make the UK join the

EEC before his end of term, if only to place his name in the history books as the British Prime Minister that negotiated on behalf of the nation to be part of this incredible moment.

Two more years of negotiations commenced, with France finally deciding that The UK should join, if only to keep the Germans in place, and the Germans wanted the UK to join, if only to keep the French in place. For the first time since 1961 the UK had gone from being vetoed – twice – to becoming a major political and commercial player in a new and exciting European club.

Churchill once said, Europe should become a United States of Europe, not unlike the United States of America. Working as one with free trade between all member countries. But there was one fundamental problem that immediately sprung to mind: USA was young, naïve, spoke with one recognisable national language and had one currency. Europe is made up of individual countries with different languages, cultures, religion, social structures, currencies, politics and conflicting industrial practices.

Europe is also ancient, set in its own individual ways and incredibly stubborn. But EEC members liked the idea of a one political authority, where each Member State contributed ideas, industrial as well as commercial innovations, border and boundary discussions, trade, and of course, loads of donated tax money. By October 1971 the Treaty of Accession was scrutinised by both sides of the Houses of Parliament, but the masses weren't too enthralled about joining a European club.

Concerns quickly surfaced as to whether UK's interests were correctly negotiated and terms met, so a public debate was aired over radio and television channels to address any issues voters may have. Nonetheless, disregarding public opinion, Ted Heath signed the Treaty on behalf of the UK 22nd January 1972 automatically introducing The European Community Bill, giving detail to parliament Britain's membership of the EEC where countless hours of debate ensued upon the House.

Britain became a full member a year later on 1st January 1973. Of course, this new club created huge discussion inside and outside of parliament. In 1974 Ted Heath was beaten by Labour leader Harold Wilson in the General Election, where Wilson promised a referendum on the EEC to decide whether we stay in the EEC should he win. Keeping his promise, in June 1975 the country had a referendum to decide whether the UK should stay a member.

The question put to the nation on the ballot paper was simple: Do you think that the United Kingdom should stay in the European Community? Yes or No. The weeks before the referendum created a storm of arguments between same party and cross party politicians, industrial leaders, unions and the voter. Print and airwave media had a field day, openly leaning towards staying in the EEC – later known as the Common Market – and papers only printed reasons as to why the UK should remain, totally ignoring reasons as to why we should leave. Remind you of a more recent European political quagmire? The situation is uncanny.

Labour party Member of Parliament, Tony Benn, predicted huge job losses should we remain, and it turned out he was right. Half a million workers found themselves out of work and predicted further job losses should the country continue its membership. But newspapers snubbed him as lying through his back teeth, ridiculing his facts with political rhetoric.

Front page of The Sun newspaper headlined: Vote Yes for a future together, and No to a future alone. The

Daily Mirror headlined: A vote for the future, then had a picture of children from each EEC country huddled together, leaving one lonely child from the UK adding: For the lad outside, vote Yes. Even the Daily Express headlined: The Express is for the Market. And with their biased view, including radio and television, a brainwashed nation voted. 17.3 million for Yes, with 8.4 million voting No.

There was also another huge and incredibly important national change, treated with suspicion of its content and timing towards joining the Common Market: Decimalisation. Even a new currency name was considered, such as Noble, Royal or simply New Pound. Thankfully it was decided that The Pound Stirling would remain, although a new unit of denomination became known as the New Pence to distinguish it from the old Penny, termed later as 'Pee.'

For those that are too young to remember old money, it had been around for over 2,000 years. Roman letters LSD (lsd) were used to determine abbreviation of old English currency with L (Librum – interpreted into English as Pound), S (Solidus – interpreted into English as Silver), and D (Denarius – interpreted into English as Pence). The Roman Pound consisted of 240 Denarius or 240 pence in old money. With me so far?

Breaking down old English currency even further, and putting it simply, starting from the lowest denominator was a ¼ of one penny or 1/16d of the old penny called a farthing. Half penny was 1/2d or 5/24 of one new pence. A penny, 1d, was 5/12 of one new pence. There was also a 3d coin (similar in size and shape of the new £1 coin) known as thrupence, making 1 ½ new pence. Sixpence was worth 6d or 2 ½ new pence. A shilling, 1/- became 5 new pence. Then there was a florin, 2/- or 10 new pence. Half a Crown was 2/6 (2/- and 6d) or 12 ½ new pence. A crown was 5/- or 25 new pence. The 10-shilling note was replaced with the new 50 pence piece. You see, easy.

After using a currency devised by the Romans and adapted for use in a British constitution, it all came to an abrupt end with the introduction of Decimal Day, 15th February 1971. Banks closed for 4-days during the run-up of the big day. Ready available coin converter tables were printed for everyone to carry in their pockets, shops and staff that worked with money were educated using the new currency, and a huge pile of media print on decimalisation was splashed around the country ready for a smooth transition. The result, pandemonium let loose upon the nation.

Although the exchange went swimmingly, and old money worked with new in unison for a while, there were those that couldn't or wouldn't embrace decimalisation, even though it was incredibly simple to use. There were even fears that shops would swindle shoppers by short-changing them and raise prices to confuse the nation's elderly. But generally the masses embraced the new and easy system. Finally, the United Kingdom, including Ireland, were the last European countries to embrace decimalisation, now having a currency with the same denomination table as the rest of Europe, and joining of the EEC was mealy a coincidence?

To be fair, conspiracy theories behind the timing of new money failed to carry any gravity. Decimalisation was first thought of during the Victorian era where a Decimal Association was put together in 1841 to discuss possibility of replacing old money. But over time it was forgotten; pushed to the back of the draw, left behind as some crazy afterthought. In 1961, however, South Africa decided to decimalise its currency, in turn re-kindled further interest with the British government to do the same by supporting an enquiry into how and when decimalisation could be possible. And on 1st March 1966 the government agreed to convert, taking a further 5-years to come to any fruition.

Whilst the masses converted old money into new, and get their heads around joining the Common Market, there was yet another bitter pill to swallow – Value Added Tax (VAT). And this particular introduction was a huge headache for everyone, yet today we all take for granted. Almost everything we purchase has some sort of VAT on it: clothes, food, fuel, electrical goods, cars, laptops, computers, smartphones, services… the list goes on and on. In fact VAT is the third largest tax income for the Chancellor of the Exchequer – only beaten by Income Tax and National Insurance. But not so long ago this wasn't the case.

A Purchase Tax was the precursor to VAT where a levy was attached to the wholesale price at source of manufacture. In other words the manufacturer was taxed on the goods they made, not at the point of sale. Due to the Second World War higher Purchase Tax levies were raised to help with the war effort, where 33 1/3 percent was initially added. Towards the end of the war Purchase Tax was raised to an incredible 100 percent.

On 1st January 1973 a Conservative government introduced VAT at a rate of 10 percent on most goods and services. In the following year, and now with a Labour government in charge, the rate was lowered to just 8 percent, but raised on fuel and expensive goods to 12.5 percent. It was then raised again later in the same year to a staggering 25 percent. It has since raised and lowered – mainly raised – ever since its introduction, standing, for now [2020] at 20 percent.

During all this palaver of a new and exciting decade, surely the country could now settle down and just get on with it. Well, no. You see, whilst the government changed its ancient currency to a new decimalised denomination, joined the EEC without a referendum, and introduced a new VAT system to sting everyone, the working masses were still in a bit of a flap over pay and conditions.

Coal powered electricity stations struggled to meet consumer demand and old technology started to breakdown and crumble. Industrial action by powerful coal unions also forced power stations to either run at a minimum or shut down altogether, causing power cuts and widespread panic across the nation. The situation became so bad hospitals had to carry out operations using emergency battery power and head torches.

Factories had no choice but stop production whilst other businesses, including shops, warehouses and offices rushed to finish off what they were doing during a dip in supply signalled by the dimming of lights before complete shut down. Within a few minutes or so the electricity supply ceased, and there was no indication as to when it would return. At home I remember watching television then suddenly it switched off, as did the lights, toaster, twin-tub, followed by a lot of swearing by mum. But just like previous generations, my Baby Boomer parents didn't panic. Instead, they lit many candles stood in saucers around the house.

Industrial action by coal miner unions in 1970 went on a 'work to rule' where other pits quickly followed suit, dramatically reducing supply to power stations. Transport unions were also quick to jump on the bandwagon, preventing delivery and causing a huge disruption of goods across the country. Conservative Prime Minister, Edward Heath, demanded a 3-day working week, only to exacerbate the problem by causing further power cuts and a lack of food reaching shops and supermarkets. Upon the eve of his demise he famously asked unions, 'who runs this country, me or you?' They replied, 'we do.'

To make matters worse there had been a global shortage of oil where petrol and diesel was rationed per vehicle – first time since the Second World War. Putting aside the immediate panic buying, remarkably, the nation organised themselves with very little argument and simply did their best to work around the problem by queuing – a craft past down from the war. The reason for the lack of oil was down to the Organisation of Petroleum Exporting Countries (OPEC).

Founded by Iraq, Kuwait, Iran, Venezuela and Saudi Arabia, they supplied Europe with most of its crude oil to produce diesel and petrol. But on 6th October 1973 OPEC introduced an embargo on the UK, USA, Canada, Rhodesia (Zimbabwe), South Africa, Portugal, Netherlands and Japan, for supporting Israel when Egypt invaded the occupied Bar Lev Line, Sinai Peninsula. Egyptian ally, Syria, then launched an offensive upon Israeli occupied Golan Heights, where Israel took both areas after the 6-Day war in 1967.

President Richard Nixon provoked OPEC further still by supplying Israel with a vast amount of weapons totalling $2,000,000,000 where OPEC retaliated by decreasing supply of crude oil to Israeli allies by a staggering 25 percent, creating a global recession. In doing so, the largely unaffected self-sufficient oil producer, USA, increased tensions with Europe, virtually reliant upon OPEC. Meanwhile, coal miner and railway unions continued their strike action.

Transport Secretary, Barbara Castle imposed a speed limit on motorways to 70mph – still enforced today – and a total driving ban (except emergency services and the armed forces) on Sundays to conserve fuel for the nations commute. During the winter months Prime

Minister, Ted Heath, advised the masses to heat only one room in houses to conserve resources, as well as stockpile on candles due to power cuts. Netherlands went one further by imposing a prison sentence should anyone exceeded electricity rations. Not quite sure how this was monitored, but there you go.

Thankfully, by March 1974 the oil embargo was lifted, taking a further 6-years to reach some kind of normality. But political unrest remained in the UK, where Ted Heath lost the 1974 election to Labour Leader, Harold Wilson, a socialist and union sympathiser agreeing with union politics, and they knew it. They also knew the government was finally held tight within the fist of their greedy hands.

Disputes for higher wages and better working conditions during the beginning of the century were necessary to fight a just course towards having a decent life, and the 1970's working class reaped the rewards. But unions were a huge money pit for Harold Wilson and the Labour Party, receiving millions of pounds in donations for propping up union support. Yet caused a massive headache for industrialists forced to agree with union working conditions, hours and impossible wage increases. Even if it meant closure for many businesses unable to afford their extortionate demands.

Industrialists verses unions of the late 19th Century had been completely turned on its head by 1970. It was now the unions that became so powerful they demanded and received almost anything they wanted. Socialism through the 19th Century had reached its pinnacle, but ruined by incredibly powerful union leaders, ignoring the fine balance deservedly reached only a few decades before. Blinded by scorn and resentment, hell-bent on destroying modern industrialists that had nothing to do with destroying their forefather's social belief, the new socialist movement completely missed the point and they themselves emerged as the greedy fat cat industrialists of old.

Disputes of this magnitude during the 1970's caused food shortages, incredibly inflated High Street prices and even starvation. One morning a loaf of bread would cost around 9p but the following morning it cost 20p and continued to rise. Fuel shortages created delivery shortages, with little or no shop deliveries for weeks. In turn shops and supermarkets had to close because shelves were empty, and the vicious cycle continued. The inevitable became reality: socialism is great, until you run out of capitalist money.

Something had to be done, and by 1976 the Labour Party voted a no confidence with Harold Wilson, replacing him with Jim Callaghan – out of the frying pan, into the fire. At first he managed to reduce inflation from an almost staggering 27 percent to half of that but at a cost for the unions. Although Callaghan was a staunch socialist he knew he had to curb spending. To do this he introduced a pay cap and, remarkably, the TUC agreed.

Callaghan's plan was working, but there was still a long way to go. Pushing his proposal further by introducing a cap of 5 percent on wage increases with the unions, surprisingly, the TUC accepted the offer. But this time the General Council didn't, demanding a return to collective bargaining. In other words, strike until union demands were met.

By 22nd September 1978 the country embarked upon another era of dark clouds no different to the 1920's. To further darken already dark clouds, the Ford factory in Dagenham, all 15,000 employees, walked out. Workers from other Ford factories around the country quickly followed suit, and within 4-days a total of 57,000 had downed tools. Of course, it was over pay and working hours, where Transport and General Workers Union (TGWU) demanded an incredible 25 percent wage increase and a reduced working week of 35-hours for their members.

With these impossible demands Ford managed to make a deal with the TGWU of a 17 percent wage rise with no decrease in working hours. This agreement made many workers from other industries incredibly jealous and wanted a piece of the fat inflation raising pie. Sod the masses, we're alright Jack, so to speak. Public sector employees, including the nationalised railways, council workers, television camera operators, set designers, electrical engineers and even ambulance drivers also went on strike demanding a wage increase.

NHS nurses in over 1,000 hospitals refused to treat patients until their 25 percent increase was met. Fuel tanker drivers demanded an outrageous 40 percent increase and held picket lines outside refineries, stopping much needed fuel reaching petrol stations until their demands were met. Other truck drivers followed suit with their demands, not wanting to miss out on tanker drivers. A total of almost 1,500,000 workers across the country were now on strike.

Schools closed due to fuel shortages – again – diesel trains were left in sidings and airports closed with airliners grounded because no fuel deliveries. Many other private and public sector workers were unable to travel, and even gravediggers went on strike as did refuse collectors. Corpses lay unburied and stockpiled in mortuaries. Industrial, commercial and domestic waste remained piled high, creating mountains of rubbish on the nations streets. Rats in their millions polluted areas, scurrying from one rubbish mountain to another, spreading disease and creating a foul stench not experienced since the Victorian era.

Queuing outside shops became almost as common as the Second World War, and rationing was considered to quell fighting over a can of beans and rioting in shop aisles. Working hours lost piled up like rubbish on the streets to a staggering 29,500,000 hours. Those unaffected by unions couldn't get to work and found themselves unable to claim benefits because, technically, they were still employed. Some employers sacked employees for not getting to work, and others made redundant due to business closures.

However, there was some rest-bite from VAT, decimalisation, strikes, industrial disputes, EEC, political carnage and high inflation, thanks to Her Majesty the Queen and her Silver Wedding Jubilee, on 7th June 1977. Everyone went wild over the celebrations, with communities across the whole country working together, including Scotland, baking cakes and making sandwiches for street parties. Yes, in 1977 and in between industrial disputes, large majority of the nation loved their Royal Family, still believed in their country, and worked together for the common good.

London alone had around 4,000 street parties, and all over the country towns, cities and villages laid trestle tables and chairs down streets, tied red, white and blue bunting across lamp posts and Union flags hung from bedroom windows. Parks, pub gardens, halls, car parks, clubs, river banks, town centres, markets, businesses and tower blocks, all held parties. Offices, factories, warehouses, derelict buildings, in fact, everywhere you looked a Union flag flew in the wind.

Crowds filled The Mall and around Buckingham Palace. RAF flew across London in vintage planes and modern jets, Royal Navy frigates, destroyers and aircraft carriers sounded foghorns, and the army held parades up and down the country. And after the Silver Jubilee, parties turned to quiet streets once again: it was back to work, strike, or whatever the masses were doing before the celebrations. And during the following years manufactures, railways, coal mines, power stations, factories and the House of Commons continued arguing, bickering and disrupting the nation.

By 1979 the 'Winter of Discontent,' dubbed by Conservative Member of Parliament, Norman Tebbitt, described the connection with William Shakespeare's play Richard III and the chaos within Callaghan's Labour government. The country was crying out for change. A huge and drastic change to rid the rubbish as well as union power that brought the United Kingdom down on its knees. And in the merry month of May 1979 the country went to the polling stations to place their vote with hope of placing the country back on its feet.

THE MILLENNIAL BUG

Chapter Thirteen

Dawn of a new era

To re-cap: The Millennial Generation started in 1980, right? Okay, but between Generation X and the Millennials, Xennials squeezed into a 10-year gap starting in 1975 last of which born in 1985. However, Latter births of Xennials were born 4-years within the Generation X era, where Generation Y started in 1980 5-years inside the Xennial Generation, ending in 1994. Then came Generation Z – or iGen in its latter years. This extremely confused generation ended in 2012 lasting a closer realistic 17-years, with Generation Alpha starting in 2013. Got it? No, me neither.

The incredible sense of community spirit lasting from the Victorian industrial era was slowly coming to an end. As factories closed and cars became increasingly ready available, commuting to other towns and cities was becoming the mainstay of working practices. Entire communities with row after row of terraced streets were now just homes for the individual family or single occupier, rather than a solid community where everyone in the street knew each other.

Generation Y walked into an era of the UK voting for its first woman Prime Minister, growing unemployment, racial and youth issues within inner cities and towns around the country. By 1981 the Conservative government continued with their promise to lower inflation, but at an enormous cost. Jim Callaghan's Labour government left the UK skint and with inflation at an incredible 27 percent due to his failed socialist policies, but by 1981 it was brought down to 11 percent. Although the severity of Thatcher's solution created a massive wave of unemployment engulfing large industrial areas and local authorities alike.

The previous Labour government, ruled by the unions, had little power other than surrender to their outlandish demands. Although creating millions of jobs, they didn't really exist within companies that employed them. Inevitably this job for the boys attitude came to an abrupt end, bringing with it high inflation, exacerbating domestic costs and mass unemployment. The effect was huge, and once again leaving the masses to face incredible hard hitting consequences.

However, another social issue was thrown into the mix, and although inner cities of Victorian and Edwardian era's had some racial tensions, they were nothing compared to the early 1980's. Black and Asian immigrants grew at a rapid pace after the Second World War, settling down and creating communities synonymous to their own culture – not unlike Victorian Jewish immigrants – where clashes between local indigenous communities were inevitable, especially when mass unemployment crept into the equation.

Cities including Liverpool, Manchester, Leeds, Nottingham, Birmingham and Newcastle suddenly erupted into unprecedented violence. Groups of youths from all backgrounds gathered en-mass to exhaust frustration, igniting riots first in London, particularly the Brixton district. And there have been many reasons as to why these riots took place: racial hatred, victimisation, police brutality, poor housing and unemployment, to name a few.

But there must have been an incident that claimed intention, and that finger of blame pointed towards the stabbing of a young black man, only the perpetrators in this particular case, were also black, so any knee-jerk racial motive was ruled out. Fighting between rival gangs increased over the decades and was slowly becoming out of control. On this occasion, however, the incident created a subterfuge for turning anger onto police.

A crowd gathered around the victim whilst police desperately tried to administer first aid, but when they attempted to get him into a patrol car and drive to the hospital they were set upon by an angry mob. Further police arrived to disperse a growing crowd but they too were attacked, believing the police were questioning rather than helping the victim. The young lad was eventually taken to hospital, but hatred towards the police was so intense unsavoury rumours soon spread throughout the black community, accusing the police of simply leaving the victim to die of his wounds because he was black.

Nevertheless, hatred of the police bore deep. Within hours crowds of all creeds, colours and cultures grew larger and larger, bringing with them total anarchy onto the streets of Brixton: turning over cars and setting them alight, smashing windows, looting shops, even fire stations were attacked with stones, bricks and petrol bombs – all in the name of racism. The riot lasted for almost 3-days before order was restored, but other cities found themselves having similar problems.

Thanks to the media, print and television alike, news reports poured in thick and fast, often exaggerated and definitely speculated with macabre undertones, pinpointing problems to racial aggression, mass unemployment within black communities and police brutality. Asian communities also rioted, highlighting their plight with police brutality and racial diversity. And there lied a dilemma: a rise in violent crime, gang-related attacks and burglaries in cities around the country resulted in larger police patrols. Stop and search procedures were implemented but young black men in particular regarded the searches as a licence to practice racial discrimination.

There was also something missing from the riots that in someway leant towards condoning the quagmire of events, and that was a considerable lack of support from the white community, in particularly from those that enjoy a good protest. Yes, them, where were they? Why weren't they out en-mass demonstrating against racism, youth unemployment, poverty and police brutality? Something they too believed was rife, coupled with their own accusations of persecution and living in a totalitarian Police State.

But no, they were nowhere to be seen. No CND marches, no anti-racist movements, not even one Socialist Worker poster was insight. And what an opportunity they missed, joining fellow brothers and sisters in their hour of need, united against police brutality and racial abuse. But that was the problem, there wasn't any emission of police brutality against white communities. And because it never entered the lives of champagne socialist anti-establishment protesters, why should they join hands with them poor, inner city rioters?

Inner city youth had little chance of employment and no hope of a better life. Pushed to one side by a society that still upheld a racial ignorance bequeathed by past generations. With nothing to do, totally renounced by local authorities, there's only so much they could tolerate. Gangs became extremely common, and with it knife crime was on the rise. Stabbings, shootings, robberies, muggings, burglaries, all on the increase, all connected with gangs and drugs.

<hr>

Throwing even more petrol onto the social fire, tower blocks of the 1960's forced thousands of growing families to live in close proximity with one another. Architects in their typical dream world didn't take into consideration family size or the fact that living so close together creates tension – we all need space. Take a look at social housing projects of the 1930's through to the 1950's where houses had large rooms, gardens were big and had enough space between roads and neighbours.

That little space made all the difference. But the real reason behind tower blocks wasn't anything to do with welfare of its occupants, it was to reduce cost on land, building materials, place as many families as possible in one area and collect as much rent legally possible. Social housing became a display of budget over people. With a combination of living in tight overcrowded communities, growing poverty due to lack of employment, in turn exacerbating petty crime, violence and gang culture. All of which we should have learnt lessons from the last century.

Early eighties music reflected the mood of poor communities. Bands from the 1950's and 1960's predominately wrote music about relationships, young love and breaking up. In the 1970's it was all about Glam rock, disco and ABBA. In the early eighties bands from inner cities wrote songs that expressed emotions on the streets. UB40 (a band title that emphasised the growing unemployed having to complete a form called Unemployment Benefit 40) wrote many songs that told a story of the times. The Specials with their hit track, Ghost Town, depicted large industries closing and communities disappearing.

The band Franky Goes To Hollywood, however, went one step further by writing a track about the Cold War. Two Tribes was a huge hit, depicting two Super

Powers finally going to war and making huge profit out of it. The band took another massive and extremely daring step with the track Relax, from their album Welcome To The Pleasure Dome. Relax was incredibly risqué for the time, as it highlighted homosexuality in such an obvious manner, subsequently banned from the airwaves. Second to the Sex Pistols in 1977 with their track God Save The Queen, during her Silver Jubilee.

Music across the eighties went through tremendous changes with many different styles, guises and fashions. Out went disco and make way for Ska, Punk, Mid-Atlantic rock, New Romantic, New Wave with annoying synthesisers, Hip Hop and Rap with its anti-white, gang related undertones. Big guys of the early eighties were Duran Duran, Madness, The Specials, Wham, Blondie – of course – Madonna and Michael Jackson. Many artists hit the airwaves during the 1980's with too many to mention, but brought with them big hair for girls and short back-and-sides with floppy long tops for the boys. Tight stretch jeans replaced bell-bottom flares, tank-tops and blouses were out, T-shirts were in – go Franky.

By far the biggest music attraction was Live Aid on 13th July 1985. The nation was glued to television screens. Organised by Bob Geldof from the band Boomtown Rats, and Midge Ure from Ultra Vox, they put together a dual event benefit concert to raise much needed cash for the famine in Ethiopia. Simultaneously broadcast from Wembley Stadium in London and JFK Stadium in Pennsylvania, USA, where the audience packed every inch available.

The original idea came from Culture Club's Boy George and Jon Moss, after they, and other pop stars, recorded the single Do They Know It's Christmas; a record produced by Bob Geldof and Midge Ure in December 1984 raising a staggering £8,000,000 far exceeding Bob's original proposed figure of £70,000. Live Aid kicked off the gig with Status Quo, and top of the bill was Queen, although had already split and gone their separate ways, re-joined to play at the concert. And thank god they did, staying together up until the sad passing of Freddie Mercury on 24th November 1991 after contracting AIDS.

Acquired Immunodeficiency Syndrome (AIDS) spread from chimpanzees that carry the Simian Immunodeficiency Virus (SIV) caught from smaller monkeys they eat. The disease spread from Africa in the 1960's to other parts of the world, including the Caribbean and New York by the early 1970's. From then on international travel between continents spread the disease, but didn't come to attention of the masses until the early 1980's.

Human Immunodeficiency Virus (HIV) is a virus that attacks the immune system by destroying T cells. Eventually the body defence mechanism can no longer fight infections, including flu, pneumonia and even a common cold, leading to further complications. At first it was thought the virus could only be caught via sexual intercourse between men, as the virus was initially found amongst the gay community. But later studies found that the virus could also spread by heterosexual relationships via vaginal and anal fluid as well as semen. Further studies proved that drug addicts sharing needles can also carry and spread the disease. But it was too late; the virus was branded a gay disease by the media, and it stuck.

Death of Hollywood actor, Rock Hudson, was the first high-profile celebrity to die of AIDS, shocking the world because everyone thought he was heterosexual. But gay actors refrained from 'coming out' due to hostile treatment evident amongst the masses. His death quickly introduced the banning of gay men from donating blood, where the media caused further panic with incredible headlines to spread fear throughout the heterosexual community that everyone wasn't safe from the gay disease.

A massive government public warning campaign was launched, with radio and television adverts, double page newspaper centre spreads and door to door leafleting to educate a concerned nation about AIDS and how it can be transmitted. The idea was to calm everyone but it had an overwhelming adverse effect by alienating the gay fraternity, causing them to secrete themselves into dark corners of communities blamed for spreading the disease.

Print and television public information broadcasts were nothing new. In the 1970's and 1980's the masses were warned of dangers of not being able to swim. Remember this line: No way man, not my thing. What he meant was, he couldn't swim, said the annoyed girlfriend waiting for him in the sea. Or, Charlie says, never approach strangers, as the boy interprets what his ginger cat says whilst eating a fish. Flying kites near overhead power cables, playing near railway lines or rivers, swimming in quarries, we were warned about every possible danger by a concerned government. But they all came to an abrupt and sudden stop due to cost of broadcasting, leaving everyone stranded with no protection whatsoever.

Television had changed beyond recognition, and with American imports such as Dallas bringing shoulder pads and bright lipstick for the girls, Miami Vice brought pastel coloured light suits and slip-on shoes of various colours, and of course, worn without socks. Not forgetting rolled up sleeves, an attempt to grow a neat stubble, and blonde highlights.

With new television programmes came new sitcoms such as the Young Ones in 1983 and was an instant success. With radical scripts by writer, Ben Elton, the show certainly reflected his hatred of Margaret Thatcher. But it also played a role testing a huge shift in politics, sociology and morals left behind by the Baby Boomers. Their steady drip, drip, drip of independence, questioning, and a search for answers, was slowly replaced by Generation X with a quest for further answers, as well as a thirst for knowledge, reasoning and global political awareness.

The new wave of comedy, dubbed alternative comedy, was mainly spearheaded by up and coming comedians such as Ade Edmondson, Rick Mayall and Alexei Sayle, all starring in the Young Ones. Ben Elton, along with Rick Mayall, were already stand-up comedians, but their material attracted only a student-like fraternity, portraying political humour and student anti-establishment rhetoric. Alexei did the same, adding Communist undertones with visible annoyance to Margaret Thatcher and her supporters.

Television adverts were still as outrageous as the 1970's but with the added difference of using modern (for the eighties) computer technology to market goods and wares. Gentlemen adverts for aftershave were telling single men that wearing their particular brand would attract girls – because a man doesn't have to try too hard. For women, Harmony hair spray sold in massive aerosol cans, giving the impression of confidence whilst swishing hair from side to side walking through a park.

Although cigarette adverts were banned from television since 1967 they remained top of any marketing tree. Tobacco companies with huge budgets to market latest brands sponsored Formula One teams such as John Player Special (JPS) and Marlboro. Other large crowd pullers including snooker, horse racing, even darts attracted tobacco companies for sponsorships, only to lure gullible 16-year olds to take up the habit.

The birth of a new Millennial Generation, although too young to realise, was introduced to another programme we're all mesmerised by – The Blue Planet. David Attenborough became our teacher of nature. First aired in 1982 he told us stories and took us places we never knew existed. He showed us exotic birds, animals, plants, trees, insects, deep ocean creatures and polar bears. We learnt about how ant and bee colonies behave, how long a Californian Redwood takes to mature, and, of course, learnt loads of facts about the blue whale. There was also one other subject he told us about – global warming.

Generation X school pupils did have the odd lesson about clearing of forests in the Amazon for crops and erosion of coastlines, but not one explained in finer detail. We only touched the effect of global warming – as it was termed – where its explanation came from an expanding hole in the ozone layer above the Arctic Circle, blamed on my mum's hairspray. Even pollution was skimmed over as a subtext to other subjects because our teachers had very little knowledge of its consequence on the climate.

Thankfully there was an incredibly knowledgeable gentleman called David Attenborough to tell us all about the effects of carbon dioxide and what mum's Harmony hairspray was doing to the planet. Chlorofluorocarbons (CFC's) is a compound gas made of chloride, fluorine and carbon, with an accelerant of highly inflammable methane, ethane and propane, depending upon its application. All aerosols had CFC's, as well as most solvents, air-conditioning, refrigerators, packaging, insulation foams, and many more applications. But the effect what CFC's had when released into the atmosphere since the 1930's remained unclear, until the early 1970's where tests were carried out.

CFC's has an incredible life span exceeding 100-years, where particles have plenty of time to diffuse into the stratosphere and contribute to the greenhouse effect as well as, in effect, burn a whole in the ozone layer by breaking it down. Thankfully, the hole is now shrinking, and we have since learnt it wasn't just down to mum's hairspray. Nevertheless, the ozone hole was plugging up so the threat of global warming was now over. Hooray!

In the meantime religious tension between inner city communities also came to a head during the early eighties, and there was one particular religion that was definitely treated with suspicion – Catholicism. And if someone spoke in an Irish accent – most definitely a Northern Irish accent – they were instantly perceived to be the enemy.

The Lost Generation, as did The Greatest Generation, hated Germans for obvious reasons. You can't blame them for that. Baby Boomers had the thought of those pesky Soviets threatening them with nuclear war. Generation X also had an enemy – threat of being bombed by the IRA (Irish Republican Army). But the majority of IRA members weren't actually classed as Catholic or Protestant. They only believed in a united Ireland.

The Northern Ireland predicament has been a headache for centuries, dating back even further than the mid 17th Century and Oliver Cromwell. Until 1922 Ireland was part of the United Kingdom, but there was a group believing themselves to be freedom fighters wanted total independence at what ever cost. Many treaties have come and gone in an attempt to keep the peace, but the troubles continued, as they do today [2020] albeit on a smaller scale of violence than yesteryear.

My Great uncle Frank was too young to join his brothers at the Somme, but as soon as he was old enough, in 1920 he enlisted into the 2nd Battalion, Northamptonshire Regiment. Within only a few months he found himself in Ireland guarding a post office van, along with a captain and a few others from his platoon. Post office vans were a prime target for the IRA and the van Frank was ordered to protect was no exception.

Coming under fire from pre-determined positions along a country lane lined with high hedgerows, Frank and his mates returned fire in an attempt to save the van falling into IRA hands. But it was no use, the IRA knew when the van would pass and executed a plan to hijack it. Consequently, on 28th October 1920 Frank, the captain and his fellow soldiers died of gunshot wounds trying to protect the van and the mail inside it.

After the Civil war Ireland regained its identity, leaving the remaining Northern Ireland politically connected to mainland UK policies. But the IRA in its many guises was adamant the whole of Ireland should be reunited. In doing so their campaign of indiscriminate bombings in Northern Ireland killed many innocent victims, exacerbating discrimination between Catholics and Northern Irish Protestants.

By the late 1960's the British army was called upon once again to help the Royal Ulster Constabulary (RUC) protect Catholics from discrimination executed by the predominate Protestants, keeping them safe from persecution living in Northern Ireland. But incredibly the Catholics quickly turned against the soldiers that were sent to protect them. Now in a difficult and precarious situation the soldiers spent most of their time in Northern Ireland protecting themselves from both religious factions, as well as disarming IRA bombs planted in shopping centres. Designed to indiscriminately kill anyone, if only to prove how far they would sink to gain complete independence.

The escalation of violence against British soldiers was also exacerbated by a vote as to whether Northern Ireland remained part of the United Kingdom. The 1949 Ireland Act recognised that the Irish Republic had no influence upon Northern Ireland, but the Northern Ireland parliament had the right to leave the United Kingdom and return to the Republic of Ireland. So the abolition of the Northern Ireland parliament in 1972 created a new Assembly. In doing so raised questions as to whether it still had the right to leave the UK and re-join the Republic of Ireland.

In true British parliament tradition to avoid delicate and potentially lethal questions, it was put to the public vote. And on 8th March 1973 the people of Northern Ireland went to the ballot box. Overwhelmingly 591,820 voted to remain part of the UK, where only 6,463 voted to leave. After which, total and bloody mayhem hit the streets. Bombing campaigns during this time remained in Northern Ireland, but by 1974 mainland UK bore witness to innocent lives taken by bombs planted by the IRA: The Tower of London bombing, where one person was killed and a further 41 were injured. Two Guilford pubs fell victim to IRA bombs, killing 4 soldiers, a civilian and injuring 65 others. Another pub, this time in Birmingham, was hit, where 21 innocent people lost their lives.

Further bombs terrorised those in Northern Ireland and the UK mainland over the following decades – well into the Millennial Generation, where the last bombs up until now [2020] were in 1996. But not until the IRA pushed harder still with larger and more devastating bombs. The Canary Wharf suffered incredible damage

---

with the use of a 'lorry bomb' packed with high explosives to kill as many as possible. Upon detention a huge area was flattened, yet with an incredible low loss of only 2 lives, but injuring over 100.

Manchester suffered the very last IRA bomb – another 'lorry bomb' with over a tonne of explosives detonated on Corporation Street. Although surrounding buildings were totally destroyed, remarkably, there weren't any fatalities, but 212 were injured. By far the most infamous IRA bomb attack was on the Grand Hotel bombing in Brighton, 12th October 1984 during the Conservative Party conference.

Designed with a crude yet effective time-delay device the bomb exploded in the early hours five floors above the suite of Prime Minister Margaret Thatcher, where she was perceived to be in bed fast asleep. Luckily she was awake preparing notes and her speech for the following day, when a huge explosion ripped through the hotel, killing one Conservative MP and four others connected with the party, one of which was Norman Tebbitt, and a further 31 civilians were injured.

Shaken but undeterred, Margaret Thatcher insisted upon giving her speech to a bewildered audience. Putting aside her expected attack on the Labour Party she turned her contempt onto the IRA. The effect of the bombing had an adverse consequence, where the IRA and its sympathisers hoped it would at least shake her into submission considering she was the intended target. Instead her popularity soared to levels last seen during the Falklands conflict 2-years prior. World leaders, including USA President Ronald Reagan, and Soviet leader Mikhail Gorbachev, praised her steadfast and steely condemnation of the IRA and the UK's resilience towards terrorism.

The IRA tried a second attempt at killing Conservative Prime Minister John Major – Margaret Thatcher's successor – a few years later on 7th February 1991 by using crude home made mortar-type bombs launched from a tube 250 meters away to attack number 10 Downing Street and its Cabinet office, the official residence of the Prime Minister. John Major and his Cabinet were discussing the progress of the Gulf War when one of the mortar bombs exploded in the garden. Two more bombs overshot the Cabinet rooms and hit a nearby green. The windows of the building were bombproof to some extent, so no one inside the office was harmed. But 4 people sustained light injuries, including 2 police officers on duty patrolling the Cabinet grounds.

Many towns and cities fell foul to IRA indiscriminate bombings, unseen since the Blitz. Belfast felt the brunt, and with no shame went about their business terrorising the neighbourhood with beatings and shooting those they deemed necessary to blame or believe were either Protestant or spying for the British Army.

IRA members, including those from other groups, raised much needed funds through protection rackets, drugs and the use of violence. Sympathisers from the USA including NORAID – the Irish Northern Aid Committee – started to raise funds for 'the course' in 1969 when the troubles escalated. Cities such as New York and Boston were favourite with large sympathetic Irish communities, yet understood very little of the history and why they fought against the British government.

Weapons and explosives were quickly stockpiled, including over 2,500 small arms and high powered rifles smuggled on board the Queen Elizabeth 2 cruise liner from New York by her many Irish crew into

Southampton before making there way to Belfast. Larger weapons such as the .50 calibre M1919 machinegun and the 7.62mm M60 machinegun, including ammunition, were also smuggled in from the USA. Even IRA sympathiser, Libyan leader Muammar Gaddafi, provided weapons as far back as 1972.

The Palestine Liberation Organisation (PLO) supplied the IRA with terrorism training, tactics and even offered weapons, but they turned down the offer in fear of Israeli intelligence keeping a close eye. Basque separatist movement (ETA) in Northern Spain, Estonia, Czechoslovakia, Lebanon, and sympathisers in Canada, Netherlands and Norway, all provided weapons, ammunition and explosives in the 1970's through to the late 1990's.

Towards the end of the IRA campaign the last British soldier killed was shot by an American Barrett sniper rifle at a Checkpoint outside Bessbrook, South Armagh, on 12th February 1997. Total killed during the 30-year unrest stood at an alarming 763 British and Ulster Defence Regiment (UDR) soldiers, where the total wounded was 6,116. The IRA also murdered over 1,800 civilians and a further 3,000 innocent bystanders tragically caught in shootings and bombings.

Sadly, in whatever guise the IRA now call themselves, continue to murder innocent victims. 29-nine year old journalist, Lyra McKee, was killed by the New IRA on 18th April 2019 whilst reporting a story of young Irish Republicans rioting on the streets of Creggan, Londonderry. Cars were set alight and petrol bombs thrown at police as a protest against Republican homes being searched prior to the Easter weekend. In March the same year, three explosive devices were discovered at major transport hubs in London. So the 'troubles' were nowhere near at an end.

Undeterred by these sick acts of violence the UK masses refused to give in and carried on regardless. Patriotism remained incredibly high throughout the 1980's. And on 29th July 1981 the streets were buzzing once again with flags, bunting, parties and celebrations, similar to the Queen's Silver Jubilee. On this particular Royal occasion, it was the marriage of Prince Charles and Lady Diana at St. Paul's Cathedral, with an estimated television audience of 750,000,000 around the world.

With so many eyes looking at the young couple the whole world heard that famous cock-up of Prince Charles's name when Lady Diana said: Philip Charles Arthur George, instead of his correct full name, Charles Philip Arthur George. She also omitted 'obey' from the traditional vows, as agreed by Charles and Diana.

Princess Diana became known as the Queen of Hearts, where her fashion caught the attention of women throughout the world, let alone the UK. And to have a Princess Di hairstyle was a must, lasting throughout the eighties and well into the nineties – until the American comedy show, Friends, hit the airwaves. Women then went wild for the famous 'Rachel' hairstyle.

British patriotism was again at its best when Argentina invaded the Falkland Islands on Friday 2nd April 1982. At the time I was taking my CSE (Certificate of Secondary Education) exams, and was suddenly distracted by the news. Before the invasion I had never heard of the Falkland Islands, let alone where they were, and I was supposedly revising for my geography exam.

Switching on the news on our incredibly large yet small 21-inch screen, now 4-channel button (one still spare) colour television, yes colour, there it was: Argentina had invaded the Falkland Islands and South Georgia in the South Atlantic. Images before me were unbelievable, taking the public, let alone the British government, by complete surprise. It was the first time since the Second World War a Sovereign State belonging to the UK had been invaded by a foreign power.

The masses were, at first, flabbergasted, and also wondered where the bloody Falklands were. The press searched frantically on maps and globes, at first believing they were a bunch of Islands off the coast of Scotland, raising the question as to why would Argentina sail so far to invade them? But once found on the map, a huge majority of the public demanded the removal of the invading Argentine Forces from British soil. By the way, so did Prime Minister, Margaret Thatcher. Not one for pulling punches, she instructed HM Armed Forces to remove them – adding, in any means necessary. And they did just that.

Putting a Task Force together, seemingly overnight, which was an amazing effort in itself, including two ageing aircraft carriers, as well as destroyers and troop carriers, it steamed south. In the meantime almost retired Vulcan bombers flew a 16,000-mile round trip to bomb Port Stanley runway on the Falklands and deny the Argentinian Airforce air supremacy. Once the British troops landed on Falkland soil, within 10-weeks Argentinian Forces surrendered and the British Task Force regained control. In total 258 British soldiers lost their lives, with over 700 wounded. Argentina lost 649 soldiers – mainly young conscripts – and 1,068 wounded. Two Islanders also lost their lives, killed by the Argentinians upon the first few days of invading.

As soon as the Islands were secure from any further invasion the Task Force sailed home, leaving behind a few jet fighters and a contingent of troops, just in case. Upon their return Union flags flew proud from houses and businesses. Red, white and blue bunting hung across streets. Church bells rang, tens of thousands lined the docks to welcome them home, and millions more cheered whilst live pictures were televised across the nation and around the world. A proud moment for the United Kingdom, united in victory. Well, sort of.

Yes, them again. Anti-war protesters had gathered momentum since the CND movement of the 1950's. And with them attracted attention from not only students, but also those from a certain political persuasion – the loony left. Ever since Margaret Thatcher won the 1979 General election the Labour Party had gone completely bonkers. Always known for their potty socialist beliefs, they decided to go one step further and lose the plot altogether.

MP's such as Michael Foot (leader of the opposition during the Falklands conflict), Tony Ben, Ken Livingston and Jeremy Corbyn, yearned for a State to be controlled by a Communist Red flag. And with their illustrious leader, Neil Kinnock, at the wheel, their shift towards Communism attracted not only hard-line trade unions but also shed-loads of students, champagne socialists and those that just wanted to protest, no matter what the agenda. And as soon as there was a mere whiff of a gathering, Labour Party members, including its Cabinet, led the way.

This particular crises, however, had Michael Foot, Neil Kinnock and most of the opposition agreeing with Margaret Thatcher, that a Task Force must be sent to the Falklands as soon as possible. Naturally, the likes of Ken Livingston and Jeremy Corbyn opposed any sort of reprisal, especially military. The usual supporters followed suit, including the CND. In fact CND marched with many protests that had nothing to do with nuclear disarmament. As did the Socialist Worker banner wavers.

Militants, socialist movements, anti-establishment groups, students, university political groups, those that opposed whatever government was in office, the IRA – purely for their anti-British policy – they were all there. All displaying their democratic right to protest against British Forces that actually protect their rights, from removing a foreign military force that had invaded British soil. To put it another way, their protests would be no different to protesting against police entering a house to arrest and remove a bunch of violent burglars.

Thankfully 99 percent of the population had common sense and totally supported military action. Nevertheless, this incredibly unbelievable mind-blowing selfish attitude bore a new gene into our society, exposing its ill-educated, puerile and pathetic infliction upon the masses, desperate to spread its existence across the nation. Although in its embryonic stage, this cancerous infection will grow into a huge nuisance for us all in later years.

Meanwhile, the early Millennial era with its grown-up Generation X continued to abide some Victorian values: manners, constraint, punishment when needed, respecting others and obedience. Many children carried out household chores, listened to elders knowing they knew best, made beds, kept rooms tidy and had pride in doing so. Patriotism remained high, although slightly scarred by a growing number of loony-left political activists, hell-bent on destroying the remaining threads of a forgotten Victorian society, unbeknown to our next problem threatening our shores – the European Union and its unforgiving laws.

EU laws in the early eighties didn't really affect the masses. Seen nothing more than, at best, creating only incredibly small ripples of interest by mainstream media. Nonetheless, slowly but surely, employment, automotive and criminal law, even local authority regulations, entered our lives drip by drip.

After I finished my last CSE exam on 28th May 1982 I left the gates of my school for the last time and into a grown-up world: it was time to find a job. After all, that's what we did in the eighties, no different to our forefathers. Of course, college was an option, as was the army, but most of us wanted a job to earn our own money and leave home as soon as possible. Question was, where were the jobs?

Unbeknown to us fresh-faced school leavers, we were walking straight into a recession. Having no interest whatsoever in politics or the government, we didn't realise how bad job cuts were and the issue of rising unemployment. At its peak unemployment figures were racing past 3,000,000. So like many school leavers in the early eighties we signed up for a Youth Training Scheme (YTS) devised by Margaret Thatcher, offering 2-years training in building technology, engineering, carpentry, catering and packing bay leaves into pots.

I was paid a wage of £25 per week, which wasn't too bad considering a packet of twenty cigarettes was around 80 pence. But mum took a tenner for board – my first lesson of being a working man living at home. Within 2-years I finished my course in building technology, engineering and packing bay leaves, eventually finding a job at a diesel engine company in Manchester, and walked straight into yet another industrial dispute: coal miners strike.

Chapter Fourteen

Fight the good fight

By 1984 Margaret Thatcher was still trying to sort out the country's mess, including destroying the unions, introduce a right-to-buy scheme – where council tenants could now buy their house – and privatise nationalised companies, including the utilities. Water, gas and electric companies were now for sale to the highest bidder, British or otherwise. British Rail and British Steel were also privatised, as was British Telecom (BT). So no more waiting an age for a telephone connection, and no more boring telephones – new models were now available, and they were funky, apparently.

Margaret Thatcher's tough policies did generate income, private investment, and jobs in the long term. In the short term, unemployment reached just over 3,000,000 unseen for decades. The next bitter pill to swallow was the closing of coal- mines that were losing money hand over fist, where the cost of these losses fell onto the taxpayer. And these costs ran into millions of pounds per uneconomical coal mine, which there were many.

In the early eighties the richest coal seams were depleting fast, becoming increasingly harder to mine and expensive to reach, so modern mechanisation for mines that remained profitable was necessary to keep costs down. In doing so less miners were needed to extract coal and inevitably job losses ensued. In 1983 there were 174 mines. Only 6 remained functional by 2009, and continue to close [2020].

The National Coal Board (NCB) announced on 6th March that due to modernisation and reduced subsidies – taxpayers money – 20 uneconomical mines would close with a loss of 20,000 jobs. First of which was the Cortonwood colliery, sparking an immediate walkout. NUM leader, Arthur Scargill, a militant trade unionist, socialist, and a strong advocate of Communism, believed the British government wanted to close around 70 pits. The government denied this and accused Scargill of scare-mongering. Nevertheless, Scargill was determined to fight against all colliery closures, where strike action quickly gained momentum.

Scargill's strategy was to cause a severe energy shortage similar, if not worse, than the dispute only a decade earlier. And like the previous strike he was determined to beat the government into submission, as it did with Edward Heath's Conservative government. Margaret Thatcher's strategy, however, was to keep as many miners at work as possible and stockpile coal to keep power stations supplied – eventually converting them to use heavy oil instead of coal. Recruit independent hauliers to transport coal just in case railway unions strike in sympathy with the miners, and use police en-mass to prevent pickets stopping other miners going to work.

Battle lines were drawn. Miners in Yorkshire were eager to strike, where Cortonwood colliery already downed tools. Bullcliffe Wood, Kiveton Park, Manvers, Silverwood and Cadeby collieries quickly followed suit, with more than 6,000 miners now on strike. Pickets from Yorkshire travelled to Nottinghamshire fearing miners would carry on working, then onto collieries in County Durham, Scotland and Kent. Lancashire miners were reluctant to strike, and some refused to stand at picket lines, only to have a sympathetic response to their cause rather than support their actions.

As predicted by Margaret Thatcher, the National Union of Seamen, Railway, Dockers and Steel Unions supported the strike, where Arthur Scargill demanded all steel workers not to cross any picket lines, only to keep furnaces burning. But British Steel was planning to close another plant, having already closed Corby plant in Northamptonshire, so workers were reluctant to strike in support of the miners in fear other closures would be made easy for their employers. Transport unions gave support, but the majority of HGV drivers didn't belong to a union.

Within 3-months aggressive picketing was out of control. At the coking plant in Orgreave, Rotherham, 5,000 picketers and almost the same amount of police clashed. Violence erupted with rocks and stones thrown by the picketers whilst police on horseback charged towards them in an attempt to break the blockade. Fights broke out where 51 picketers and 72 police officers were treated for injuries.

The Communist Party supported the strike and opposed Thatcher – naturally – but shied away from Arthur Scargill and his strike tactics in fear of losing public support. The same fear pointed towards miners using aggression, believing it divided a nation's sympathy. South Wales miners wanted to return to work providing all miners sacked during the strike were reinstated. Their proposal was rejected by the NCB so Yorkshire and Kent miners voted against any return to work until their demands were met. It never happened. And with no hope of the NCB or the government caving in to demands, the strike eventually ended on 3rd March 1985.

Margaret Thatcher not only beat Arthur Scargill, he was publicly humiliated. Having promised a win for the miners by using power cuts, cross union support and national shortages, his strategy was no match for Thatcher. Public support was also never really there at the beginning, where those that did support the miners dropped dramatically towards the end. And the socialist movement of the 1980's was nowhere near as large as it once was in the 1970's.

From March 1984 to March 1985 miners and their families also became divided over the strike. 11,291 people were arrested, where 8,392 were charged, and 200 served prison sentences. Coal mines inevitably closed and bulldozed to make way for other developments. Communities disappeared and mining towns went into decay. Even today [2020] some of these former mining communities still hold antipathy towards the police. And tensions between strikers and those that carried on working also continued for years after the dispute ended. Photographs and posters of miners and their families were displayed for all to see in an attempt of naming and shaming those that continued to work or broke picket lines. Even the NCB was accused of deserting the striking miners.

With the collapse of UK coal mining industry in plain sight, many miners deserted their trade to seek other work, often in neighbouring towns to avoid contempt from the striking miners refusing to believe their jobs had been made redundant. However, offers of redundancy payments by the NCB were accepted, even by the most militant of miners, usually behind closed doors and out of sight of other striking miners.

With the collieries closed Margaret Thatcher and her government could now carry out their energy plan: intermediate stockpiling of cheaper coal from the USA,

Columbia and Australia, whilst slowly introducing gas and oil fuelled power stations – a cheaper and cleaner option for the environment. The remaining coal industry, incredibly smaller than it once was, became privatised by the end of 1994. In total 168 mines were closed since Thatcher's government, where the 'so called' sympathising Labour governments closed a total of 252.

In the 2016 Brexit referendum, many former colliery towns voted by a majority to leave the EU, including Arthur Scargill, believing the Brexit vote and leaving the EU would resurrect the UK coal industry to its former glory. But this could never happen, especially within a lean, green environmentally obsessed modern society. The UK government, whichever party in power, was then, and still is committed to rid all coal fuelled power stations by 2025 where natural clean gas will be used instead, along side nuclear, wind and sea turbine, even solar generated electricity. And on 9th May 2019 the UK produced 190 hours of coal free power for the first time since 1882. Although it did return during the winter months and the inevitable increase of demand.

With the coal miners strike over surely industrial disputes were finally at an end. Surely we had reached a time of social evolutionary harmony between employer and employee. Surely, since the industrial revolution, strikes, disputes, working relationships between employer and employee were now able to work together? Well, no, not exactly. Unfortunately, and depending upon how you look at it, the 1970's disease lingered around for a little while longer. Dock yards, airport traffic control and baggage handlers, ship yards, even the newspaper print industry had industrial disputes as the country went through its radical employment changes.

Latter part of the 1960's and the decade of the 1970's goes down in history for being the strike era of the

20th Century. From 1965 to 1969 there were 2,397 industrial disputes that led to strikes involving 1,215,000 workers, losing almost 4,000,000 productive days. From 1970 to 1979 there were a staggering 5,262 industrial disputes involving 3,231,000 workers, and losing a total of 13,140,000 productive days. Throughout the 1980's industrial disputes were slashed. Taking into consideration the miners strike, there were 2,258 industrial disputes involving 2,081,000 workers, and losing 1,879,000 productive hours.

One of the many reasons why industrial disputes and strikes almost disappeared was Margaret Thatcher shifting balance of union power, breakdown of traditional large industries and a government determined to destroy unions by making it almost impossible to strike without breaking the law. In effect the outrageously greedy and selfish attitude of unions that strangled many large and small industries in the 1970's was finally beaten into submission.

Smaller disputes certainly continued but took a considerable decline towards the end of Thatcher's government in 1990. And when John Major took her place, strike action became less and less. Overall, from 1990 to 1999 – two years into Tony Blair's New Labour government – there were a total of 274 industrial disputes that led to strike action involving 223,000 workers. Most of which were down to public sector staff – civil servants, teachers and council employees. Whilst some still believe Thatcher destroyed the UK, the masses now had opportunities once thwarted by previous governments to better themselves and create their own wealth. Some took this to the extreme. In walked the Yuppies.

The term Yuppie came from America and first used in 1982 from the term Yippie: a business networking group founded by Jerry Rubin, a radical leader and formal member of the Youth International Party - Yippies. In the UK newspapers termed Young Upwardly mobile Professionals as Yuppies. They were usually well educated – often university graduates – arrogant, selfish, money-driven, pretentious champagne swiggers. Their attitude certainly met the criteria and became synonymous with young city merchant bankers and stock market traders.

Expensive cars, such as Porsche, Lamborghini and Ferrari were a must purchase. Savile Row suits, Omega watches, Gucci belts, gold and diamond studded jewellery, even second homes and holiday retreats were also on Yuppie shopping lists. And of course, buying houses to either rent or sell, increasing the value of houses in and around London. So further North became the perfect target to buy cheap houses and sell at enormous profits thanks to the rail link into London. Buckinghamshire, Bedfordshire, Northamptonshire, even Lincolnshire were perfect counties to expand the Yuppie empire.

Before they reached Grantham, Lincolnshire, a friend of mine bought a mid-terraced Victorian house for £14,000 in 1984. Within 4-years Yuppies finally reached Lincolnshire, where the same terraced house was now valued at £40,000 by 1988. Second homes bought and sold became third, fourth and fifth houses. Terraced were incredibly common to buy, some as cheap as £1,000.

The likes of B&Q and Texas (Homebase) made a fortune out of kitchen and bathroom sales as DIY Yuppies renovated cheap houses, only to sell to make a quick buck or two. Local builders and DIY enthusiasts caught on what was happening, and with local knowledge knew the bargains. Towards the late eighties value of houses within the 1-hour train commute to London tripled, even quadrupled, depending upon which catchment county. But wages remained pretty much stagnant, causing the start of unaffordable housing across the nation.

In 1980 the national average house price was twice the national average salary. Within a few years the property boom increased house prices to 3 times average salary. By the early 1990's it had increased further still to 4 times, where today [2020] it sits around 6 or 7 times the national average. Across southern and east midland counties many 16-year old school leavers that took the trade route became self-employed thanks to government incentive schemes and the Prince's Trust. First taking college courses to become bricklayers, plasterers, carpenters, electricians, plumbers & heating engineers, Yuppies were desperate to hire the lot and renovate their money making houses.

But as the sun shinned for home-grown entrepreneurial tradesmen, the odd cloud spoilt their clear blue sky. National building projects were non-existent, where thousands of bricklayers and other building tradesmen once reliant on large construction companies for employment had ceased trading. For a while in the early eighties the construction industry in the UK was knackered, so thousands of tradesmen headed to West Germany, where huge national building projects were underway, but had a shortage of builders. In walk the UK boys.

Television drama, Auf Wiedersehen Pet, depicted a bunch of odd-ball characters with various building trades leaving Thatcher's Britain, desperate to seek work in Germany. And Boys from the Black Stuff, a compelling drama about a bunch of Asphalt tarmac spreaders, suddenly finding themselves on the dole. Desperate to earn money, they'd try their hands at anything to earn a crust and feed their families. To many these two dramas alone reflected the harsh reality of the early eighties. On the flipside, Margaret Thatcher's Britain produced thousands of new small businesses sprouting everywhere.

Computers became essential with negotiation and bargaining between new businesses, where computer hardware and software companies grew ten-fold around the nation. The Service industry exploded across the industrial spectrum, where small companies were now outgrowing the diminishing industrial giants. Cleaning businesses, repair and servicing centres, workshops, fashion boutiques, trendy eateries, wine bars, cosmetic surgery clinics, all private and trading across the nation, not dissimilar to businesses and entrepreneurs since lost during the Victorian Era.

With new businesses came new technology to smooth company chores and administration. A new machine full of magic and sorcery hit the market that could send whatever was printed, written or drawn on a piece of A4 to anywhere around the world as a facsimile of the original message. This magic box was called a fax machine. It didn't take long before most, if not all businesses owned one.

Another invention that had been around since the late 1970's was now available for all businesses, as well as home use: the Personal Computer. Computer manufacturing giant IBM supplied mainframe computers for many years before modern technology allowed the shrinking of computers into a single box. By the early 1980's companies from around the world begun installing personal computers en-mass to help with invoicing, calculating and storing information rather than using reams of paper. It was said that by the turn of the 1990's paper would become redundant. Guess we have since learnt computers create an enormous appetite for paper, and we now use far more than we ever did.

Another leap in technology was communication without using wires: the hand-held portable telephone, also known as the mobile telephone. Actor William Shankner – Captain James T Kirk of the USS Enterprise from the original 1966 Star Trek Sci-fi series – once said, tongue in cheek, that it was he who first thought of the handheld portable communication devices. Of course, he was referring to the iconic communicator he and is crew used on the television program.

Children of the 1980's first became aware of mobile telephones when highlighted on shows such the iconic television programme, Blue Peter, where Leslie Judd stood outside on her bicycle and called Peter Pervis on his normal landline telephone inside BBC television centre. We were amazed, if not stunned by this incredible technology. How could this be possible, and with such a small device? When I say small, it was the size of a shoebox. Nevertheless, these remarkable devices became popular with small and large businesses alike, becoming a prominent fixture within only a few years, made famous by Yuppies.

Another great invention for businesses was the telephone answering machine, to the point of doing without the humble secretary. Well, not quite, but they were a must item for small businesses, and of course, for those that hadn't caught on with the importance of mobile telephones. Answer machines were also used at home, but they didn't really catch on due to the increasing popularity of mobile telephones.

Meanwhile, at home, personal computers were beginning to catch on with the incredible Sinclair ZX Spectrum. A cheaper option than IBM costing around £400 where the IBM computer cost anything up to £1,000 and the ZX Spectrum used the humble audio cassette tape to record data. Naturally a 90-minute magnetic cassette could only hold so much information, but it didn't stop budding computer whiz kids learning about writing programs.

My stepdad tried in vain to write a program of a flight simulator. He was a pilot in the RAF flying Victors and then F4 Phantom fighter jets, so naturally his idea of a great game would be of those with aeroplanes in them, in particular Phantoms. But his frustration was evident every time the computer crashed simply because it couldn't handle the required data. Even the slightly more powerful IBM personal computer didn't have enough memory for the type of game he wanted to write. To get anywhere near writing such a large software programme the masses had to wait for Sir Lord himself, Alan Sugar, bringing to the market his Amstrad personal computer that had the first in-built screen and keyboard.

Home Entertainment was growing fast by the 1980's and many homes could now record television programmes with the use of a video cassette recorder. Video recorders had been around for a while in the US but took an age to catch on in the UK. This was mainly due to cost and nothing really worth recording. But with video machines came video rental shops, and they sprung up everywhere. So rather than going to the cinema, you could watch your favourite film by hiring a video for a few quid to watch in the comfort of your own home. You could even watch it over and over again and pause it whenever you liked so to make a cup of tea. Isn't technology marvellous.

The downside was these machines were huge, clumsy and controlled manually by pushing down big tough buttons. But when more slim-line versions came to the market they had a remote control. When I say remote control, it was a small box attached to the Video player via a cable. But hey, saved time and energy getting up to press buttons. Video tapes also jammed from time to time, where the removal of the cassette after jamming meant miles of video tape had to be pulled out or cut from the spools inside the machine.

Portable hand-held video recorders, or camcorders as they became known, could capture personal videos of family parties, events and holidays. Throw away that tatty old-fashioned 1960's home entertainment silent film cine camera played against a white screen in a darkened room. Make way for the new camcorder that recorded sound as well as colour vision onto a re-useable tape the same size and format used for the VHS video player. And watch recordings instantly, either direct from the camcorder or by inserting the tape straight into the video player. I wonder what else mummies and daddies recorded?

Vinyl grew increasingly popular throughout the 1980's with thousands of artists producing 7-inch singles, 12-inch Extra Play (EP) and 12-inch Long Playing (LP) albums by the million. And the best way to complement these albums was by cataloguing and storing them under a stack system. These music-playing marvels were part of a youth culture as well as the furniture – literally. A beautiful machine that played music through ever-increasing powerful loud speakers equally cased in a wooden(ish) surround.

When Steve Wright played the Top Twenty on a Sunday afternoon teenagers around the nation tuned in, tape wound on ready, fingers poised over the record and play buttons, ready to record their idols latest single. But this wasn't totally legal. Nevertheless, we were young teenagers so didn't either care or understand copyright infringements. However, disc jockeys had a trick up their sleeve, particularly noticeable by Radio One DJ Steve Wright. And that was to introduce the new single by talking over the first few bars, only to talk over the ending. But Mr Wright sometimes went one further, and that was to talk over part of the record somewhere near the middle of the track.

In 1983 something else came along that totally radicalised the music industry, making enthusiastic vinyl collectors ambivalent about its quality and performance: the Compact Disc. Supposedly scratch proof, waterproof and marmalade proof, this digital music playing disc gave a crisp, clear sound quality unheard of before. No more jumping records due to scratches, no more static and no more removing fluff from the player needle, the CD was perfect in every way.

The new music concept didn't catch on at first, but when the word spread about the clarity of the sound music lovers embraced its performance. And the icing on the cake was the CD players were small and portable, and even playable in cars. Further amazement was that it didn't wear either. The thin plastic cover protected millions of tiny packed lines of digitalised data stored in a series of zeroes and ones – the digital language. So no more stretched and tangled tapes getting stuck in cassette players.

As the eighties drew to a close, whether young or old, rich or poor, we had experienced an unprecedented change throughout the decade. From socialist ruled unions causing havoc to voting for a woman Prime minister determined to put the country back on an even keel, no matter what the cost. From rockets to space probes landing on mars, expansion of the international space station to shuttles taking astronauts into space and back again. From micro technology making it affordable to buy must have small gadgets, to larger television sets. We thought science had reached its limits and technology couldn't possibly go any further.

From vast unemployment to jobs for all, as long as you got on your bike to find one – thanks to Mr Tebbitt. Easy credit and having the largest expendable cash society had ever enjoyed – but with quite high interest rates. From a huge expansion of car ownership to council tenants given the right to buy their own house. From easy mortgages to even easier hire purchase.

Thanks to a strong and stable economy anyone could have a private pension and dabble in the stock market. From the use of an almost perfect National Health Service (NHS) to Top of the Pops with mullets, Wham and A-Ha, we could finally, after centuries of demonstration, demand and debate, live the dream and enjoy a prosperous UK. We never had it so good. It was our second chance; an extended renaissance last experienced in the mid sixties.

In the meantime there was something else that happened right at the end of the 1980's catching us all by surprise. Something that happens to be the most important and significant change since the rise of Soviet Communism in 1917. Something that at the time was thought to symbolise the end of any possible global annihilation. Where world peace could finally be restored. But it didn't take long for suspicion, distrust and tension to seep through once again, causing ripples of circumstance across the world, involving many nations, creating further conflicts and division not seen
since the Second World War – fall of the Berlin Wall.

Chapter Fifteen

Just another brick in the wall

When Germany surrendered to the Allies 8th May 1945 its Capital, Berlin, was carved up into different sectors between Great Britain, USA, France and the USSR. Germany was then cut in half, where the Soviets took the slightly smaller slice to rule the German Democratic Republic – East Germany, under its Communist flag. The West was carved up into zones, occupied by the Allied Forces.

In 1948, as potential hostilities became a real threat from the Soviets, Allied Forces united their zones creating a new Capital, Bonn, and a new country, Federal Republic of Germany – West Germany – in May 1949. Berlin remained in East Germany, causing a huge headache for Westerners travelling to and from the Soviet sector. In response to the new free West Germany the Soviets instructed a blockade of West Berlin in an attempt to drive out its citizens from the Soviet occupied sector.

Great Britain and the USA equally responded with an unprecedented rescue mission by flying in all supplies necessary, including medication, clothes, food and fuel, where the rescue became famously known as the Berlin airlift. In May 1949 the Soviets were defeated and had no choice but end the blockade. The Cold War had begun.

As tensions rose between the Soviet East and Democratic West, East German citizens, still recovering from huge poverty Hitler left behind, were now, once again, battered and bruised, but this time by a Communist dictator. Many fled to the West to live in a free society, and from 1949 to 1961 an estimated 2,500,000 people made it across a dangerous border into the democratic West. Most of which crossed the border from East to West Berlin.

To prevent further loss of much needed labour, Soviet leader, Nikita Khruschev, ordered the construction of a wall between East and West Berlin, and during the early hours of 13th August 1961 hundreds of soldiers rolled out a 30-mile barbed wire barrier whilst Berlin slept. He then ordered a closure of checkpoints, leaving only a few to control. When Berlin woke to start a fresh day they faced yet another era of separation and division. Citizens of East Berlin were then ordered not to cross the barrier, where any attempt would result in being shot on sight. But threats of death didn't stop the desperate, and many were either shot as they ran towards the barrier or became tangled in the barbed wire – then shot.

Within only a few weeks a huge 15-foot concrete wall was erected, spreading across the border and even cutting through gardens and dividing streets. The Soviets told citizens the wall protected them from the decadent capitalists spreading their cancerous culture pouring into a pure Communist way of life. But they knew it was to prevent further loss of citizens, more importantly much needed labour and stop the dwindling economy of East Berlin.

Upon completion it not only stretched across 28-miles of Berlin, but also a further 75-miles around the entire city, completely enclosing the democratic society within the Eastern Bloc. Barbed wire was placed along the top with observation towers and machinegun emplacements placed at strategic positions, and anti-personnel mines buried in no-mans-land between an electrified fence and the wall. Soldiers also patrolled the entire perimeter armed with machineguns and dogs. A fortified barrier was then constructed along the 850-mile border between East and West Germany, with patrolling soldiers, machinegun emplacements and anti-personnel mines.

The Berlin Wall became a symbol of oppression and the evils of Communist rule, but it didn't prevent a further 5,000 East German Berliners risking their lives to cross into West Berlin. But thousands more were captured and arrested, and a further 191 killed by patrolling soldiers. In 1989 the last Soviet leader, Mikhail Gorbachev, portrayed a more lenient approach towards Soviet citizens than previous leaders. He also recognised the West and the importance of working closer with US President, Ronald Reagan, whom publicly told Gorbachev to tear down that wall.

Behind closed doors Reagan was concerned with a possible unification of Germany after Gorbachev said he had no interest expanding Eastern European borders and had a close relationship with the West FDR Chancellor Helmut Kohl. This soft approach and the 2 leaders working together prompted fears that FDR would open its borders and invite the Soviets to reunite Germany as a whole once again, but solely under Communist rule.

The fear of any such unification quickly subsided when in the late hours of 9th November 1989 crowds of West German citizens suddenly started to knock lumps out of the wall using pick axes and hammers. Within a few hours heavy machinery arrived and pneumatic Jack hammers battered the tough reinforced concrete into rubble. Holes and gaps started to appear big enough to crawl through, where many East Berliners poured into the West cheering and crying, but why weren't they captured or even shot on sight?

It was all to do with the Strategic Arms Reduction Treaty, where negotiations had been underway for quite a while between the Warsaw Pact and NATO to reduce nuclear arms on both sides. Part of the negotiations was to relax border crossings and on 6th November a draft of the new travel law for GDR citizens could now pass over the border into West Berlin individually, but had to return or risked leaving remaining family members under observation and threat of arrest.

In reality, the law was designed to prevent a mass of GDR citizens from crossing into Czechoslovakia with their families in fear they would abscond. When the new law was published GDR citizens renounced the terms and demonstrated against it, so a revised law was hastily passed, including the right to a visa issued for private travel too and from either side of the border without restriction.

Upon premature announcement on the evening of 9th November 1989 there was some confusion over its conditions, as it was interpreted as permission will now be granted immediately for private trips across the border without notice or requirement of proof or reason of travel. Even border guards were at a loss having no instruction with what to do or how to react as thousands of East German citizens hearing the announcement gathered at checkpoints, waving passports, demanding their new right to cross into West Berlin unhindered.

Crowds gathered at the Bornholmer Strasse checkpoint eager to cross, where guards tried to elevate pressure by waving the first few through. But passport officials, confused and frustrated at what was happening, stamped passports as invalid, preventing holders to cross. But the crowds kept growing, creating further pressure on the checkpoint. Eventually, guards had no choice but raise the barrier and let people pour through without visa checks, where an estimated 20,000 crossed in the first hour.

News quickly spread and within a few hours all border crossings opened to allow thousands of people walk through unchallenged. Equally, and surprisingly, peaceful demonstrations within East Berlin carried on without interference from GDR officials, and even stepped aside when West Berliners turned up with machinery to tear down the wall. Communism in East Germany had come to an abrupt end, signifying a new unification of Germany on 3rd October 1990 and the true official end of the Second World War, as well as the Cold War. So now you know, David Hasselholf had nothing to do with the fall of the Berlin Wall after all.

With a New Year just around the corner 1990 also witnessed the collapse of Communism in the USSR. Meanwhile, on the other side of the world, the Orient bore witness to a similar demonstration of unity – the Tiananmen Square Incident in Beijing, China, 4th June 1989. The obvious difference was democracy didn't exactly win over oppression, no matter how hard demonstrators tried. But it was a significant start to an unbelievable change within the regime.

Western democracy and the freedom it offered, along with its technology and gadgets, encouraged a huge Western hungry Chinese following, predominately from students, and they were desperate for a piece of that freedom pie. Becoming increasingly frustrated with oppressive leaders, Chinese youth demanded political and economic reform. A brave or stupid – depending how you look at it – display of anti-Communist sentiment.

The spark that fuelled a fire of mass demonstrations was death of the Chinese Communist Party (CCP) General Secretary, Hu Yaobang, who tended to lean towards a more democratic reform of China's regime.

Because of this he was forced by hard-liners in government to resign in January 1987. Hu died in April 1989 making him a martyr towards the student democratic cause. Soon after his death mass demonstrations gained momentum in cities across China, including Beijing and Shanghai, where thousands of students gathered in Tiananmen Square chanting for reform.

By May Martial law was declared, where Tiananmen Square attracted an incredible 1,000,000 demonstrators. Soldiers tried to keep growing crowds away from city borders by building blockades, including around the Square itself, but the crowds kept coming, many gathering around the statue, Goddess of Democracy, a prominent symbol of their cause. But the Communist government was in no mood to put up with disobedient citizens, so they poured thousands of soldiers into the Square to disperse them.

By early June, as demonstrations increased momentum, police and the military lost patients so the army called in tanks, but crowds were determined to stay put and chant demands. Inevitably, on 3rd June the government ordered soldiers to open fire with live ammunition and tear gas on the remaining demonstrators that refused to heed warnings. Tanks ran over demonstrators as they tried to flee the carnage of dead or dying citizens.

By the morning of 4th June the demonstration was over and the military gained control of Tiananmen Square, including Shanghai and Chengdu, where soldiers also opened fire on demonstrators. This led to an iconic film clip on 5th June of a lone Chinese man walking in front of approaching tanks standing steadfast, refusing to budge as they came to a halt only feet away. As the lead tank tried to divert around the young man he simply shuffles to one side preventing it from moving forward. He then climbed on top before saying something to the tank commander through the open turret capola. What happened to him afterwards isn't quite clear, but more than likely he was arrested for his display of non-conformity.

The film clip of his incredible bravery and refusal to move out of the way went viral on news channels around the world, including the death toll. Chinese authorities reported 241 killed and 7,000 injured. Devastating as it was, the actual number massacred by the Chinese government was much worse. As for the thousands of demonstrators arrested, they were either given long prison sentences or the death penalty, executed for daring to speak out against the regime.

The Chinese government has since ordered a complete ban of any gathering or Commemoration of the demonstrations. In response to the massacre USA carried out economic and political sanctions upon China, and many other Western nations, including the UK, voiced their discussed of the way Chinese officials handled the demonstrators. But with the dawn of 1990 witnessing an end to Communism in the USSR, and the Chinese students demonstrating for reform, the Western world at least breathed a sigh of relief. Peace was fully restored.

Well, no not exactly. Unfortunately, the idea, even dream of world peace, was shattered once again by a region that fails to understand the concept of peace and been fighting one another for over 2,000 years – the Middle East. The Soviets were at war with Afghanistan from 1981 to 1989, Beirut and Lebanon continued their arguments with Israel, whilst Iraq and Iran tore colours out of each other in the early eighties.

Saddam Hussein, the dictator of Iraq, was placed in position of authority by the CIA (Central Intelligence

Agency) supposedly to control him and the country, decided that he was no longer content with just his own oil fields. He also wanted the rich oil reserves in Kuwait to help pay off his war debt. And his feeble excuse to invade Kuwait was that the oil fields belonged to Iraq, accusing Kuwait of stealing them from him.

On 2nd August 1990 his army crossed the border into Kuwait, spreading havoc around the country with sporadic killing of men women and children, including rape and torture, whatever age or gender they took a dislike to. Many were even set alight and left to burn alive in the middle of the street in front of passers-by. The West had to intervene and put a stop to this outrageous invasion of a Sovereign State and callous act of wanton destruction.

By January 1991 NATO put together a huge Task Force involving over 30 countries, spearheaded by the powerful USA. UK also sent a considerable amount of troops and hardware not seen since the Second World War, with different armies gathering in Kuwait and Saudi Arabia under the banner of Operation Desert Shield – UK Forces using their own Operational name of Operation Granby.

UN sanctions had no effect on Saddam Hussein, so on 21st January Desert Shield turned into Desert Storm. Unprecedented air and naval sorties destroyed hundreds of military targets in Iraq within the first few hours, disabling reinforcements and denying air supremacy. In fact, the only Iraqi military jets taking off headed to Iran in fear of being shot down by allied jets.

By 15th February 500,000 coalition ground troops, majority of which made up of US, Saudi Arabian, Egyptian and UK forces – largest of the European contingency – forced the Iraqi army to withdraw from Kuwait. An unprecedented task taking only 100-hours to complete. Overall, from 17th January to 28th February the entire conflict lasted only 5-weeks.

President Bush, Commander and Chief of Desert Storm, gave an order for all coalition forces on the ground to halt at the Iraqi border, leaving a somewhat bemused Kuwait thinking a perfect opportunity was going to be missed to topple Saddam's evil regime. But President Bush was adamant not to create tensions between Arab States by invading another, so war ended at the border, only to leave Saddam to lick his wounds. As for his army, it was estimated that over 60,000 military combatants were killed and a further 100,000 wounded.

Casualties on the allies was considerably lighter but nonetheless devastating to families and friends back home, with USA suffering the brunt at 148, of which 35 were killed by 'friendly fire'. UK troops suffered 47 killed with 9 due to 'friendly fire'. The term 'friendly fire' became synonymous with the Gulf War, where almost a quarter of US battle casualties resulted in deaths this way.

Back home the usual demonstrations were out in force no matter what the reason or belief as to why war started, or indeed what the troops went through and their incredible achievements ousting an invading army from another country. Thousands gathered in London outside parliament and the US Embassy, chanting 'not in my name' and 'troops out'. Other demonstrations gathered in towns and cities up and down the UK, USA, France, Germany, Netherlands and many other European countries. Clearly they must have either been strongly against liberation of any kind from an invader or were supporters of Saddam Hussein. Otherwise, why demonstrate?

Although there has always been an argument for and against war, we were now entering a new era of demonstration carried out predominately by students and those growing into adulthood too young to experience or understand threat of War, invasion, terrorism or Mutually Assured Destruction. These horrors were now cast to the history books, as far as they were concerned. Deemed obsolete to an up and coming youth of the Western world. After all, we were now living in a time of unequivocal security, freedom and liberty. Remind me, where did our freedom come from?

Most of us realise this and are incredibly thankful for the sacrifice made on our behalf for our protection and safety. Sadly a growing number of this new modern society thought different, and were not so obliging in any shape or form. Security was there as a matter of fact, to be taken for granted and even ridicule; bite the hand that fed them freedom and liberty, so to speak. There were even signs of actually blaming the armed forces for carrying out incredible crimes against humanity, when in fact they were ousting an invading force on behalf of a country that begged for help. But there was still a little way to go before this new wave of anarchist wreaked havoc upon the masses.

There was, however, still good reason for the masses to demonstrate; to revolt in huge crowds when they could no longer tolerate outrageous government policies, especially when it concerned all those of a voting age. A demonstration not seen since the industrial revolution where a nation once gathered in desperation to plea for a reasonable wage and better conditions. Kids, welcome to the introduction of the Community Charge, dubbed the dreaded Poll Tax. The most stupid, corrupt and devastating policy the Conservative government at the time could ever bestow on the nation.

Margaret Thatcher was forced to submit her Premiership 22nd November 1990 as she walked out of number 10 Downing Street for the last time, where John Major took her place as Prime Minister. She certainly left an incredible legacy – good and bad – where her final encore became the worst decision she ever made, and all 3 contenders for her position pledged to abandon the infamous Community Charge.

Thatcher previously introduced to the Conservative manifesto a new local taxing system when she was the Shadow Environment Secretary in 1974. The old system, where a notional rental value of a house determined a rateable value, could now be replaced with a Community Charge for all adults over the age of 18-years old living in the same household.

By 1986 a green paper was published – Alternative to Domestic Rates – that lowered income tax but created another tax to fill the Chancellors coffers by taxing every adult, working or not. Four years later it nationally replaced Domestic Rates on 6th April 1990, first introduced to Scotland the previous year. We all had to pay it, home owner, tenant or otherwise. The unfairness of this tax was incredible. Over 18-years old and working had to pay 100 percent of the Community Charge, where those claiming benefits or in full time education only had to pay 20 percent of the full demand. So a household with working parents and any children over the age of eighteen living under the same roof, working or not, had a Community Charge bill.

The masses quickly dubbed this Community Charge as the poll tax. It was also called a living tax or air tax due to everyone had to pay it regardless of rental or home ownership. It followed you everywhere. This caused a huge headache for local authorities chasing unpaid bills and defaults, where parents failed to register their adult children on the electoral roll, or moved house but failed to register in an attempt to evade detection. In doing so, anyone that wasn't on the electoral roll couldn't vote in local or general elections, where it is believed so many didn't register the consequence was a fourth victory for the Conservatives in the 1992 General election.

The poll tax quickly became unpopular upon its national introduction, where it was perceived to be a tax for the poor to pay for the rich. At the tender age of 23-years I remember my rates suddenly doubling overnight, and I had no choice but pay or receive penalties and inevitably have bailiffs knocking on my door to collect. But how on earth could I possibly afford to pay?

I earned £7,200 Gross per annum, but my 20-year old wife didn't work. She stayed at home to look after our young son and didn't claim benefits, therefore wasn't recognised as unemployed. But she didn't want to be recognised and placed as a statistic on a depressive system. She took pride not drawing the dole, and knew within a few years would start work again when our son was old enough to go to nursery. Nevertheless, she was legally bound to pay the Charge in full, even though she wasn't working. But regardless not being registered as unemployed, how could she possibly pay?

Well, I had to, as well as my bill. The only option we had to reduce the bill was for her to sign on, but it wasn't as simple as that. To sign on for unemployment benefit without proof of previous work within a given period, she had no option but wait 13-weeks before any payment of benefits could be awarded. Until then I had to pay both Charges in full. But we couldn't afford to, so fell into arrears. In turn we received countless threatening letters from the local authorities for non-payment, including threats of penalties, even prison.

We were now desperate. In an attempt to prevent any process of local authorities taking both of us to court we took drastic action by missing a rent payment, leading to another, then another, just to keep up with poll tax demands. In doing so we received an eviction notice from the housing agency the same morning receiving a letter from the Council confirming we had finally caught up with our Community Charge payments. And should we fall into arrears again, we must contact them immediately because they were there to help. Meanwhile, my Ford Cortina became our home.

Most, if not all local authorities around the country were just as callus. Millions of households struggled to pay the Charge, and not unlike my young family, many were forced to make drastic changes, including losing homes, face eviction, procure arrears, penalties and even served prison sentences for non-payment. A few weeks before release of the new Charge, huge protests were co-ordinated by anti-poll tax groups including 3D (Don't Register, Don't Pay, Don't Collect) and local Anti-Poll Tax Unions (APTUs). Protests around the country grew larger and larger, and on 31st March demonstrators estimated to be around 250,000 gathered in Trafalgar Square.

Inevitably crowds started to riot. Police struggled to keep control and called for a further 2,000 officers to suppress trouble, but it was too late, even for the mounted police pushing rioters back from any advancement. Within only a few hours West End shops were attacked, windows smashed, cars overturned and set alight, but the majority of demonstrators had nothing to do with the rioting. Once again, it was the usual bunch of anarchists and anti-establishment groups simply attaching themselves to another demonstration and exploiting its cause as a catalyst to inject their own agenda – disrupt the nation.

When the dust settled 340 were arrested, 113 injured and just as many police required medical treatment for cuts and bruises. But protest by the masses was far from over. Local authorities up and down the country faced thousands of non-payers, raising concern for Central government. Some local authorities were left with a whopping 30 percent deficit. Thousands more refusing to pay also refused to attend court for non-payment, creating further strain on local authorities unable to contend with a considerable increase in arrest warrants. Police even refused to arrest those issued with warrants simply because it was impossible to achieve.

When parliament settled down with its new Prime Minister, John Major, he instructed his Environment Secretary, Michael Heseltine, to replace the Community Charge with a new domestic tax. And on 21st March 1991 it was announced that the Community Charge would be replaced with a fairer taxing system. When the general election of 1992 was over, and the Conservatives found themselves still in power, legislation was passed, replacing the Community Charge with a new Council Tax.

Not dissimilar to the old rates system, it returned to one bill, one dwelling, with a category of Bands to determine amount of tax depending upon size and location. Central government also introduced a cap on banded dwellings to prevent local authorities charging what they deemed fit. And a 25 percent discount with dwellings housing single occupants, for those receiving benefits, tax credits and students. But it was too late; the damage had been done, ripping families and communities apart.

Chapter Sixteen

Things can only get better

With Generation Y drawing to a close, Generation Z was born as the Balkan troubles started to brew. Due to collapse of the Soviet Union a void was left behind, instantly opening old wounds and past hatred between former Eastern Bloc European countries. The first to fall was former Federal Republic of Yugoslavia. Before it was torn up Yugoslavia was made of smaller provinces: Bosnia and Herzegovina, Serbia, Croatia, Montenegro, Slovenia, and Kosovo, most of which didn't exactly see eye to eye.

New elected Serbian President, Slobodan Milosevic, enhancing his leadership in March 1989 with many votes from Montenegro, led to angry reprisals from other opposition contenders and voters. But his leadership allowed the new government to rule over provinces in Kosovo, where before the election decision making was carried out by their own government. Meetings were held between other Yugoslavian leaders in an attempt to avoid possible war. And the UN passed a Resolution imposing an arms embargo on all provinces, but Serbia already had a large cache of arms, and Croatia could easily smuggle weapons across its coastline.

Peace talks inevitably collapsed, and on 9th January 1992 Bosnian Serbs proclaimed a Republic of the Serbian people in Bosnia. There was no declaration of independence, so a referendum was called for 29th February but the following day talks ended when Serb officials withdrew when the Bosniak-Croat delegates turned it down, so the Bosnian Muslims adopted the process, creating a clash between the Bosnian Serbs. Oh, it gets much more confusing. During the referendum on 1st March Serbians flying their flag was interpreted as provocation to the Muslim population. But the smaller Bosnian Serbs population had the backing of Serbia and a much larger army so had no fear of any reprisals.

Clashes between Serbia, Croatia and the Bosnian Muslims begun soon after the collapse of Communism in Yugoslavia during Premier of John Major and US President George Bush senior. By April all-out war broke out after the UK, Europe and the USA recognised Bosnia and Herzegovina as being its own country. And the war between the 3 former nations was almost a religious war with Bosnia receiving help from Islamic States including al-Qaeda, Saudi Arabia and Hezbollah. Croats from Catholic countries, and Serbia receiving help from Eastern Christian countries. This included money, supply of arms and freedom fighters.

At the start of the war Bosnia managed to gather around 250,000 men to fight for their cause, with over 10,000 fighting in Croatia. The following year the war created 2,500,000 refugees, where Croatia accepted just over 330,000 from Bosnia, and Serbia took a tenth of Croatia. Other provinces accepted around 150,000 combined.

The horrors of war soon materialised with Croat Forces disallowing much needed oxygen for newborn babies in incubators, leaving them to die. And 24 Serbian civilians were killed at a Bosnian Serb village by Bosnian soldiers. Even Bosnian Muslims and Serbian civilians killed each other. As the war spread towards Northern Herzegovina civilians fled in fear of their lives. Those captured were either raped, tortured or shot on sight, and Bosnian Serb Forces killed 15 Croat civilians, along with prisoners of War. Appeals from the Bosnian Forces for the West to intervene and help was returned with the United Nations sending troops from the US, France, Denmark, UK, and other NATO countries.

US and UK troops quickly found themselves under fire when defending civilians after the UN passed Resolution 836 to use force when necessary and protect safe zones. NATO Naval blockades prevented arms smuggled into Croatia and air strikes by the US and UK targeted military sites. Eventually UN intervention somewhat forced a cease-fire between Croatia and Bosnia by 25th February 1994.

Although an agreement was reached between the authorities, Bosnian and Croatian civilians didn't agree, where divisions between the masses remain [2020]. During the peace process the RAF were forced to shoot down 4 Serbian fighter jets as they defied the UN no-fly zone over Bosnia, deliberately targeting United Nations Protection Force (UNPROFOR) delivering aid, doctors and medical supplies to the besieged city of Maglaj.

The amount of casualties varies, but it is estimated that 330,000 were caused by war, hunger and biting cold winters. Of which, military casualties were around 82,000 but concise figure are difficult due to confusion with combatant and non-combatants actually fighting. Other casualties include an outrageous 20,000 women subjected to rape by Bosnian Serbs and the Serbian police, where some were used as examples to terrorise civilians.

There was also mass ethnic cleansing and genocide of Bosnian Muslims, unseen since Nazi Germany. Concentration camps were hastily constructed to cage thousands of Bosnian Muslims doomed to slaughter. Many were subjected to starvation, torture, rape, and forced to dig their own grave before shot in the back of the head. Others were shot en-mass standing next to bulldozed ditches, similar to the tens of thousands falling victim during those dark years of Hitler and his ethnic cleansing. Others were simply left to starve to death.

Thankfully, peace held – generally – and the Balkans could concentrate on rebuilding its towns and cities. Remarkably, anti-war protesters, CND movement and university students were out once again, marching en-mass outside the Houses of Parliament. Even when Serbian concentration camps were discovered and aired on news channels across the world, crammed full of Bosniaks and those that fought against the Bosnian Serbs and Serbia. Meanwhile, celebrities, pop groups and idols jumped on the merry bandwagon to support demonstrators, in turn encouraging young followers and fans to do the same.

But hey, chin up, a saviour was just around the corner, in the guise of a new Prime Minister, Tony Blair, and his New Labour government. Yes, in May 1997, as the sun shined through a clear Spring blue sky onto apple and cherry blossom, the nation elected a new leader to take the masses out of a tired and fusty old Conservative administration that had lingered since May 1979. And with a Commons majority of 179 seats 18-years of Tory rule came crashing down after taking its toll upon the nation. It was time for a change.

With a landslide victory, Tony Blair shook hands with jubilant crowds as his adopted theme tune by D-ream singing 'Things can only get better,' with professor Brian Cox on keyboards, played in the background,. We were saved – hooray! The masses assumed for the first few years nothing would happen. But they were wrong. With a 47-year old Tony at the helm (youngest Prime Minister since Pip the younger), things certainly started quickly, for better or worse. He wanted a country fit for the many, not the few. A country fit for the up and coming Millennium.

Tony inherited a prosperous United Kingdom with money in the bank, a strong economy and little threat of unions threatening large mass walkouts. Computer technology was running wild with enthusiasm, banks were healthy, high business investments swamped the market, incredibly low unemployment across the nation, and a fit Western Europe on our doorstep. The Cold War was at an end and living standards were at an all-time high.

Tony wanted to show willing straight away; get one over the old Tories as quickly as possible. To show them how it's done, and with some ease by all accounts. That first important task was to take 1,000,000 unemployed off the dole in one quick swipe of his magic wand. But how did this amazing man achieve this? Well, he didn't, but he did manage to create 250,000 jobs out of thin air, most of which were for the under 25's and within the public sector, thus reducing unemployment to an even better all time low. Hail, the magic work of Tony.

His next brilliant idea was to spend even more billions of tax payers hard earned money on the National Health Service; commonly criticising the previous Tory government on how they mismanaged the NHS, patient waiting lists and accusing them of failing to invest money. He also used pot after pot of public money to open children day care centres, help with child-care costs and benefit welfare reform. Meanwhile, Chancellor Gordon Brown introduced a minimum wage with no rise in income tax, at least for a while. So far so good, eh? After all, it was springtime for Blair in Britain, and all was well.

To accomplish his many tasks he needed a solid following of loyal Members of Parliament and shunt his government away from far-left politics, renouncing die-hard old Labour members from his Party. But there was one small problem. A few remainers lingering in dark corners of the House of Commons refused to budge, determined to keep the far-left flame alight. And not really having a choice, some even sat in his Cabinet, including Deputy Prime Minister, John Prescott.

Blair, however, was undeterred by old Labour rhetoric, and made a point of surrounding himself with yes men and women. He also appointed more females into his Cabinet than any other previous government, providing they displayed his kind of socialist views, such as Harriet Harman and Margaret Beckett. To ensure he was popular with the youth of the nation he got darn wiv da kids by playing his electric guitar in front of a young crowd of amazed onlookers.

Not realising their new cool Prime Minister once played lead singer and guitar in a student rock band – Ugly Rumours – he also invited guests from the Rock n Roll world, including the band Oasis, to number 10 Downing Street. Where the delighted crowd stood cheering as he played host at the reception.

From the early 1990's Britain was going through a music revolution, and bands such as Oasis, Blur and Pulp, created a new sound called Britpop. Although some of these bands played different types of music, they all came under the same banner, much to the annoyance of Oasis, as they perceived their music to be light-years ahead of mainstream pop culture. And of course, not forgetting the Spice Girls. Yes, even them, all part of the Britpop clan, making the UK centre stage once again for popular music.

A decade earlier British music reflected the mood of the nation with its high unemployment, disappearing industries and rising poverty. By the 1990's there was a completely different atmosphere, with a definite sign of confidence and optimism amongst the masses reflecting the economy, and it showed in music. Tony knew this and wanted to ensure his New Labour government was part of the youth and music scene by inviting pop groups to Downing Street and Chequers – the official home of the Prime Minister. In doing so he developed a huge following from youth culture, and, of course, created future voters. With a large House of Commons majority and the youth on his side, what could possibly go wrong? His political future was secure – zig-a-zig-ah.

Students were a big attraction for Blair, and they would be. After all, he was once an annoying, nice but dim, champagne socialist student. And he saw other students as potential voters, so he prompted change with the expansion of further education, including higher education, universities and academy schools. In doing so the university fraternity became a frenzy of excitement for information and literature on New Labour policies. Socialist lecturers now had a leader they could rely upon to spread their political agenda, and teachers felt more autarchic than ever to teach pupils left wing policies.

Student movements and political groups grew exponentially since Margaret Thatcher's government, and expanded further still with the New Labour movement. The question was, could it continue? Slowly but surely New Labour began to unravel its true colours with a quest to control the masses, naively unnoticed by up and coming young voters. However, older generations remembering what it was like to live under previous socialist governments, slowly injecting far-left policies drip by drip, could see right through him. But New Labour gained the trust of a young nation, spoiling them with what they wanted rather than what is needed for the nation.

One of Blair's early policies was to, somehow, put an end to the troubles in Northern Ireland and bring peace by negotiating the Good Friday Agreement between the Nationalist and Unionists, effectively creating an elected Northern Ireland Assembly not seen since 1972. He also organised Referendums for Scotland and Wales, creating devolved Assemblies in both countries.

Blair and his Chancellor, Gordon Brown, continued dangling bangles and baubles in front of the masses in between their clandestine policies, if only to throw the nation off scent and into a false sense of security, such as handing control of interest rates to the Bank of England. A remarkable diversionary tactic, but it upset his Cabinet as he never discussed it with them. Well, he wouldn't. After all, the plan was to keep the elder nation busy and pre-occupied with moaning about it whilst he set his sights on total social control of the nation, including without hindrance from his Cabinet.

In the meantime, to cement the diversion, Brown sold all of the UK's gold reserves when gold prices were at an all time low. Would have got a better price from Cash Converters. Nevertheless, in doing so it raised much needed immediate cash required to fund New Labour's real policies. Both radical decisions created a few quid to supposedly spend on the people, but it was inevitable such decisions were going to eventually have dire consequences in later years. But for now, and with everything seemingly going swimmingly, what could possibly go wrong for New Labour? After all, he'd just received a shiny new credit card to spend, spend, spend, on the strength of the previous government's credit reference file.

Blair was about to make his first drastic mistake, as far as his young followers were concerned, and that was to agree with the UN and send troops to Kosovo. His young followers found themselves between a rock and a hard place. They felt cheated and turned their disgust into hate – not yet old enough to know the difference. But how dare he agree with war-mongering Tory policies by sending scary British troops to a conflict. He was supposed to be on side of the anti-war fraternity. Full of love, peace, music, picking daisies, skipping through meadows and everything paid for by mummy and daddy. Even supposed to be a political advocate for those displaying loud, unequivocal, anti-war chants.

Young supporters wondered around like lost sheep baying a desperate plea for leadership, but from where, and who? Ah, that'll be from the likes of Ken Livingstone, Tony Benn and Jeremy Corbyn, that's who. All opposed any sort of military intervention, which was tantamount to supporting the Serbian invader, thus seemingly against protecting the oppressed Kosovo citizens. Far-left politicians welcomed young lost sheep with open arms, eager to inject loony-left policies into a vulnerable youth and turn their allegiance away from New Labour.

Nevertheless, Blair, as would any grown-up with an ounce of compassion, couldn't let Serbia destroy another neighbouring country and spread Nazi-style ethnic cleansing across the region, as they did only a few years previous in Bosnia. In a heartbeat he sent British troops to the Balkans for the first time under New Labour and join NATO allies to oust Serbians out of Kosovo. The last tinderbox of the Balkans, comprising of Muslim Albanians and Serbians, where the Serbs were a loud and arrogant minority.

Serbian leader, Slobodan Milosevic wanted the Albanians out of Kosovo, and set about cleansing the country the same way he tried in Bosnia. By 1998 tension grew to breaking point between the two factions. Serbian police and Milosevic's Yugolav Forces set about controlling the majority Albanian Muslims using heavy-handed force and fear, killing thousands from the offset. In response the Kosovo Liberation Army fought back, sparking a new war with the Yugoslav Forces of Serbia.

Grown-up international condemnation soon gathered pace, and the UN passed yet more Resolutions for NATO to force the former Yugoslav army and Serbian paramilitaries out of Kosovo, demanding an immediate ceasefire. The coalition of allies, once again comprising of US and UK troops, with France, Italy, and surprisingly Germany. A somewhat hesitant country to send troops to a war zone, believe it or not, and actually fired their first shot in anger since the Second World War when they came under attack from former Nazi allies, Serbia. The newly formed Russia also sent a contingent of troops, although disrupted NATO rather than help, as they predictably would.

Allied Forces continued a relentless bombing campaign of strategic Serbian military targets over a 3-month period, creating irreparable damage to ammunition and supply dumps. The Serbs retaliated by displacing hundreds of thousands of Albanian Muslims out of Kosovo into neighbouring Albania, creating a massive humanitarian crises around the border region. NATO continued with its bombing campaign whilst ground troops under the UN peacekeeping flag supplied safe zones and humanitarian aid to all civilians caught up in the conflict.

By June 1999 Serbian troops were forced out of Kosovo when their leader, Slobodan Milosevic, signed a peace agreement with NATO ending the war. Albanian refugees returned to their homes in Kosovo, where 1,000,000 were displaced. Most Serbian civilians decided to leave Kosovo in fear of reprisals from the Muslim

Albanians, but some of the even more arrogant refused to move. To this day [2020] tensions prevail between the two factions. In February 2008 Kosovo declared independence from Serbia, internationally recognised as a country, but Serbia remains steadfast in their refusal to accept any kind of independence whatsoever.

Out of those caught and tried for crimes against humanity include the former Serbian President, Radoan Karadzic, and Ratko Mladic, arrested for the siege of Sarajevo and the Srebrenica massacre, where both were found guilty of all crimes, sentenced to life imprisonment by the Hague. Biljana Plavsic, Momcilo Krajisnik, Radoslav Brdanin and Dusko Tadic, all former Serb leaders, were also found guilty of all crimes and given life sentences. Slobodan Milosevic was found guilty in 2006 but died before the tribunal could come to a close. Many others were found guilty of crimes against humanity, sentenced from 10-years to life in prison.

The Balkan war brought its attention to a world-wide audience via a new concept of communication. A revolution in media broadcasting technology with the capability of transmitting data and information instantly. This incredible invention was the World Wide Web. Invented by Tim Berners-Lee, a British computer whiz kid working at the European Organisation for Nuclear Research (CERN) in Switzerland, invented a new communication system in 1980 using hypertext to talk to each other. His invention, however, wasn't entirely a new concept. NATO first used data sent between computers in the 1960's where a vast amount of information was transmitted in a short burst between Navy vessels. But the coding used was, in comparison, ancient and slow.

Scientists at CERN needed data from experiments sent to other scientists around the world using a communication system adapted to suit different computer and software programmes. Tim designed user-friendly software that stored a large hypertext database with typed links that can send data to different computers by using ready available telecommunication networks. Six years later he had everything in place for a fully functional operating system to send linked hypertext information to other computers using the internet – a communication system already available.

By developing the first computer system with HyperText Transfer Protocol (HTTP) and the HyperText Markup Language (HTML) he could send text pages over his web browser to other computers on the internet around the world. His new browser was called, after much thought, the World Wide Web. The first HTTP server on his World Wide Web had the address, http://info.cern.ch, and carried the first web pages to explain what it is and the massive project Tim was working on.

With US backing it was tweaked and improved so that everyone with a computer could use the same software design developed with programmes that send and receive HTTP web pages. And in 1993 Tim announced at a CERN conference that the World Wide Web should be accessed by anyone for everyone and free of any charge. In May 1994 CERN held its first WWW conference, and has done so every year since.

By 1995 media outlets and news broadcasters caught on incredibly fast with this new technology and its ability to send attached information to a recipient almost instantly, using electronic mail (email), including photograph and video files – although with limited capacity in the early days. Media companies also found a new niche with marketing and advertising, as did other companies, and those with an entrepreneurial flare soon constructed websites to advertise their services and wares.

In 1998 I bought my first home computer, kick-starting my writing career with a popular Packard Bell package, and continue to write books on it, including this one. However, although my home computer was at the pinnacle of cutting edge technology, it didn't have a built-in modem. When curiosity got the better of me I bought a modem and a long telephone cable so I could connect to the internet using dial-up, taking several attempts to make a connection – my first lesson with using the internet. Second lesson was annoying the wife because I was using the telephone line.

Lesson 3 was to join a server to connect to the World Wide Web. I chose AOL as their details came with my computer. Once connected I discovered AOL chat, which was handy because I had so many questions about my new toy, and there were loads of other users willing to answer them. Within a few weeks I was a diva on the net. Well, I thought so. And I quickly realised the importance of this technology and its potential. If only I was more entrepreneurial and knew how to write a website or envisaged the popularity of digital auction houses or social media sites.

When I joined the internet village there wasn't nowhere near as many web users as there are today. But the World Wide Web quickly caught on, creating the dot-com revolution. New internet start-up companies hit the web with a vengeance, inspiring many other whiz kids to do the same. And when the bubble burst in 2001 it most certainly didn't mean the end of the internet. New companies, and those that rode the dot-com storm, such as Amazon and Ebay, have grown beyond their wildest dreams. More about this phenomenal worldwide communication technology later, because Tony, much to my dismay, and surprise, insists that you must know more about his fantastic leadership and how he was the creator of the Millennial generation – in his mind.

Chapter Seventeen

Seriously, more Blair?

Yes, I know, but his long serving regime had a huge influence upon modern day society and the Millennial generation. So bear with me and read on. You will soon understand where I'm coming from.

New young voters, as well as older supporters of Tony Blair, were beginning to notice New Labour had similarities to previous Tory rule. His 'Third Way' policy reflected this when he renounced old Labour and adopted a more centre philosophy by dislocating himself from previous political directions. In a sense he gave the impression – at first as being A-Political: neither left or right, placing his values close to Liberal Party policies, but with a twist. Needles to say, he strived for globalisation, recognised the importance of small start-up businesses and was determined to make the UK a fully integrated member of the European Union. So on paper he appeared fantastic.

Blair could see what the far-left was doing and knew he needed to win back confidence from his young admirers no matter what the cost, but was running out of ideas. He was already half way through exhausting a 2-year exclusion of raising income tax – a previous Tory proposal should they have won the election. In the meantime tax payers money was running dangerously low due to his freeze on many tax revenues, yet increased public spending on NHS funding, tax credits, introduction of the minimum wage, amongst other expenditures. So what could he do?

In 1998 Blair deployed a white paper on asylum seekers: European Convention on Human Rights and immigration in UK law. Inevitably hoping to sway young voters to believe in his policies and regain confidence. In doing so he assured the masses that his immigration policies were the right approach for Great Britain towards a united Europe. And if repeated enough times on television, radio and the print media, be it interviews, television panel shows or political programmes, the public will eventually believe what he says.

Although totally unaware of the consequences, Millennials loved the idea of a European Union having control over its members, including the UK, and embraced the idea of helping those from war-torn European countries by inviting them into the country. The masses from an older generation, however, and with a little more experience, were not so accommodating. Fearing overcrowding, threat of losing jobs to cheap labour, and for those on Council housing waiting lists denied privilege over foreign needs. As well as a huge cost to the taxpayer and a sudden drain on NHS resources and welfare.

In 1997 the EU had 15 member States, where EU net migration stood at around 48,000. Within a year the figure rose to an astonishing 140,000 where most of the increase came from Kosovo, Bosnia, Serbia and Croatia, not including thousands more smuggled in as illegal immigrants. Most of which were sold a promise of money and jobs by gangs, but found themselves sold as slave labour on the black market.

Thanks to New Labour policies there was a large jump in asylum applications, rising to a whopping 42 percent in 1998 on the previous year. There was also a huge increase on visa applications to join spouses already living in the UK or about to marry into British families. Before 1997 there were around 1,000 applications, but once again within one year of New Labour, there were an astonishing 32,000 and all granted entry into the UK unhindered and without question. With an already overcrowded population of 60,000,000 in 1997 the national figure increased to a staggering 70,000,000 by 2019 and continues to grow.

With collapse of Soviet Communism and peace – almost – in the Balkans, Blair's naïve observation of the real world also failed to recognise that the majority of Eastern European immigrants were young men. That is men of conscription age that faced a call-up notice in their former Soviet State enforcing a military deterrent should neighbouring reunited countries create a fracas, as they did in the Balkans.

But these draft dodgers didn't want to fight for their country. After all, they were not only Millennials, they saw themselves as Western Millennials but ruled with Communist undertones. So they opted to leg it to a ready-made freedom in Western Europe, offering asylum from donning a uniform. After all, why be forced to protect your country when you can live in the West and have their own Forces protect you from potential enemies without having to integrate within a new social system.

Young New Labour followers, however, also naïve about the real world, loved this new influx of immigrants. But the original issues remained: where do you house millions of immigrants coming into a small country already brimming to capacity; where are the jobs going to come from when there were already 1,500,000 signing on; and where will the extra tax payers money come from to pay for a sudden increase in welfare handouts? But that didn't matter to up and coming young voters, because they didn't pay taxes, have rent or mortgages and bills to pay. Mummy and daddy did that.

By the end of New Labour rule in 2010 the official government total migration figure to the UK was 3,600,000. However, due to the government losing count and having no idea how many actually poured into the country, further figures suggest closer to 12,000,000. To put this into comparison, the 1960's gave a net immigration figure at a negative against the minus 60,000 emigration figure leaving the UK.

Whilst the elder masses feared a sudden influx of immigrants, their concerns were renounced by Foreign Secretary, Robin Cook, as nothing more than a small insignificant amount of the nation expressing anti-European racism refusing to adhere to Labour policies. His words resonated with young New Labour voters, and they embraced every challenge from anyone that dare say otherwise.

Blair had won back his young followers, slowly indoctrinating his regime into their psyche ready for his next General election. But the fact remains you cannot get a quart into a pint pot, no matter how much political rhetoric is poured onto it. In other words overcrowding on such a small island has become a significant problem ever since. And not unlike overcrowded tower blocks of the 1960's and 1970's, being on a much larger scale there are going to be problems, often controversial and sometimes explosive.

Approaching a new Millennia, Blair's vision of dragging the UK from its steadfast Victorian attitude towards his personal vision of a modern European-mentored Britain led by a European President – him – was slowly becoming a reality. Anything else didn't matter. But Blair's New Britain was put to the test once again on 11th September 2001 when the Twin Towers of

New York were brought down by a new enemy of the West, al-Qaeda.

Using four hijacked civilian airliners, al-Qaeda leader, Osama Bin Laden, targeted the World Trade Centre Twin Towers, by deliberately crashing the aeroplanes full of innocent passengers into them. Where the third airliner hit the Pentagon – US headquarters of Defence – and a fourth crashed in fields south of Washington, originally targeting the White House. The hijackers were heroically overwhelmed by passengers, and knowing they faced their fate, fought the terrorists so they would crash the aeroplane clear of any civilians and prevent further casualties.

Within only a few hours every single civilian international flight from around the entire globe were suddenly grounded, and the blank radar screens shown on television news channels were eerily silent of any traffic. President George W Bush Junior stood amongst the Twin Tower rubble alongside New York fire fighters and pledged that he will not stop until those responsible were brought to justice. In saying so he implied that those countries that didn't agree were against the US, instantly making them the enemy.

Although it was interpreted as those countries refusing to stand shoulder to shoulder were enemies of the US was in fact imposed by the media and political opposition groups that used his words against him – a sickening notion considering what had just happened. He was actually reiterating the anger of the world to those that could plan and execute the murder of almost 3,000 innocent civilians, many of which were from other countries.

Using Bush's term 'shoulder to shoulder' was quickly exploited by journalists to grab instant media attention, and also used by many other nation leaders, including Tony Blair, whom was the first to offer assistance, be it military or otherwise. As intelligence was hastily gathered, by 7th October US and UK military Forces begun targeting al-Qaeda military training camps and communication facilities in Kabul, Afghanistan, using laser guided bombs and cruise missiles.

And guess what? Yes, yet another bunch of anti-war protestors hit the streets of the UK as well as other European countries, and unbelievably the US. But despite the use of UK Forces in Afghanistan, Blair managed to explain to his young followers why they were sent, narrowly clinging onto a majority confidence. Nevertheless, as he headed towards a second term he attracted hundreds of thousands of under 25-year olds suddenly becoming interested in his politics. And these young supporters of Blair's Britain were having children of their own, only to grow and nurture into believing Blair policies.

Student followers were also attracted to New Labour for similar reasons as any other young voter, but being university students they had to go one step further with voicing their own naïve left-wing political views, apart from actually bothering to place a vote into a ballot box. University students up and down the country expanded a deeper interest with politics during the early years of Margaret Thatcher, but for completely opposite reasons: accusations of nothing less than branded a Nazis and Fascist by the younger fraternity. But then again, that was bound to be the case, especially with a surge in 'alternative comedy' hitting the airwaves, attracting student humour to bash Thatcher and her Conservative policies.

When Blair replaced the old stuffy Tory rule, his politics was most definitely a fresh of breath air for students as well as the younger generation. But he did manage to upset the 'alternative comedy' scene, where up and coming comedians had to drastically change their material due to Thatcher's absence. Fortunate for Blair, youth culture changed considerably since 1979 where many of his votes came from those that had never served their country – voluntary or National Service. They had also grown in a household with a steady income, full of labour-saving devices, gadgets, electronic games, colour television and music centres. Not forgetting food on the table and clean clothes every day, holidays, easy credit, full time employment, and of course, safe from invasion and the Luftwaffe.

Blair also gained votes from immigrants thanks to his immigration policies. It was suggested that he planned a mass immigration policy with a belief that once integrated into British society they would return the favour by voting for him in future general elections. Some did, but many didn't, of which most were from the former Eastern Bloc, and simply had no interest in British politics or joining the British Armed Forces. But Blair did gain a considerable amount of votes from the gay community by relaxing and even rewriting many laws, including amending the age of consent.

Remarkably, the 1967 Sexual Offences Act remained at the consent age of 21-years for homosexuals, where all consensual sexual acts had to remain behind closed doors. This included without showing any affection in public, kissing or even holding hands. But in 1979 there was an attempt to update the 1967 Act by reducing the age of consent to 18-years of age, but negotiations never even reached the House of Commons, so the reduction debate was dropped.

By 1994 the Criminal Justice and Public Order Bill was raised to reform the law on rape and sexual offences, where the debate on lowering the age of consent for homosexuals returned once again. Only this time to bring the consent age in line with the heterosexual age of 16-years. The consent age, however, remained the same until a case was raised against UK Parliament where upon European Convention on Human Rights was breached by UK law for maintaining a discrimination of a higher consensual age for homosexuals.

It took a further 3 years for parliament to propose the European Court on Human Rights with a Bill to reduce the age of consent to 18-years. But this was rejected insisting that the age be the same for all, be it 18 or 16-years of age, but could not be favourable in any way to one or the other. Blair pushed for a Bill that would be agreeable with the European Courts and UK Parliament, but the House of Lords rejected the motion.

Eventually the House of Lords had to bow down to Europe and after 33 years the Sexual Offences Amendment Act was passed in 2000 becoming law January 2001 lowering the age of consent to 16-years of age to suit all. This included lesbians, although there was no previous law in any Sexual Act because lesbianism was never recognised. Nevertheless, so they didn't feel left out, they too were added to the Amendment, although there was nothing to amend.

New Labour won its second term 7th June 2001 by another landslide victory, and with the war in Afghanistan starting the same year there was also another headache for Blair, and that was the growing tension in Iraq. Saddam Hussein, the dictator of Iraq, paid billions of US dollars to the French government for them to commission French scientists design and build a nuclear reactor. But the rest of the world knew this was nothing but a subterfuge to develop weapons-grade plutonium for producing nuclear warheads so to, as he clearly and deliberately put it, destroy Israel. Israel bombed the reactor, but his James Bond style villainy madness didn't stop there. Oh no.

He waged war against Iran, attacked the Kurds in northern Iraq, used chemical weapons on his own people, invaded Kuwait and was close to finishing a pair of super-guns: huge canons with a one-metre bore designed to launch nuclear shells, strategically pointing in a pre-determined fixed position towards Israel. A large section of the gun is on display at the Imperial war museum, Duxford, Cambridgeshire. He was also a notorious mass-murderer of millions that dared oppose his regime, so he simply had to go.

By February 2003 NATO Forces, spearheaded by the US military and with huge support from the UK, gathered in a spars Kuwaiti desert whilst last ditch negotiations carried on between the UN and Iraqi officials. Meanwhile, Tony Blair convinced the masses that Saddam Hussein had stock-piled weapons of mass destruction with a capability to reach the shores of Europe, so he had to be stopped before gaining any possible chance to use them.

Yes, of course there were demonstrations against any possible escalation of war, only this time there was something different about the protestors. Although there were the usual bunch of anti-war fanatics, amongst them was a new kind of demonstrator that seemingly came from nowhere; quietly incubating over the past few decades to grow and develop into a vicious protestor. A kind that fed on extremism and radicalisation originally seeded by Thatcher and Blair, yet raised by liberal parents within a passive society.

A kind that grew into adulthood with little experience of compromise and never needed to beg, steal or scavenge for food. Always expected a full belly every day, preferably cooked, prepared and served by mummy and daddy. A kind that knows their Human Rights, yet struggles to recite even one, and has very little reason, understanding or even cares how they got them. A kind that no longer wants to just demonstrate, they want to destroy anyone that dares disagree with them. Willing to employ gratuitous violence to put their point across, and there were thousands of them sprouting everywhere. The masses started to question their existence: where did they come from, why were they so angry, and why didn't society see them coming?

Meanwhile, after losing patients with Saddam, clearly unwilling to cooperate with the UN, in the early hours of 19th March 2003 US and Allied Forces started their advancement into Iraq to finally put an end to Saddam Hussein and his evil regime. Reflecting UK's operational name Operation Telic: Ancient Greek mythology meaning to change. Certainly better than the US name of Operation Freedom, although it amounted to the same. And by the 16th April, 1,000,000 Iraqi crack troops and Saddam's formidable elite Republican Guard were beaten to a pulp, only to officially surrender to the allies on 26th April.

However, during the conflict it wasn't just a uniformed enemy the allies fought. There were also Saddam's Fedayeen Militia – Gestapo – dressed in civilian clothing, running amuck, throwing babies off roof tops and burning children alive in front of parents as a warning to those that dare report to the allies where they were hiding. These were the bastards to be weary of. They would eventually call themselves other names, including ISIS. And during the following decade Iraq became the most dangerous country on earth as religious factions continued to fight amongst themselves whilst attacking UN peace-keeping troops.

Although simplifying this conflict, the casualties during the war on the allied side were considerably low with 214 killed and 606 wounded. But the Iraqi's suffered much worse at over 26,000 deaths, proving they were no match for NATO Forces. By the end of operations in 2011 the allied total had risen to almost 4,800 casualties, and Iraqi insurgent casualties exceeded 150,000.

Back home Tony Blair suffered wounds of his own, having to explain to parliament and the nation why weapons of mass destruction (WMD) were never found. Although there were plenty of residual evidence the media decided to ignore it, only to concentrate on emphasising the lack of WMD scenario and shame Blair as being a bit of a fibber.

Anti-war protestors, including the new radical kind, were now becoming anti-Blair protestors at an alarming rate. Demonstrations grew larger and larger around the country, including Europe and the US. The media, in particularly the BBC, poured an endless supply of rhetoric over the airwaves – radio and television alike – spreading rumours and obvious hatred towards the government, allied soldiers, even the liberation of Iraqi civilians from an incredibly evil dictator. And with the anti-war socialist media jumping on the bandwagon, Blair never stood a chance.

The most gullible of the masses were now so brainwashed by the media they materialised into an enormous hatred for Blair, even worse than Thatcher during the miners strike. And because of the way media outlets spread anti-war stories, once moderate level-headed citizens were now confused by the likes of ITV and BBC news reports.

Red-top tabloids, such as the Mirror, convinced readers into believing lie after lie after lie of allied soldiers either abusing Iraqi prisoners, raping women or murdering innocent civilians. The damage was done, and now, for the first time in history, the masses turned their media-adopted hatred into a witch-hunt towards British and allied troops sent to Iraq to oust Saddam Hussein.

When I returned home from Iraq the aeroplane landed towards the rear of Birmingham airport well out of sight of the chanting and spitting demonstrators baying for our blood outside the terminal. After instruction we were then sneaked out of the airport and ushered to awaiting unmarked civilian cars to take us home. It was almost a covert operation to avoid enemy detection, so a tad different to those returning home from the Falklands conflict. I didn't expect any yellow ribbons tied around an old oak tree, but certainly never expect to be ripped apart from an angry mob of anti-war peace protestors. There's an irony hidden here somewhere.

Within 24-hours landing on Blighty soil a young man walked past me as I carried shopping from the car, and started to shout at me with accusations of being a child killing rapist murderer and even a racist. I didn't know who he was, and he didn't know me, but he knew I was a British soldier that went to Iraq. I was even spat at and called a murderer during a trip to my local Co-op, but I couldn't understand why, until my wife explained.

She told me about the television, radio and newspaper reports, in particular a picture of British soldiers urinating on an Iraqi Prisoner of War (PoW) held captive in the back of a troop carrier that was splashed on the front pages of the Daily Mirror, but the photograph was proved to be a fake. Yet the editor, Pierce Morgan, was determined to show the world, if only to sell more newspapers, with no care, admittance or acceptance of responsibility whatsoever. And due to his incredible and outrageous behaviour, he turned many of the masses against the British Armed Forces, only to face ridicule and fear from our very own country when we returned home, now hated and renounced from society.

Other print and airwave media outlets quickly followed suit, injecting the word 'allegedly' to cover their arse, yet poured unfounded stories of allied atrocities onto the masses. Completely swamping and hiding true reports of how we liberated the country – all explained in my book *Weekend Warrior: A Territorial Soldier's War in Iraq*. The aftermath of the war and how British troops struggled to cope with this unexpected invasion upon our delicate psychological situation is also explained in my book *PTSD: Living comfortably numb*.

The yet to be coined 'fake news' phrase was already exploited in 2003 as it spread to television and radio talk shows discussing the war. Carefully selected celebrity guests with strong anti-war beliefs and no military experience whatsoever, were evidently chosen over professionals that understood what was going on. These included radical politicians, biased reporters, even pop stars and poets.

In a typical BBC tradition, they vented ill-educated anger towards British and allied troops simply because they wanted to air their anti-war rhetoric. Young naïve fans and followers of these celebrities immediately emulated similar views, believing that they must be right in what they said, otherwise why be on television to sell their belief to the nation? Remember the Beatles and their ant-war rhetoric over Vietnam?

Blair was now in so much deep water he would do anything to divert attention away from a nation that now hated him, as well as Her Majesties Armed Forces, thanks to the British media. To try and win back his young and trusted followers from the ever-increasing anti-war far left movement he used his humanitarian trump card by publicly repeating his signing of the

Lisbon Treaty with hope of putting the Iraq war behind him, thus out of minds of angered young voters that tend to have extremely short memories.

The Maastricht Treaty was originally signed by former pro-union Conservative Prime Minister, John Major, where he predicted a future for the UK to be, as it was, within the European Economic Community (EEC). But the European Community, as always, changed their Treaties as many times they changed shirts, and came up with yet another treaty – the Lisbon Treaty – so to streamline a more effective platform to pass laws and regulations around its growing member States.

In effect it created 2 positions of power within the Union – a Foreign Secretary to oversee all member State foreign policies and make sure they upheld EU agreements. The President of the EU – a position Tony Blair saw himself – was proclaimed to be a similar position as the President of the United States. However, there is a fundamental difference: US citizens vote for their President, the EU President is appointed by fellow EU members, not a public vote from member State citizens. And he can make life extremely difficult by blocking any member State that disagreed with any EU legislation that he himself passes. Call me paranoid, but I'm pretty sure a large European country once had one of these leaders with a desire to rule Europe.

The un-elected EU President – in effect a dictator – serves for two and a half years with a salary exceeding £250,000 employing 20 full time permanent staff and political aides, also with large salaries, paid for by EU member State taxes. Your taxes. It also comes with many perks including free travel around the world – first class, of course. And the gravy train doesn't stop there. Oh no. State banquets and dinners by the dozen, top-star hotel accommodation on numerous country visits, all-expenses paid that would turn any Tory back bencher green with envy, and a pension so fat it could support an oil tanker across the Atlantic without losing a single Euro whilst negotiating a Force-9 gale. So you can see why Blair set his sights on the position.

Surprisingly, or maybe arrogantly, young and not so young EU supporters have no problem with such extravagant behaviour, costing the taxpayer tens-of-millions in Euros and Pound Sterling. Yet throw their dummy out of the pram when a train ticket is bought for the Queen to use, even though she alone brings into the UK over £6,000,000,000 in tourism.

The elder generations were at a gasp when Blair signed over the UK to the European Parliament with one stroke of a pen. And Foreign Minister, Jack Straw, had the bare-faced cheek to say over the airwaves that the signing of the Lisbon Treaty will have little effect upon UK Parliament and its citizens. Blair even offered a referendum – a Peoples vote – on the Treaty, but quickly denied any option after Holland and France rejected the draft. Even Ireland's citizens voted no, but quickly held another referendum until the nation voted yes. Don't you just love democracy.

Chapter Eighteen

Freedom and Liberty for all, but don't blame me when it goes tits up

Labour back-benches joined Liberal Democrats and Conservative opposition criticising Jack Straw and Tony Blair's position on denying a referendum. Conservative Party leader, Iain Duncan Smith, accused Blair's White Paper on the Lisbon Treaty as nothing more than a white flag surrendering UK rights over to the EU. But Jack Straw insisted it was in the UK's national interest and the population's patriotic duty to stay within the EU.

Slowly but surely Blair's young lost sheep came back, but by no means all. Many remained annoyed of the fact their illustrious New Labour socialist leader waged war upon nation after nation. But Blair managed to win his second election with or without the young vote. And similar to last elections, votes were cast by electorates that bothered to register in the first place and were over the age of 25-years, which has always been the case, but why is this?

Since the abolition of conscription, growing up in a safer and carefree world with everything on instant demand, suffocated by a liberal society, deters under 25's ever needing to vote because parents do everything for them. However, within Blair's beloved New Labour Party, the natives were getting restless; he was losing grip on his leadership. And the elder voting masses were also losing confidence due to his rapid, yet expensive social projects and careless immigration policies causing problems within communities up and down the country.

Totally oblivious of his unpopularity, he continued with his social reforms, undeterred that he ever failed to please the masses.

Remarkably, New Labour won a third term of office 5th May 2005 but his own Cabinet voted a no confidence in his leadership, eventually replacing him with old Labour dinosaur Chancellor, Gordon Brown, on 27th June 2007. Meanwhile Blair's policies remained for a little while longer, including giving a sense of freedom but with a subtle hint of hidden oppression and obsession to control the nation with small yet social penetrating policies.

From creating a maximum hot water temperature that must not exceed government guidelines, or specifying how hot a summer temperature is before you are officially hot, to the compulsory use and possession of identification cards. A particularly sneaky piece of dictatorial legislation sneaked through the parliament back door in the guise of a new credit card style driving licence governed and dictated by the EU.

Many more obscure rules and regulations were secreted into law, funded by extra taxes and legislation on private transport owners and commercial hauliers. This included taxing those with company cars and vans, which was the final nail in the coffin for the British car industry. Up until his great idea in 2001 to heavily tax individuals that had Company cars, the biggest customer of any car manufacturer was fleet sales to private businesses. Some manufacturers heavily relied upon these sales to keep afloat. But Blair put a stop to all this malarkey by deciding to levy a further 20 percent tax on those that had Company cars, on top of an already 20 percent income tax.

The outcome: a massive drop in fleet sales, causing huge job losses across all British car manufactures, as well as related industries. But Teflon Tony wouldn't take the blame, and spun the lack of sales on a lame excuse by turning the car into a machine against the environment. Yes, Blair started the hate-trend towards the motorist so to clandestine his grand-plan of raising further taxes and help fund his social reform plans, including secure his vote from the young and gullible.

Environmentalists, especially from his younger easily led followers, loved Blair's idea that cars were the cause of all global pollution, no matter how ludicrous it sounded, and set about spreading his word around schools and universities, exacerbating the issue if need be. After all, it must be true. The Prime Minister said so. And of course, when naïve students get wind of Blair's radical solution to global pollution, biased media groups soon raise an interested eyebrow.

The first and easiest target for Blair to pick on was the notorious gas-guzzling 4X4 owners of Range Rovers, Toyota Landcruisers, Mercedes M class and BMW X5 cars. They became New Labour's public enemy number one and an excuse to raise even further taxes through the road fund licence to the maximum possible at £550 per year for this particular type of car.

Radically changing rules and regulations so all motorists suffered, Blair decided to go one step further – again – by changing the road fund licence from charging a levy on vehicle weight per axle, thus its wear and tear on a road surface, as it had done since 1935, to his new vehicle emissions scale. The road fund licence was then completely reinvented from raising revenue for road maintenance, to taxing a vehicle on its emissions and spending the income elsewhere, offering only a token gesture towards filling potholes. Next brilliant tax raising idea was to place a huge levy on petrol to an all time high, exceeding £1.50 per litre at many service stations.

Blair certainly gave a cast-iron impression he hated the car, if only to use the perception for raising revenue and promote public transport. But there was one fundamental problem with this particular socialist philosophy. Apart from that there London, the amount of buses and trains available to ferry the masses too and from work was – and always will be – nowhere near enough, let alone to include the various shift patterns, distances and locations.

There was also a catastrophic cost issue, let alone a massive lack of government subsidy – the preverbal putting money where ones mouth is. Even deputy Prime Minister, John Prescot, once said in front of a pact House that everyone will soon be using buses too and from work under a Labour government within a year of next turn in office, otherwise he would eat his hat.

But it didn't matter. The whole rhetoric was a smoke screen to simply steer attention away from Teflon Tony's disguised agenda to destroy the British car industry once and for all, and continue nurturing young voters to naively believe New Labour actually cared about the environment. He even conned the masses to believe petrol cars were the worst contribution towards air pollution and raised a purchase tax, as well as further tax on petrol, accordingly. In doing so diesel powered car sales dramatically increased.

Blair had finally found a niche in the political market to increase votes. It was a win-win situation: tax the hell out of millions of car owners and company car users, and get away with it because the ever-increasing far-left socialist movement shouted louder with their new hatred of the car destroying their fluffy planet, inevitably bringing them media attention. The seed was sewn, and Blair was on a roll, going one further against the motorist with his next weapon in his arsenal: tax everyone that travelled into London, regardless of vehicle, be it coach, truck, car or motorbike.

The new tax included everyone that dared to drive or travel in a dirty polluting vehicle in Blair's fairy-tale London. To offset any connection with his hatred of motorists and to please his young followers, the new tax would be known as a congestion charge: a fee to enter London for no other reason than raise a tax for the Capital and do bugger all with it. Certainly not used to eliminate congestion in the city.

Hang on a minute, he must have thought, it doesn't have to end there. So he extended the congestion zone further still to engulf even more thousands of motorists, grabbing even more tax from drivers already paying higher road tax, fuel tax, and insurance tax to run them. Then came yet another brainwave: emissions tax. Yes, of course, add further charges to vehicle owners heading towards the city with a levy reflecting the amount of emissions they produce. Brilliant. Another kick in the bollocks for the motorist and one huge tick in the box for the tree-hugger vote.

Whilst on a high with winning hearts and votes – in his mind – he set about probing for votes from the gay community when he recognised many laws didn't exactly compliment gay relationships, including common law. So in true New Labour style, he set about pleasing the gay fraternity by getting them on board his 'vote for me' express by pushing for the Civil Partnership Act, which was passed and became law in 2005, giving most rights and responsibilities as a Civil marriage, but not all.

Although not under a New Labour government, same-sex marriages became law with the Same Sex Marriage Act 2013 having the same responsibilities and rights as the previous 1949 Marriage Act. However, the Church of England and Catholic churches weren't so obliging with marrying same sex couples, employing their right not to marry them should the church disagree. And should a same sex marriage end due to adultery, this act of infidelity is not recognised in the divorce courts for gay couples [2020]. It is only recognised as a definition of unreasonable behaviour, thrown in as a law stop-gap to cover the gay infidelity issue.

After Blair opened this particular can of worms, they all came out demanding their legal rights, whatever they were, or where they came from, and that is the right for transgenders to marry – because gays can, so why not us? Not fair! Oh dear, Tony, you see what happens when you try and please everyone. Nonetheless, it is the right of every man – or woman – thanks, Reg (sorry, couldn't resist a reference from Monty Python's Life of Brian), to be whoever they want to be, thanks to the 2004 Gender Recognition Act. Either way, the law is now set in stone, so we can all carry on regardless and be what ever we want to be. Hooray! Well no, we can't.

You see, because Blair naively opened an exceptionally hostile floodgate the transgender community was not happy because they wanted more rights, such as protection against persecution with the use of discrimination laws. Okay, so New Labour policies sorted this out and we're all happy once again. Actually no, we're not, or at least the gay community wasn't, because they also wanted more, and that included rights for protection against religious and employment discrimination, and for the masses to accept their way of life without ridicule. Well, maybe in Europe, or at least most of it, and other parts of the Western world, probably. Well, maybe. But anyway, all happy now.

Er, no. And that's because the gay community decided to go all out and push the boundaries of social acceptance to the limit by insisting upon having the same rights as traditional couples to have a baby. Well, that isn't going to happen, is it, because it isn't a right, otherwise everyone can have a baby, which is what a right is – for everyone, not just a chosen few. Ah, but it appears the Lesbian, Gay, Bisexual, Transgender (LGBT) community haven't quite thought through their demands. But once correct terminology was explained, or was it manipulated, and the over-excited screaming boys and girls calmed down, transgender couples now have the right to adopt. Hooray, although confusing for the rest of us, we got there in the end, didn't we? No, we didn't.

You see, there's more: Equal Pay and Employment Rights, Racial and Religious Hatred Rights, Marriage and Civil Partnership Rights, Gender Reassignment Rights (banning of), Disability Rights, Sexual Orientation Rights, Equality and Human Rights, recognition within the European Court on Human Rights, Criminal Justice Act to include homophobic crimes, changes in the Local Government Act to include banning of public or private promotion of prohibiting homosexual teaching in schools by any local authority, Ethical Standards in Public, amendment to the Public Order Act, and the ban of conversion therapy as recognised by the European Court on Human Rights. Most of which come under the umbrella of the Equality Act of 2010 but some Acts are still being tweaked or renewed altogether to keep the LGBT community happy [2020]… and breath.

Hard to believe, I know, but once upon a time, not so long ago, life was so simple with only 2 genres recognised by the masses: male and female, whatever sexual orientation. But with this new-found non-negotiable Millennial ideology came a sudden deluge of unexplainable genres in the guise of gender fluidity: the ability to freely and knowingly become one or many limitless number of genders that doesn't recognise borders or rules. But there's one small problem. One of the Millennials unbelievable list of 112 – yes, that's 112 – genders is this non-binary bunch: a spectrum of gender identities that are not exclusively masculine or feminine where identities include transgender. Kind of cocks up (pardon the pun) their gender soup a little.

The amount of fuss and media attention the gay community brought upon the masses, let alone itself, no matter what preference or favoured gender, certainly gave an impression of a huge explosion of homosexuals, trans this, fluid that, suddenly appearing from nowhere. Swamping the media airwaves with a deluge of screaming and wailing for rules and laws they demanded to protect themselves. In doing so, a lasting expression became permanently engraved upon the masses, believing a large proportion of society were, in fact, gay, lesbian, trans – whatever. Thus entitled to the same laws as everyone else. But there was yet another small problem.

Whilst the gay, lesbian, bisexual and trans-thingy society marched in bright vibrant colours, blowing whistles and chanting equal rights, the Office of National Statistics carried out a survey on behalf of the Labour government to enlighten a true count, if you will, on what percentage of the population were actually gay. The result of which was remarkably astonishing, but not exactly in favour for the gay community or the government.

Only 1.5 percent out of a population of 70,000,000 were in fact, gay, lesbian or bisexual. A surprisingly low figure considering the huge amount of fuss and nonsense the masses had to endure from a very loud and shouty brigade on television, radio and the print media. Not to mention the millions of public Pound Stirling spent on promoting, lobbying and passing laws for the gay community. But no matter, the gay movement set a president for all minority groups that if you shout, scream, stamp your feet and display childish tantrums loud and long enough, you too can get what you want. Especially when there's a Prime Minister at the helm determined to please the minorities.

With a growing obsession of minority groups determined to dictate the importance of political correctness, Blair's government loved this type of social obedience, if not for its own means. New Labour policy of a nation obeying new political correctness was working. But the term Politically Correct, or PC as it's known, has been around for quite some time, way before Blair's regime hijacked the meaning and gave it a facelift.

Back in its day being called PC was an insult to describe those from the far left as being a bit namby-pamby; too weak and feeble to accept the true nature of any given situation. Or divert attention away from any discrimination against minority organisations. Fast forward to 1997 and the New Labour era, the PC brigade could now develop into something new: the anti-whatever got in their way brigade, sponsored by Blair, certain radio and television presenters and the print media.

Within an incredible short space of time PC grew at an extraordinary rate of knots. And with it came fast promotion from the small groups within its core that thrived upon its popularity amongst the younger, and a most definite naïve generation with little or no understanding of its true meaning. Yes, them, the student. And because many students studied topics of no interest, value or contribution towards industry and commerce – social and media sciences – quite a gaggle of these post-graduates end up working for that most tempting of socialist employers – the media. A perfect breeding ground for naïve students, describing themselves to know everything there is to know and spread their vast knowledge and experience of noting by dictating the importance of political correctness to the elder and wiser masses.

The irony is, actual definition of PC is to live within its own rules by controlling the masses with lies and censorship to protect its own means. In other words PC is an ideology: to be totalitarian and govern by oppression. It is a kind of cultural Marxism that defines its own recognition of race, colour, creed, sexual orientation and religious following. Nothing more than a cold and rigid entity that has no feeling, emotion or awareness of pain, suffering or discomfort. It has to be completely independent and impartial of any human intervention or reason.

Digging a little deeper into its true meaning, being Politically Correct has to be able to define what is good and what is bad by its own written definition dictated by those that have a belief in its biased rules. For example: students that believe PC is correct and true generally define those that are black as victims, therefore they are good and cannot be wrong. So Political Correctness must protect them in whatever means and ways possible within its own rules. Therefore, by its own definition, those that are white must be bad, as defined by Political Correctness ideology.

Taking PC to its weird and quite obvious outrageous extreme, it includes rules and regulations on how we live our lives. Putting aside the obvious – obscenities towards anyone that is fat, thin, short, tall, bald or ginger – it also wants to control our everyday actions, movements and even thought processes. To give an example: October 2018 a student and even a lecturer from Manchester University were interviewed on BBC breakfast television promoting the banning of clapping. And their reason behind the ban – you're going to love this – because clapping upsets those that are sensitive to sudden bursts of noise, so we should all use 'jazz hands' instead. By which you wave each hand simultaneously in the air to avoid clapping and making a noise.

University students, as we know, moan, cry and complain about how hard their lives have become due to, as they see it, an uncaring, Nazi government. And because they want to spend most of their time sleeping until noon, getting drunk with tax payers money, and thinking of a new craze to spread around the playground, such as pretending to be politically correct, they believe us grown-ups must play the same game. But what they really want is free money to piss up the wall. Money that you get up early to earn, only for them to demand the cream off the taxable top because it is their right to do so, apparently.

Meanwhile, before PC got completely out of hand, Teflon Tony (by-the-way, just in case you didn't know, Blair was known as Teflon Tony because whatever he did wrong never stuck) as a trained lawyer, and maybe a little influence from his left-wing lawyer wife, relaxed laws so anyone could afford a solicitor on a 'no win no fee' basis. In doing so there was a huge influx of claim companies taking advantage of the new laws, quickly advertising on independent media channels for anyone to claim against employers, councils, even individual family members for accidents caused by neglect. The 'where there's a blame there's a claim' culture was now adopted from the US and embraced on UK shores. But hold on tight, there's more.

When Blair extended the Licensing laws in 2003 allowing licensed premises to apply for 24-hour serving of alcoholic beverages, the nation thought he'd gone mad.

Up until he changed the licensing laws pubs stopped serving at 11pm and 10.30pm on Sundays, but his new extension caused a little concern from organisations such as Alcoholics Anonymous and other groups. Alcohol-related violence and abuse being the brunt of many issues raised.

Blair, on the other hand, believed that the masses on the whole were sensible drinkers and should be allowed to drink around the clock, and the extension of opening hours wouldn't raise any concern or cause problems within communities. As far as he saw it, bringing the UK closer to Continental Europe habits and drinking culture was the right thing to do. He added that the law should also come down hard on those that spread violence through alcoholic abuse. In reality, Accident and Emergency departments up and down the country were inundated with more alcohol-related incidents than ever before.

Changing gambling laws was another part of his social reform to please the masses and gain votes, and in 2007 it certainly took off with the exploitation of the internet and 24-hour gambling. Websites quickly appeared with clever video clips advertising easy to play games, enticing existing gamblers, as well as new ones that had never gambled in their life, but liked the idea of winning a few quid on a turn of a digital roulette wheel. Inevitably, many became addicted, including children due to an unregulated internet.

What seemed overnight, his new gambling laws attracted the masses with clever enticing advertising on television, radio, newspapers, in fact everywhere, increasing gambling advertising 100-fold, but that wasn't the initial problem. It was the fact that advertisements were viewed 1,500,000,000 times by children under the age of eighteen in the first year, where 500,000 were aged from 4 to 15-years old.

To make matters worse the advertisement viewing figures didn't include the internet, where a further estimated 2,000,000,000 views were made by children as the internet became a larger attraction. These staggering figures continue to grow. The consequence of Blair's relaxed attitude towards gambling has created a figure of over 25,000 children now registered as having a gambling problem [2020] and continues to rise year on year.

Towards the end of Blair's reign, he was remembered not only for exacerbating alcoholism, gambling addiction, exploiting the taxpayer, skinting the country into submission and creating outlandish socialist projects. Not forgetting enforcing outrageous laws upon the nation and renouncing a majority belief – even though he needed one to win the election. He was also remembered for his close relationship with US President George W Bush, seen as nothing more than a right-wing war-mongering pact by a growing far left-wing support.

However, ignored by New Labour socialist supporters, Blair actually ordered British Troops to war an incredible 5-times in his first 6-years of office. More so than any previous Prime Minister. Even more so than President Bush Senior and Bush Junior combined. And they were accused by the loony-left as being warmongers.

Chapter Nineteen

Project Alpha: Indoctrination made easy

You may have noticed the odd war and conflict mentioned throughout the book, and with good reason. Wars have winners and therefore losers, where enormous dividends are rewarded to the victor in one way or another. But the winner, as well as the loser, will always be left with a national debt created by funding the conflict, only to repay loans and not forgetting counting the human cost. Wars – win or lose – also define countries, boarders and territories, which in turn creates societies, law, government, religion and cultures.

European countries, for instance, have counted the cost of war ever since man first ventured north out of Africa and set foot onto the plains of Spain, France and Germany around 60,000 years ago as the ice age retracted, only to start the odd skirmish with a neighbouring tribe along the way. From these early disputes to the Baltic wars of the 1990's pencil lines have constantly changed or erased entirely between bordering countries. And that is the true definition of Europe: nothing more than lines on a map, only to shift a few miles either way, up or down, left or right, after an opposing country takes a dislike to its neighbours.

Then there is the United Kingdom. A small insignificant piece of rock poking out of the Atlantic Ocean, separating it from mainland Europe. And it's that water, folks, that defines the UK as a nation; a country without lines and artificial borders drawn in pencil that cannot be rubbed out and repositioned by an invading greedy neighbour. Oh, they've tried, and some almost succeeded, but the natural border remains the same, no matter what, providing Scotland, Wales and Northern Ireland remain within the Union. Yep, kind of spoilt my point a tad. Nevertheless, the UK does have its own natural border, separating it from that lot over there.

What on earth is he blabbering on about now? I hear you ask. Well, bear with me, because being an Island nation also separates UK society and beliefs from them Continental folk. Politics, laws, social policies, education and personal morals became unique and poles apart from that lot across the English Channel. As an Island race the UK had an entirely different outlook on life and the challenges it bestowed, lasting for well over a thousand years.

I say had, because as you have read, certain developments over the past decade or so has created a new era totally alien to previous generations. The otherwise stagnant DNA of past societies has mutated into a generation with a completely different generic make-up. You may have also noticed I mention politics here and there throughout the book, with the odd politician mentioned – some more than others – and there is a very good reason for this: there are certain attributes from every generation, past and present, that has a profound effect upon our society. And like it or not, war and politics are major players. For any given nation they have shaped, produced, challenged, defeated, won and lost its identity. Even fed yet starved, housed yet made homeless, created wealth yet caused poverty, united yet divided. Get the picture?

From the ashes of Margaret Thatcher her influence upon modern society certainly left its mark. Everything in society has changed, be it for the best or worse. Nevertheless, Thatcher managed to oust the suffocating unions that ruled with Communist aggression – disguised as a Labour government – by reintroducing a recently forgotten attribute called freedom and allowing once again a society to express its own self determination.

The nation was reunited with skills once lost to look after itself and promote a decent way of life – to a degree. Allowed to re-educate and make independent decisions without interruption or oppression from iron fist unions, and take responsibility for their own mistakes rather than blame others. When you think about it, all this free and self-determination came from a Tory Prime Minister, where a century before it was the Labour movement that wanted to do the very same.

Then came along another Labour leader, Tony Blair, but with a twist. Inheriting not only a nation with money in the bank, but also a country that thrived upon patriotism and surprisingly managed to preserve the odd good old-fashioned value. Yet with his exciting New Labour policies for the masses, his inane grin and chirpy optimism, it didn't take long for the champagne socialist attack Tory policies and replace them by enforcing his personal idea of modern socialism to change attitudes of future generations.

And with a blasé demeanour with most New Labour policies, his amateur approach towards the up and coming technological renaissance was a tad lame with its consequence. In other words, he had little or no understanding of its influence upon the masses and the indifferent social behaviour he created for future generations, let alone a huge drain on energy resources. Will explain about that particular issue later. But can we blame Thatcher, Blair, or any other Prime Minister before or since for radical change in social behaviour that had a profound effect upon today's society?

As a whole, society either rebels against or enjoys its freedom and liberties during all government terms of office, regardless of political party. And yes, there has been the odd bump or two in the road during our long journey. However, since the 1950's – and to coin a phrase – we've never had it so good. And that, kids, is why we are in such a political and social quagmire today. To pick on the two main Premiers since Churchill, true legacy of Thatcher and Blair wasn't beating the coal miners, introducing poll tax, destroying the car industry or turn a nation into alcoholic gambling addicts. Above anything else, between them, they literally killed liberalism, only to give birth to 21st Century political and social extremism.

Their influence over 3 decades fundamentally changed society and how we live today. Include the slow drip drip-drip of taking the piss out of freedom and liberty since 1945, combined with a new selfish and carefree attitude since the baby boomers, with pathetic arguing and bickering, we're no different to those spoilt brats we now sneer and condemn. We have become a nation – no – world of want, want, want, now, now, now, take, take, take. Rather than give, help and share. We have become narrow-minded and above all suspicious beyond belief. To the extent we no longer trust anyone, offended by everything, and drive like Germans – impatient and arrogant to the point of unable to understand courtesy, politeness and give way. Drive through Cambridge, you will see what I mean.

The result of our suspicion and distrust has escalated out of control, exploited by modern technology, such as miniature cameras recording our every move. And not just by the authorities, insurance groups and traffic lights. Dashcams in our cars, trucks and buses, helmet cams used by bicycle and motorbike riders,

CCTV installed on trains, aeroplanes and emergency vehicles. Even home cameras are mounted not just on external walls, but also inside rooms. They're hidden in offices, warehouses, shops, restaurants, cash machines, hospitals, retirement homes, all secreted in every nook and cranny to catch someone out.

Police, paramedics, fire fighters and soldiers on operations wear them on uniforms to record every action should they find themselves in court having to prove themselves either a victim or innocent of all accusations brought against them. And yet, the younger generation growing up with this constant interference has accepted it as the norm. To the point of constantly using them on laptops, tablets and smartphones, recording their every move, event, mood or situation.

For elder generations they are still a little confused with this weird obsession, and most definitely disgruntled by Big Brother peering down recording everything and anything from every angle. After all, they remember going about business unhindered, only to now feel as if their freedom has been violated to the extreme. But to the younger generation they not only accept it, they no longer fear it. In effect its so-called security aspect has created the exact opposite.

Putting aside the ignorance of being recorded whilst pissing up a shop window or a war memorial, Millennials of even school years record their own criminal acts. Only to download footage on social media for all to see, not caring about the consequences as they grow in a world believing they're beyond contempt. And the introduction of 'black boxes' in cars by insurance companies to record every move of travel – predominately for recording speeding offences – is yet another attribute towards modern life accepted by Millennials to be the norm. But how has it come to this?

Our political backbone has become so weak after decades of nipping away at laws and past morals that were once effective, influencing discipline and punishment where necessary, have since become bullied into believing to be unlawful. Classed as cruel by recent governments and society, accusing them to be vulgar and inappropriate for modern cultures. Such carefree attitude only reflects a lack of responsibility, recklessness and unbelievable blatant arrogance, with a stench of selfish greed, disassociating themselves from reality.

Instead a social fungus, spawned by previous governments, has infected old laws originally designed to protect us, not realising the threat it carried to destroy any past remaining thread of liberty and freedom. Our easy living and everything we have developed, invented and improved to make our lives better over the centuries, has simply exacerbated extremism by radicalisation in every possible crevice of modern society.

An example of this modern social disease: Barak Obama becoming President of the United States on 20th January 2009 and the black community going wild with excitement. Strangely, so did other black communities around the world, including Europe and the UK. But why? It simply defies sense. He wasn't President of every nation, and had, as predicted, little interest with other countries, especially the UK. So why the euphoria?

What followed in the US and soon after in other countries was a sudden hatred of anything Right Wing, including those that voted for the previous President, George W Bush. But where did this surge of hatred towards Right Wing politics from a progressively loud audience come from in an incredible short space of time? Or was it in a short space of time? After all, the masses around the globe have always been at loggerheads with anyone that showed the slightest glimpse of anti-union or profit over workers rights. Nonetheless, the former mind-set defies sense, or more likely lost within the denial of Millennial interpretation of history. But history is history; no matter how much modern political fashion you wish to interpret to suit political persuasion.

For example: the USA, along with many other Millennials in other countries, still believe the British Commonwealth is the old Empire, which couldn't be further from the truth. For one, all countries within the Commonwealth wanted to join, and were definitely not forced. Nevertheless, many Millennials express strong feelings of contempt towards the British Empire with its use of black slaves from Africa to work on plantations across the length and breadth of the Caribbean and Southern States of the USA. And within their pathetic mind-set, all this happened last week.

Although the use of slaves was abolished in the UK in 1772 it carried on within the British Empire until the Abolition of the Slave Trade Act in 1807. But traders continued to ferry slaves from Africa illegally until it was forced to stop by the powerful Royal Navy by 1860. And within those 47-years of patrolling the African coastline, a total of 1,600 transport ships were seized – including those destined to French, Spanish and Portuguese colonies – where 150,000 slaves were liberated. But what isn't recognised – or conveniently ignored – is the African political leaders from many African States that profited using slavery condemned the actions of the British and refused to accept the abolition.

In the meantime, Republican President Abraham Lincoln certainly did not agree with slavery and declared slaves free on the shores of North America in 1863. It took a further 2 years for the Thirteenth Amendment to be added to the American Constitution when passed by the Senate in 1865. And yet, it was a Democrat government – US Millennials saviour – that invited slavery into the USA in the first place.

And why just pick on the British for using slaves to build its past Empire? What about the Roman Empire enslaving those from every country it conquered, including the British. And not forgetting Genghis Khan and his enormous Mongolian Empire in the 12th Century. He was one of the most evil leaders of any Empire. Or the Egyptians, Chinese Dynasties and the Ottoman Empire, all using slaves. Going too far back? Okay, what about the French, Portuguese and Spanish that used slaves to build their Empires in the 19th Century.

How about the Japanese during the Second World War using PoW's as slave labour, only to torture and starve to death thousands. Or how about the Chinese slaves the Japanese used, and the 250,000 civilians they slaughtered. Still too far back? Okay, what about the white slave trade still going on today [2020] in the former Soviet Bloc, the Middle East, even the UK? But no, never mentioned, and all because of a new social ingredient mixed into the modern society disease – fashion politics.

With the unbelievable seismic change of political fashion that only believes in its own individual opinion rather than the masses, the loud bleating of modern gossiping, and the naïve social sheep that follow, owes its rhetoric from the early years of gossip from the domination of print. Then came along the exploitation of the airwaves – radio and television – carefully interjecting a political persuasion for the masses to react upon, but taking weeks, if not months to filter through into hearts and minds.

But a certain technology took a further gigantic leap in technological achievement – Social Media – allowing political fashion to not only thrive, but travel at such speeds around the globe there is no longer any control.

Unfortunately, this was during the manifestation of a recent social disease festering around every corner, fed on past fears, ignorance, and a rise in self importance, sensationalism, narcissism and shallow-minded pretentious arrogance.

Social Media websites, although in its infancy, grew incredibly fast during New Labour's third term at Number 10. And with this new way of communicating on such a vast scale the entire world could suddenly write comments, pass views and try to persuade, if not brainwash everyone to believe they are right in every way.

It is argued that the first Social Media site to be constructed for use on the internet was in 1997 titled Six Degrees, used for profiling its members with school affiliations. Although there are further arguments that earlier sites were already using the internet in 1994, such as GeoCities regarding itself as a social networking site. But it wasn't until the early to mid 2000's where social sites started to gather pace: Linkedin and Myspace in 2003, Facebook in 2004, Yahoo in 2005, and twitter in 2006. But it was Facebook that had the edge on all others, quickly spreading an interest on a global scale.

During the early years of Facebook laptops and desktop computers were predominately owned and used by mum and dad. Kids only had access when given permission to use for homework, but in reality they quickly realised the attraction of mum's social media websites. And due to no or very little restrictions, guidance or policing from parents and website servers, children faked their age to join them and 'chat' with friends. But these early days were the pre-cursor towards virtual social behaviour issues affiliated with Millennials today, feeding its sensational appetite on a raw, misguided, unrestricted youth and their confused outlook on what is real and what isn't. And all from the comfort of your own living room or bedroom.

Then a new concept of communication hit the streets – the smartphone – exacerbating the new social disease into a global pandemic. Armed with a handheld device that linked to the internet is a marvel in itself; saving shed-loads of time communicating between businesses as well as private relationships. It also expanded the internet a thousand-fold with websites adapting to this exciting technology, enabling wireless interaction without the use of a home computer. Brilliant. But there was one small problem: a younger inexperienced narrative. And when I say younger, I mean pre-teens, even as young as 7-years old, demanding their very own smartphone. The latest victim to fall foul to this unprecedented and now uncontrollable global social disease.

The smartphone was invented during an era of a growing selfish youth culture and its modern social demands. Everything was now available at a touch of a button, click of a mouse or swipe of a screen. Instant dating, countless reality television programs and shopping channels on cable or satellite, 24-hour supermarket and internet shopping, fast food with immediate home delivery, 24-hour home shopping with next day delivery service – even same day – computer games online 24/7... the list goes on and on and on. Instant demand, demand, demand, now, now, now, want, want, want.

With this wanton and crass demand came an explosion of advertisements suddenly exploiting the mobile internet frenzy, selling useless offers, services and goods to exploit the increasingly expanding Millennial market to part with cash, earned or not. This constant demand for anything and everything straight away without waiting was something new to elder generations, but for Millennials they welcomed it with open arms, as if it was expected to feed their sensational on demand appetite. It became the new way of life, but fundamentally, yet silently, rubbed the wrong way against their virtual transparent interpretation of peace and global harmony.

As far as Millennials were concerned waiting is for those from a bygone era. And with a rapid expansion of a social media revolution the under thirties quickly dominated this potent renaissance of communication with the use of smartphones. And the incredibly inflammable fuel that powers the engine of this particular technology is gossip. Millennials can't get enough of it.

The root cause of this epidemic emanates from a social migration induced cancer called reality television. Reality TV is certainly nothing new. As far back as the 1940's programmes in the US hit the airwaves, such as Candid Camera: previously a radio show titled Candid Microphone – not sure how that worked – was turned into a television programme in 1948. A canned laughter programme of gags played on an unexpected public whilst filmed by hidden cameras.

The UK took a little longer to catch up, but by the early 1960's overtook the US by steering reality TV away from comedy and turning it into a serious documentary, such as the Up series. A programme first aired in 1964 followed a bunch of 7-year old children across the social spectrum, watching them grow up with various interviews regarding every day life issues. The success of this plotless programme returned to the same children every 7-years, lasting way into their adulthood. In a way they were the first 'reality television celebrities' in the UK.

Fast-forward a few decades and the sensational appetite for reality television by the masses – young and not so young – has not only travelled beyond the boundaries of sanity, it has gone completely bonkers. The only way is Essex; Big Brother; Love Island; Geordie Shore; Made in Chelsea; The Kardashians; Jeremy Kyle Show, there are hundreds of them. Whether exploiting simple folk in front of millions to dangling your bits on Dating Naked, they all had the same theme: desperate, attention seeking, talentless, pretentious, ill-educated, shallow-minded nobodies, where unbelievably some were, and still are, exploited by clever marketing guru's and made into national celebrities.

To add insult to injury, awful talent shows of yesteryear have also been blown way out of every possible proportion by today's modern up-take with tempting would-be singers and performers to chase their pipe dream. Bygone programmes such as Opportunity Knocks and New Faces from the 1970's have been replaced with Pop Idol; American Idol; Britain's Got Talent, and the biggest of them all, The X Factor. All exploiting wanna-be fame and fortune seekers, Millennial or otherwise, disillusioned with the thought of their screeching and wailing will make them an instant success.

Another aspect of modern pretentious television has to be mainstream news presenters interjecting their own self-importance on subjects they no nothing about. But over the past 20-years or so presenters continue to emphasise their point of view to be unequivocally correct, and we must take heed and hang on to every single word. In doing so their reckless attitude is nothing more than an added infectious ingredient that has had a profound effect on Millennials naïve mind-set struggling to absorb the incredible amount of garbage they spew over the airwaves, feeding their unguided and ill-educated interpretation of the real world. For the rest of us with an ounce of common sense, we know they're talking bollocks.

Realising it or not, mainstream presenter's self-important nonsense is simply adding their poisonous ingredient to the soup of modern social change, un-noticed by Millennials whilst incubating a hatred towards past generations for destroying the planet and their future. Intoxicated with extremism, radicalisation, complete lack of discipline, yet full of self-opinionated political persuasion. The easily offended, including very loud university students obsessed with political correctness, shout even louder unhindered, protected by modern political rhetoric and mainstream media hype. With a fashionable socialist-led biased support, their sticky tentacles spread across new territories, penetrating an even younger audience: Generation Z and the new up and coming Alpha Generation.

To pick one name out of the enormous hat of many self-righteous national presenters, Jeremy Vine springs to mind. Yep, I know there are many, and Pierce Morgan is a strong contender, but for now, Jeremy will suffice. Although I may have agreed with some of his opinions, albeit on the most rarest of occasion, he has caused some quite exasperating arguments, including the encouragement of horse riders and cyclists to wear similar clothing as police uniforms to slow down traffic. And whether or not venting his own opinion on a national lunchtime radio show has influenced naïve Millennials with vulnerable, easy influenced political and moral direction, well, you decide.

He also displayed disgust with soldiers firing at a picture of Jeremy Corbyn on a live firing pistol range, emphasising the Millennial attitude by ignoring the fact that he is an IRA sympathiser. Jeremy also only interviewed left wing Millenials believing they fully understood squaddie humour yet turned it around to suit their own anti-armed forces rhetoric. Jeremy, however, failed to add that cut-outs of Margaret Thatcher, Donald Trump and Jerry Adams were also used as targets, yet never mentioned one of them during the interview.

On another occasion he believed that those over 50-years of age are responsible for the state of the planet. And with vegan guests talking about veganism, he allows them to complain about the slaughter of pigs, linking meat eaters with changing the environment on a global scale. Although denying Jeremy to get a word in edgeways – as they had a great deal to say about global destruction by car drivers – they conveniently diverted away from the subject of Halal slaughtered meat. Displaying Millennials taboo discussing Muslim practices in fear of branding themselves racists, quickly using their trump card – political correctness.

On this occasion, Jeremy implied he could not see the problem with throwing a milkshake over former UKIP (United Kingdom Independent Party) leader, Nigel Farage. Considering the news at the time [2019] was full of headlines with innocent victims having acid thrown over them during street robberies, callous acts of revenge, even terrorist attacks, Millennial left wing political activists – mainly university students – arrogantly carried out supposedly innocent attacks using milkshakes. To the victim, however, by which I mean anyone that disagreed with the assailant's left wing political views, could have easily had acid thrown over them. And even the mention of a pregnant woman or child victimised by a milkshake attack didn't change Jeremy's sadistic attitude towards this mindless act of violence.

Jeremy certainly lost the plot with his continued stance and support for bicycle riders. He actually told millions listening to his show that it was okay for children to pull wheelies on bikes whilst riding on roads and even pavements. He says, in a feeble attempt to justify his bicycle stance, that these kids were keeping fit and carbon neutral, thus saving the planet. To add insult to injury he continued by adding cars were the problem because they cause accidents. He went on to say it's good that these kids do wheelies in front of cars to slow them down as drivers are bound to otherwise speed.

Well, do you think Jeremy's comments are fair and balanced? Of course, they must be. After all, he would never advocate any immoral judgement, instruction or take side on any particular social or political spectrum on a show where all ages can tune in and listen to, would he? And not just Jeremy. Surely all radio and television presenters take into consideration for all, not a chosen favourite few. Can you remember a time when a presenter from any of the mainstream news channels interjected a personal view, political or otherwise? Be it Jeremy Vine, Robert Peston, Tom Bradby, Krishnan Guru Murthy, Jon Snow, Laura Kuenssberg or Piers Morgan?

Whatever your thoughts and opinions on television news presenters, the bulletins they report across the airwaves certainly reflects modern social issues with its profound strangulation of actual truth modern society denies or dares not to broadcast in fear of condemnation from the shouty few. Whether its politics, crime, budget cuts, unemployment, war, the NHS or child obesity, you are sure to receive outrageous exaggeration and personal comments to appease the media conception of mass belief.

Nonetheless, presenters have since learnt to prefix a headline with 'so called' before any sensationalism of a story. A somewhat transparent and pathetic attempt to cover and divert any bulletin – and their arse – away from complaint, offence, and most definitely responsibility. Covering ones arse with this limp assurance seems to be an industrial norm across the board.

Take child obesity and other social touchy subjects. There will be a few facts and figures thrown around from some recent unheard study, in essence avoiding blame in haste of any reference towards calling someone fat or, god forbid, attaching a genre or minority group. Once again, bowing to a non-existent political correctness. As for global warming, or as it is now fashionably dubbed by the media, climate change, is a quagmire of obscure and massaged facts and of course mainstream presenter's personal opinion and political persuasion. So it must be true, right?

Chapter Twenty

We didn't start the fire

Global warming: a subject shouted from the rooftops with such anger, blame and passion by university students and environmental activists alike to express an unrecognisable political persuasion by exploiting a very recognised global issue. Or as it is now dubbed – climate change. First of all, the term climate change became fashionable from around the late 1990's when scientists discovered that the already over-used term 'global warming' failed to convince the masses of its effect upon the planet.

Putting it another way, their interpretation of blame was outrageously incorrect. However, it cannot be ignored that the earth is getting warmer, so tweaking the expression a tad to 'climate change' offered a more favourable and equally global acceptance in a more modern society by diverting blame from the scientists should the new interpretation be incorrect once again. With me so far? Read on.

When David Attenborough hit the airwaves in the early 1980's to explain a new juicy media-grabbing headline called 'global warming' he went into detail as to why the world was warming up and what were the main contributors for this phenomenon. Yes, I said phenomenon, and that's because it is. After all, the earth has had many catastrophic climate changes over the past 4,500,000,000 years, billannials (is that a word) before the industrial revolution, invention of the internal combustion engine, coal fuelled electricity power stations or even curling tongs.

Regardless of fossil fuels, cars, curling tongs and cows farting, the biggest contribution towards climate change isn't man-made, it is cosmos made. The earth takes one year to travel around the sun, right? But the undulating wobble of the earth as it circumnavigates takes 200,000 solar years before returning to the beginning of its wobble cycle, only to repeat its long journey again, creating climate change on our delicate blue planet as it travels. In effect it kick-starts natural warmer periods between ice ages that have continued since the birth of the earth. Ask Professor Brian Cox, he'll explain it better than me.

There has been around 5 full-on ice ages since the earth was created, the last starting 3,000,000 years ago, where it is currently approaching its end, placing the planet in another interglacial period that started 12,000 years ago. This means global temperatures naturally rise due to the earth wobble cycle. Whilst all this is happening the effect of the sun, its ever changing spots and solar flares upon our already incredibly complicated planetary climate cycles, continue to cool the higher atmosphere – the stratosphere – whilst the lower atmosphere – the troposphere – warms slightly due to reflection from the oceans and landmass. And yes, that includes trapped carbon dioxide.

Wind back the clock to around 200,000 years ago early human tribes in Africa enjoyed wetland far and wide across the continent. But the climate continued to change due to the earth's wobble, and gradually yet naturally, wetlands of the Sahara became dry deserts we know today. 140,000 years later – and without a car in sight – those early tribes ventured north into southern Europe to escape the scorching sun and baking soil, once fresh and moist back in the good old days. Wonder who they blamed for that particular climate change?

Fast forward to present day the effect of climate change has been recycled somewhat by modern man and clever marketing. From Tony Blair and his car hatred campaign to chocolate bar wrappers, junk food to even holidays, all have exploited the latest global warming scare-mongering fashion as a catalyst to advertise re-packaged wares and services to suit the latest global hysteria. Remember the Millennium bug? A mass ploy by marketing a non-existent event yet successfully achieved to make us believe computer timers will turn to 0000 at the stroke of midnight 31st December 1999 and automatically switch themselves off because they will have no recognition of the new Millennia.

All media outlets grabbed the story with both hands to sensationalise and spread chaos around the world. The havoc about to bestow upon the globe will cause millions of deaths around the globe; hospitals unable to cope with countless casualties; aeroplanes will fall out of the sky; banks and commerce will grind to a halt; global communication will suddenly stop; satellites will burn up in the atmosphere; food stocks will rot… so on and so on. The media simply went bonkers over this story. And what was the outcome? Nothing.

In the meantime computer IT companies were employed by businesses and even governments around the world to supposedly prevent computers from switching off at the stroke of midnight 31st December 1999. Billions of pounds, dollars and many other global currencies, spilled into bank accounts of 'so called' computer expert companies to repair a problem that never existed in the first place. And where was this media-hyped world catastrophe first created? Social rumours shared between armchair warriors on an infant internet, only to catch the eye of mainstream media outlets to exploit a huge sales opportunity in front of an easily persuaded and confused audience.

One easily persuaded emotionally-fuelled naïve Millennial was Swedish school girl, Greta Thunberg. A young up and coming environmental activist first hitting our social and mainstream media headlines in 2018. A member of Generation Z who has developed a passion for saving the planet against climate change by influencing schools around the world to go on strike and reverse a global phenomenon by standing on the shoreline and demanding the tide to turn back, as it were. And of course publicise her inherited hysteria-inflated interpretation of blaming elder generations for the damage they have done to the planet and ruining it for her and future generations.

Greta became an immediate overnight success on all social media platforms, grabbing particular attention from her own generation. In doing so she grabbed further attention from mainstream media to interject their self-opinionated attitude and political persuasion. The outcome was Greta becoming an immediate hit after raising the odd eyebrow amongst leading climate scientists and political leaders. She also addressed a United Nations summit, accusing world leaders for leaving climate change for her generation to deal with.

Greta believes past generations have failed to recognise the global problem, and the planet is running out of time. She also said that unless we recognise the overall failures of our current systems we most probably don't stand a chance. Her young shoulders also believe that older generation's interpretation upon everything isn't simply black and white is a very dangerous lie. We – the older generation – should open our eyes, see the crises, and do something about it.

In February 2020 she continued her quest to belittle past generations by calling on the school children of Bristol to go on strike and join together to blame their parents for ruining their future by destroying the planet. And as she spouted her rhetoric in front of 26,000 children enjoying an excuse to skive off school, star-struck by their latest idol speaking from a solar-powered platform – albeit unable to power the public address system because it was pouring with rain, so used a back-up diesel generator – her young naïve shoulders failed to recognise the facts of her crusade.

As much as I applaud Greta's efforts, and yes, it has to be accepted that man-kind has contributed towards climate change, past generations since the baby boomers are, in fact, doing shed-loads to clean the environment. And you can't blame certain older generations for not doing anything to help because they were too busy dealing with real issues of their own, such as saving Greta's freedom and liberties so her country continued to speak Swedish rather than German, even though Sweden remained neutral during the war. And yes, if Hitler hadn't been defeated, he would have most certainly invaded her country. Going further back, her great, great, great grandparents had to endure problems I'm pleased she will never have to experience, such as trying to stay warm, keep a roof over her head or search for scraps of food to simply stay alive.

Greta's generation are full of accusations and ask many questions, but are too young to understand and raise a single responsible answer or conceive any possible solution to any sustainable or environment issue. Let's face it, they can't even decide whether or not to be Arthur or Martha, believe in veganism but love a burger, and cry at even the thought of someone disagreeing with them. However, since the 1970s mankind has taken a huge leap towards cleaning the environment – technology and materials permitting.

You only have to fly over countries and continents to see the shear number of wind turbines sprouting around coastlines, let alone in-land. And that doesn't include thousands of hectares of farmland taken over by solar and hydroelectric power stations. Businesses are converting to incredibly low powered LED lighting, placing solar cells on rooftops to power computers, printers and telephone systems, cutting back on waste, water usage and even introducing recycling programs. But these projects cost billions, if not trillions of Pounds, Dollars, Yen, Yuan, Euros, Dinar, Rand, Dong, Rupee, and even the Kip. Yes, Kip is a currency.

The automotive industry has also changed beyond belief in the past 50-years or so. Introduction of the catalytic converter in the early 1970's has been modernised with the added introduction of EGR (Exhaust Gas Recirculating) valves. And since the Euro 6 emission laws, an injection cooling system is fitted to vehicle exhausts catching 99 percent of diesel particulates through a DPF (Diesel Particulate Filter). The result is recirculated and filtered gasses from the exhaust are actually cleaner than city air sucked into the engine. But that's not enough, apparently.

Automotive manufacturers continue to put up with relentless nagging from governments determined to be better than their political counterpart by enforcing outrageous and often impossible clean air targets. The response was a hydrogen-fuelled car exhausting gases into the atmosphere consisting of nothing more than water. But the cost to produce hydrogen-powered vehicles, as well as extracting hydrogen from water to fuel them, is astronomical. So as it stands, the only option is all-electric vehicles, including cars, buses, trucks, trains and maybe one day, passenger-carrying aeroplanes. But to make and produce these green, polar bear friendly, battery-powered vehicles is a colossal drain on resources and the environment on a global scale.

Batteries that power electric cars are set to increase by enormous proportions, and by 2025 will engulf 90 percent of all Lithium-ion battery production. From its raw material state to end production, this 'so called' environmentally friendly automotive alternative actually produces twice as much carbon footprint than conventional internal combustion engines. Let me explain.

From mining of raw materials, they travel around the world to battery manufactures, only to travel back around the world a second time to car manufactures, remarkably travelling around the world yet again to car distributors. And this is before a single turn of an end users brand new wheel. The new owner then has to keep recharging the battery, where more often than not, the electricity used to charge it comes from a fossil fuel powered electricity station. To add a further problem, the UK alone produces only 5 percent excess electricity before any influx of battery powered vehicles taking over internal combustion power. And the USA actually produces a deficit of 14 percent electricity [2020] so has to import more power from elsewhere in the form of fossil fuels.

Ah, but if all power stations produced green energy, then surely the carbon footprint to produce and run electric cars will eventually off-set conventional vehicles, I hear you say. Well no, not really. Firstly, there is simply nowhere near enough solar, wind, hydro-electric, renewable or even nuclear fuelled power stations on the planet to produce enough fossil fuel free energy for other uses, let alone recharge battery powered vehicles.

———

Secondly, should all vehicles be miraculously replaced with battery power tomorrow, the amount of Co2 poured into the atmosphere would send Greta and Jeremy Vine into a frenzied panic. And forget garbage-fuelled DMC DeLorean cars, even with Doc's capabilities going back to the future.

Thirdly, and to rub battery acid into the environmentally friendly activist wound, on paper it will take 9 or 10-years for a battery powered car to off-set any carbon footprint. But this falls into insignificance due to the fact car batteries only has around a 7-year life cycle, so a replacement is required. And because batteries to power car motors cannot be fully recycled, where technology to do this has a little way to succeed with this conundrum, the replacement battery will have to be a new one. And the manufacturing cycle from raw material to end product begins all over again.

To add another conveniently brushed under the carpet problem, most new cars are replaced within 4 or 5-years, especially by the largest end user – fleet markets. And should a recycled system miraculously appear out of thin air, it wouldn't be needed due to demand for replacement new cars, where, yes you've guessed it, the entire manufacturing process begins again. Only this time a used unrecyclable battery mountain of huge proportion will quickly appear, leaving the industry to store around 10,000,000 tonnes, or over 40,000,000 inefficient, environmentally damaging, soil polluting, fluffy squirrel killing Lithium-ion batteries by 2025. And that's just car motor batteries that have drained fossil-fuelled power for charging on a daily basis.

Boat and yacht builders, plant and agricultural machinery, even HGV manufacturers are developing fully electric vehicles, including tractor units to haul goods in 50-feet trailers up and down motorways.

Doubling the size of an unregulated growing mountain with quadruple sized batteries weighing in excess of 4-tonnes. And these colossal industrial batteries require considerably larger quantities of raw materials, creating larger mines, demanding further fossil-fuelled energy and increasing further pollution to produce them.

In 2015 Cobalt – one of many materials used to make Lithium-ion batteries – rose considerably in value within 12-months by a staggering 80 percent. And in 2020 almost 200,000 tonnes of this precious material was processed and shipped to manufactures, inevitably increasing the cost, where, as always, paid for by the end user. Then there is Lithium; a rarer material than Cobalt, yet just as important towards the manufacturing of these 'so called' environmentally friendly batteries. And by 2025 almost 800,000 tonnes will be mined to keep up with demand, where it takes 1,000 tonnes of ore to extract only one tonne of Lithium.

Further materials such as Chromium, Copper, Graphite and Nickel are also needed. Mined in Russia, the Philippines, Indonesia, China, Australia and Canada. One mine in Australia alone produces 100,000 tonnes of Nickel Sulphate per year, generating incredible toxic issues for the environment. Spewing tonnes of harmful gases and dust clouds into the atmosphere, as well as sulphuric acid and other oxidised Nickel waste into nearby rivers and streams, turning them red and killing wild life. Respiratory and cancer illnesses, child deformities and premature deaths are a contributing factor of living near these dangerous areas, and are on the increase.

Graphite is predominately mined in China, where strict regulations on air and water pollution are a tad different to some other countries, such as Canada and Australia. Pollution from mining and processing Graphite has caused local health issues and damaged surrounding crops by poisoning the soil. Combining all materials and its processing to extract these precious metals from ores has created an outrageously devastating environmental impact. Add the destruction of land and the stripping of forests covering thousands of acres, the green solution to create a cleaner environment is seemingly tarnished somewhat. But surely the sacrifice is worth it?

Those employed by mines from poorer countries suffer worse health problems, where it seems employers have mislaid the memo on Health and Safety. Thousands of incredibly low paid labourers are treated no different from those during the industrial revolution. And yes, that includes incredibly long shifts, working 6 and even 7-days per week, using a large number of child labour. And let's not forget powering the enormous energy used to extract and process these precious metals are mainly sourced from coal fuelled power stations. Still want an electric car?

In the meantime governments around the world exploit the situation by hitting consumers with higher taxes and charges to combat climate change. Oh really. Like that is going to help. Or is it to raise a few quid for the exchequer? After all, how can charging customers a few pence for a plastic bag save the planet? They're still bought and discarded, paid for or otherwise. And the idea of swapping plastic for paper bags endorsed by some climate activists is preposterous. Surely they know to produce a paper bag or cardboard packaging creates harmful toxic gasses that produce 85 percent carbon footprint against its manufacturing process, as well as costing more in production and materials. Yet plastic packaging only produces 7 percent of its carbon footprint to manufacturing process and costs are incredibly lower to produce.

The sudden panic behind this interest in discarded plastic bags destroying our oceans, and the animals that live beneath, was only brought to our attention thanks to David Attenborough. The sight we witnessed on television shocked the world. Inevitably mainstream media, as well as the new infectious social media, once again blew the plastic bag crises way out of proportion, contributing towards the resurrection and biblical escalation of climate change rhetoric. And with it came billions of self-opinionated comments, as well as blame, along with the natural marketing and advertising exploitation of goods and wares suddenly becoming environmentally friendly. You've seen the adverts.

Of course, although we're all to blame, the main culprits for discarding not only plastic bags, but many other harmful bulk waste products for land and marine use, including fishing nets, concentrates around other countries. India, Africa and East Asia to name but a few, dumping huge amounts of waste into rivers and seas, finding itself in oceans around the globe gathering in tides and currents, creating floating islands, some as large as France and even the State of Texas.

Discarded plastic is certainly a global issue and most definitely a man-made problem. But it also promotes a conundrum defining the true definition to the cause of climate change exacerbated by a Millennium-made interpretation to suit their, once again, unrecognisable political fashion. A classic example of this marketing exploitation strategy to appease the young Millennial was when McDonalds replaced plastic straws with paper ones. But environment conscious Millennials complained they became too soggy, especially when drinking milkshakes. McDonalds responded almost instantaneously by reinforcing them, but the problem was they could no longer be recycled, having to be disposed of in general waste or even burned. In other words, when it suits a certain PC generation, re-defined or not, has to be right.

In the early 1980's when David Attenborough told us about global warming, the young generation at the time – my generation – didn't jump around pointing fingers or blamed elder generations for destroying our future whilst desperately searching for the nearest crying room to sob uncontrollably. And marketing companies didn't exploit the latest media-hyped world catastrophe to advertise goods and polar bear friendly services. Instead we listened whilst deciding what this new global warming thingy was and what can we do to combat it. After all, it was new to us. And the plastic issue wasn't nowhere near as bad as it is today, having taken a good 30-years to reach its critical level [2019] ironically all within the Millennial generation.

Fast-forward a few decades and into a Millennial society, with its plastic – pardon the pun – whiter-than-white modern environmentally friendly political correctness, they have simply tied themselves in knots. And that is because they dare not voice the truth and blame themselves in fear of breaking their own rules, thus branding themselves racist, fascist or Nazis. So instead Millennials had to invent an alternative truth defining their very own existence: blaming previous generations that are, in their eyes, detached from their own political agenda by exploiting political correctness as a moral persuasion. Remember the definition? A bit of Nero playing his violin going on here.

Climate change did in fact begin to slow down around the early 1990's, albeit by a tiny fraction indicated by human interaction. Yet with a far better economy, almost zero carbon particulate emission engines, cleaner gas powered electricity stations, a massive increase in railway electrification, global expansion of wind, solar and hydroelectric power, and the ban on CFC propelled Harmony hairspray, surely the climate must have started to stabilise.

In some cases, yes it has, depending upon which report you believe. UK household emissions dropped dramatically [2020] by 40 percent within 30-years thanks to more efficient gas boilers and government insulating incentives. And carbon dioxide emissions dropped by a massive 6 percent within a 2-month period, thanks to an unprecedented global lockdown of almost 7,000,000,000 civilians due to the Covid-19 virus pandemic [2020]. More on that later. But on the whole, no, climate change didn't slow down further, even with all these new environmentally friendly inclusions.

Should the reason for climate change be solely man-made, as dictated by a very shouty lot, the blame has to sit with, believe it or not, yes, your lot, Greta: The Millennial Generation and its wanton lust for modern, cheap, throw-away goods. Manufactured by using coal burning, child labour exploiting, resource raping materials, causing a global spike in carbon dioxide and a warmer climate since the slow down in the 1990's.

It is Millennials that are killing polar bears and causing mass extinction of bees and butterflies. It is Millennials contributing towards the melting of ice caps and raising sea levels. It is Millennials causing a huge expansion of coal-powered electricity stations springing up in China, Asia and even the USA to fuel demand for the young global consumerism. It is Millennials creating the outrageous waste of plastic packaging floating around our oceans. It is the Millennials incredible arrogant greed and sensational appetite for anything and everything never seen before in consumer trends, ever.

The amount of waste Millennials have created has been an enormous drain on our precious earth, causing a huge headache for recycling companies to recycle modern plastic goods and packaging previous predictions on shear volume alone could never envisage. Clothing has become cheaper due to imports from India and the Far East where child labour is deemed legal, ignorantly forgotten or shamelessly cast aside by Millennials to bear witness because of their relentless need for the latest fashion item, trend, cosmetic, or mobile phone.

Using child labour naturally encompasses cheap power from fossil fuel burning factories to produce even cheaper goods and garments Millennials are desperate to parade around clubs, pubs, bars and restaurants. And not just clothing. Take the Glastonbury Festival, where tens of thousands of Millennials create tonnes of plastic waste. The irony was when David Attenborough attended the festival in 2019 to advocate his young audience and promote environment awareness, believing they too are doing their bit to save the planet whilst blaming previous generations for the carnage.

And how did these thousands of green supporters thank their illustrious leader? By leaving behind almost 20-tonnes of cheap tents, sleeping bags, cartons, food waste, clothing, flags, cardboard, cans and plastic bottles, all discarded by 'so called' environmentally friendly Millennials. And not just at the Glastonbury Festival. All festivals, gigs and concerts turn into nothing more than general waste dumps, including tonnes of fast food take-away packaging littering pavements, roads and ditches, leaving a tell-tail trail miles away from the original venue, predominately caused by Millennials that eat the crap wrapped inside it.

Cosmetics and body lotions for young women, and even men, has also increased ten-fold in popularity since the 1990's thanks to fashion trends spearheaded by athletes, sports personalities and reality television celebrities. Mascara, lipstick, eye shadow, body sprays, fake tanning creams, all contribute towards climate change thanks to production methods, where a supposedly modern environment caring attitude conveniently cast aside the plastic container storing the product.

By far the biggest contribution to the rape of resources and waste is global expansion of electrical goods. Again, since the 1990's electrical gadgets have increased 100-fold, only for Millennials sheepishly diverting blame from their conscience. However, any consumer that plugs a device into a socket is equally to blame: hair dryers, straighteners, curling tongs, shavers, wax heaters, chargers, laptops, computers, smartphones, tablets, huge flat screen televisions, satellite and cable television decoders, DVD and CD players, washing machines, tumble dryers, freezers, refrigerators, even the internet burns electricity and contributes towards climate change. The internet, I hear you question?

Ever since its invention the groundwork and infrastructure to create a global World Wide Web has been phenomenal to say the least. Raw materials such as copper, tin, gold, silver, aluminium and platinum has been a tremendous drain on resources in itself to build and maintain this incredible monster. Savagely mined from our planet by stripping forests, jungles and farmland so to pillage the rare minerals and metals to create the internet. Even environmental harming chemicals have been developed and used across the world in the production of high-tech communication electronics, only to pollute and poison soils, rivers, streams and coastlines.

The burning of fossil fuels to clear these gigantic man-made landscapes to mine for precious materials is

---

phenomenal, and it doesn't stop there. Fossil fuels continue to burn ferociously to manufacture thousands of masts, mile after mile of copper and digital cable, hundreds of orbital satellites and huge buildings just to switch the internet on is staggering. And that's before actually using computers, laptops, tablets and smarphones to access it.

Rare metals used to make these devices, such as Indium, is stripped from the earth for the construction of solar panels, tablets and smartphones, estimated to run out by 2040. And to extract it from only one kilogram of zinc produces a poultry 2mg of Indium whilst using vast amount of fossil fuelled energy in the process. Other precious metals such as Lanthanum, Praseodymium, Neodymium, Terium, all used in the production of smartphones and tablets, consumes fossil fuelled energy to extract from its ore.

Even Strontium is needed to create back lighting. Most of which is mined in Africa using child labour to extract it without the use of PPE (Personal Protective Equipment) or basic adequate clothing, such as boots and gloves. Many dig for these materials barefoot, wearing nothing more than a T-shirt and shorts, using only blister causing manual tools. Yet earth loving, environmental sympathising, anti-slavery activist Millennials continue to upgrade mobile phones within a single heartbeat as soon as a new model is released.

To power the internet is simply mind blowing. And sending an email sounds simple enough. So surely sending one via a handheld device is environmentally friendly because no electricity is used. Well, putting aside plugging in a device to charge it in the first place, the amount of electricity used to send an email is the equivalent of running a 60-watt bulb for one hour. And with an attachment it requires the energy equivalent to running a considerably higher wattage bulb.

Within that one solitary hour 10,000,000,000 emails are sent across the globe [2020] requiring the entire output of 15 coal-burning power stations. And that is just for emails. Attachments and downloads including photographs and video, requires much, much more power, where Google alone gobbles up enough electricity to supply a large city the size of Manchester. Then there are social media companies, data centres, schools, hospitals, local authorities, military, national security, businesses, manufactures, offices, warehouses, air and sea ports, governments, all using huge amounts of extra power since the birth of the Millennial era.

Volume of data from the internet also doubles every 2-years, where 100 hours of video are posted on YouTube, 2,000,000 searches made on Google and over 650,000 messages sent on Facebook alone are carried out in just one minute [2020]. And as the digital clock ticks an ever-increasing appetite for electricity is required to power the internet. Facebook, Google and Apple, just 3 internet companies out of thousands are based in North Carolina, where they alone consume 5 percent of all electricity produced for the entire State from its 11 coal powered electricity stations.

Mobile telephone communication companies also use vast amount of fossil fuel power so you can send and receive text messages from their orbiting satellites and hundreds of thousands of masts dotted around the globe. Then there are the add-on services such as Twitter, Facebook, Whatsapp, Snapchat, and many more, all using an incredible amount of power so you can message friends, argue, comment, send photos of pouting teenagers or of a environmentally sustainable vegan meal.

Websites, such as Ebay and Amazon, have a massive global market creating millions of purchases every week, where all of their customers – that's you and me – use the internet to buy wares. Adding further billions of emails and filling virtual shopping baskets to send across the internet and burn fossil fuels so you can have that next day delivery of a new laptop, mobile phone or an environmentally friendly bicycle. Then there are other global internet companies, including entertainment sites, such as Netflix, Amazon, Apple, Sky and Virgin. The amount of data used over the internet to globally stream all the films and box set uses the equivalent of a coal-fuelled power station alone.

Then you have all the internet consuming towns and cities around the world, including London, Paris, New York, Berlin, Shanghai and Moscow, in other words millions of them. Most of which are powered by fossil fuels, including coal. A fuel that emits 50-times more carbon dioxide than any other fossil fuel, producing other toxic gasses and ash deposits that contaminate soil and rivers, causes asthma, cancer and many coal polluting deaths. It is also the largest contribution to global warming, according to Greenpeace and other environment groups. So the next time you send an email, order something online, or stream a film believing you are being environmentally friendly, you are in fact contributing to climate change.

Another contribution to electronic and internet consumption happened in 1990 – the sudden collapse of the USSR releasing a mass migration from Eastern to Western Europe never seen before. Over a 30-year period former Eastern Bloc countries, originally starved of gadgets and computers we in the West take for granted, suddenly craved the same, and certainly made up for lost time. Like starving children let loose in a sweet shop, they alone caused one of the largest spikes of electrical gadget consumerism and internet frenzy.

Add this gigantic migration influx into Western society, with their sensational consumption prompting an increase use in tonnage of fossil fuels manufacturing televisions, computers, tablets and game consuls, the environmental damage caused is added to the long list of man-made carnage. Still, at least recycling will save the planet, won't it?

We know recycling is nothing new. Archaeological digs have discovered waste dumps predating the Romans, filled with relics of recycled items originally made for other uses. I have already mentioned the Victorians, Edwardians, consequence of rationing during world wars influencing the baby boomers and even Generation X to do the same. Rising costs, including water and fuel rationing, and the odd energy crises in the 1970's certainly laid a permanent foundation for Generation X to make do and mend. But then the EU and other governments intervened, with the intention of streamlining recycling with guidelines, rules, regulations and laws.

Government interference – I mean legislation – is really a political tool to increase recycling quotas by demanding minimum quantities, procurement, utilisation rates and labelling. In other words force manufactures to create, maintain and reach enforced recycling targets, including variable percentages of recyclable materials into new products, if only to brag to other governments with what they're doing to save the planet. Meanwhile, in the UK incentives to recycle have since materialised into nothing more than further taxes and law, thus a criminal offence – at least by local authorities for throwing away an empty can into the landfill bin. And what happens to household recyclable waste? A large quantity will become landfill or shipped across the other side of the world to be dealt with – out of sight, out of mind.

However, some plastics, glass, wood, paper, cardboard, and even oil products are recycled in greater quantities than ever before by using better recycling methods. And new technologies continue to find even more applications for recycled material: ash moulded into building blocks, bottle glass made into road surfacing composites, scrapped fire engine bodies into sewerage cleaning rods, and old wheelie bins into traffic cones. Expensive metals such as aluminium can be recycled into lesser pure products such as utensils, window frame strengthening bars and toys. Sounds terrific, doesn't it.

Unfortunately, the majority of metals and plastics used in everyday manufacturing cannot be recycled due to 21st Century demand for applications required to satisfy the increasing appetite of today's society and its sensational greed to make life easy. This includes the construction of the internet, telecommunications, road developments, bridges and tunnels, expansion of railways including the manufacturing of electric trains, carriages and rolling stock. Electric car manufacturing, for instance, has caused one of the largest mining spikes of raw materials in human history.

Glass, although recyclable, is actually more expensive to implement and uses far greater energy than producing from its raw material – sand. Wood chippings are made into chipboard, hardboard and MDF (micro density fibre) board for the building and construction industry, but rendered useless for recycling. Plastic has become a taboo word, thanks to David Attenborough, yet almost every product we use has some kind of plastic integrated within its manufacturing process, including the innocent teabag. And most plastics can only be recycled 2 or maybe 3 times before the degradation of its composite materials breaks down to the point of having no use at all, other than contributing towards landfill sites.

Electrical goods can be dismantled into individual component parts consisting of precious and toxic materials, either disposed of in, let's say various ways, or smelted into ingots to resell on the recycle market. Much can be said for television and computers, including lead from CRT (Cathode Ray Tube) monitors and mercury from LCD (Liquid Crystal Display) screens. Both materials extremely poisonous. And most of the dismantling is carried out in poorer countries using child labour without the use of PPE because small naked hands are better suited for stripping smaller toxic components than protected Western adult hands. But surely there's someone out there that can clean up the environment. Oh, of course, them.

Extinction Rebellion, also known as XR, inadvertently portray the pinnacle of Millennial youth culture: demonstrate against anything and anyone that disagrees with their polices. Predominately supported by students, they are the hardcore of disruption. Whether its chaining themselves to railings or invading runways at Heathrow airport, they will stop at nothing to vent their very extremist and very loud stupendous voice to the nation.

The organisation started in the UK by a bunch of, yes, you guessed again, students, in May 2018. And by October had over 1,000 supporters congregating at Parliament Square in London to pledge their declaration of rebellion by occupying the entrance to the Houses of Parliament. Soon after they caused huge disruption by gluing themselves to railings outside Downing Street, blocking London bridges spanning the Thames, then spread their sticky student know-it-all tentacles further afield in Scotland and other counties.

Their principles include: Government must tell the truth by declaring a climate and ecological emergency, working with their institutions to communicate the urgency for change, must act immediately to reduce greenhouse gas emissions to net-zero, must be led by a Citizens Assembly on climate and ecological justice. And it doesn't stop there. Oh no. They also state: A shared vision to create a world that is fit for generations to come; mission to immobilise 3.5 percent (that's around 2,500,000 people) of the UK population to achieve system change; actively mitigate for power to break down hierarchies for more participation; avoid blaming and shaming living in a toxic system but no individual is to blame; a non-violent network using non-violent strategy and tactics as the most effective way to bring about change; collectively create the structures.

When, why and how they can achieve these incredible, yet stupendous principles is beyond me. But with a student following, or at least whilst they are still students – until they grow up and enter the real world – their recruitment tactics have become a tad more cynical to fill the void, reflecting similarities no different to the Hitler Youth of the early 1930's. XR youth wing – yes, youth wing – created to target vulnerable children aged between 10 and 16-years old.

Ever since their birth the organisation has grown exponentially by the usual mob of anti-government, anti-war, anti-work and 'anti-mummy and daddy finally seeing sense by stopping to pay for their credit cards, rent and wasted student fees.' In other words Extinction Rebellion is nothing more than a following of spoilt, over-protected and over-grown children, throwing temper tantrums because they cannot get their own way in the real world. Governments of Western countries, however, believe a zero emission environment will be possible to achieve by 2050. The Green Party believes it is possible to achieve by 2025. XR believes it is possible, today, this minute, right now.

Although spearheaded by a bunch of easily persuaded immature university students, high profile support also came from healthcare professionals, NASA Scientists, professors, predictable music artists and tinsel town actors such as Jane Fonda, Sam Waterston and Emma Thomson. In the meantime XR has partaken in unprecedented mayhem. Extremism is certainly a precursor used by XR to try and break UK's liberal lifestyle, democratic society and law. In other words, create complete anarchy in the UK. Nevertheless, they unconditionally deny any involvement using violence to put across their grievances, only to arrogantly blame others that conveniently demonstrate such behaviour, as students do.

Extinction Rebellion believes their demonstrations should create mass arrest of its members to grab national media attention by using non-violent methods of attraction. In doing so their message is broadcast to the masses with hope of highlighting the inevitable end of the world caused by previous generations, industrialists, coal power and car owners – in their mind.

These mass arrests tended to include those that wanted a little more action: burning cars, buildings, smashing windows, throwing bits of pavement, bricks and even fireworks at police blockades are some of their 'so called' non-violent methods. And the Millennial generation, including Greta Thunberg, with their must-have latest mobile smartphones, tablets and laptops, LED smart televisions and access to the internet, even demanding mummy and daddy drive them everywhere, have the bare-face cheek to say we, the elder generation, have ruined the planet with our ignorance towards climate change.

Chapter Twenty one

Stop feeding the puppy!

So where does this incredible journey of Millennials end? At the point of being totally controlled by mobile phones and incapable of looking up from them when at the dinner table or walking down a busy street ignorantly bumping into pedestrians? Or instinctively pressing the button at pelican crossings without noticing only one vehicle approaching? Or governments hell-bent on bowing to their every tantrum and demand?

Maybe it ends with students ranting and raving because they can't get their own way, or whilst studying to be a doctor publicly wishing a new democratically voted Prime Minister a painful death, yet can't be bothered to vote themselves? No longer engages in conversation, orders fast food online as part, if not all of a staple diet, or sends text messages to mum from a bedroom rather than talk to parents? Continuously posting photos of themselves next to huge meals mum and dad paid for, prepared and lovingly cooked, but has no intention of eating them. Instead blames older generations for not doing enough for the starving millions in Africa?

I could carry on, but no, the journey doesn't end quite yet, and it will certainly get worse should moral standards remain unsupervised. Otherwise the likes of Jeremy Vine, Pierce Morgan and other high profile social figures that are most definitely unsupervised will continue to exacerbate Millennial behaviour whilst mainstream media exploit it and the masses with more than 2 brain cells grow ever more frustrated.

Thwarted by intrusion of idolised celebrities has always disrupted younger generations of any progression towards social acceptance, if only for selfish means, and will continue to do so in its many modern guises. Over time their own naïve bubble wrapped tinsel town view of the world has sadly influenced millions of easily led young naïve minds over the decades, represented as nothing more than navigating modern society without a helm. Tossed around on a crawl and merciless stormy sea of self-inflicted extremism, leaving behind valuable lessons untapped in its wake. But are celebrities to blame?

Well yes, at least partly. As are mainstream media – print and airwave alike – for sensationalising stories to attract the easily persuaded masses by injecting their own political and moral persuasion, encouraged by the Victorian newspaper editor, William Thomas Stead in 1884, the inventor of sensationalism. Since, newspapers, television and radio presenters do exactly the same, honing their skills over the past decades.

Past governments also have to take a bite from this huge social shit-stirring sandwich for softening laws, ignoring the masses once voted in, only to listen to minority groups that shout the loudest rather than the majority that are now silenced by the former because of soft governments. In the meantime, wrist slapping them pesky kids committing crimes that would have previously been awarded with a custodial sentence infuriates us elder generations.

This outrageous kick in the teeth for the elder masses reflects modern knee-jerk reaction laws passed to over protect children whilst condemning all parents to be nothing more than child battering thugs. Kicking in a few more parental teeth, since 1989 in the UK it has been illegal to smack children, exploited to the point of any slight of hand inflicted on any child. And has since been defined by the print media and highlighted by very loud self-opinionated – yet childless – Millennial politicians previously arse wiped by their parents.

This confused law highlights those in appointed positions influenced by others with a similar upbringing that shout the loudest rather than representing society as a whole. But it doesn't end there. The UK government moved the goal post yet again in 1993 by increasing the child age from 16 to 21-years of age with the introduction of the CSA (Child Support Agency) influencing a continuation of child-like behaviour with the added protection of child laws to exploit in their favour.

The age of consent to buy tobacco has also increased from 16 to 18-years of age. Okay, not a bad thing, but having to prove you're over eighteen by appearing to be over 25-years of age to purchase a packet of cigarettes is preposterous. Nevertheless, the overwhelming impulse over the past few decades to continue to wrap further layers of cotton-wool around children, including those up to the age of twenty-one, but allow them to still vote from the age of eighteen, is confusing to say the least.

Of course, modern governments went one step further to appease that shouty few by supporting child abuse charities such as Child Line, and quite right to. They do fantastic work, and have helped thousands of young children suffering from abuse. But the amount of wasted phone calls by a modern legally recognised child upto the age of 21-years moaning about mummy and daddy not allowing them to have a birthday party is surmountable to abuse of the child protecting laws.

As the decades unfolded allowing children to get away with murder, influenced by soft laws and strangulated social change, so did the quality of education and its even softer attitude towards history. In 2008 3,000 teenagers were asked if they knew who Winston Churchill was. Unbelievably 20 percent said he was a fictitious Edwardian superhero. Yet another classic reflection upon the modern British education curriculum, where many teachers lean towards socialism and left wing beliefs, hell-bent on teaching pupils their own political persuasion. In fact school pupils know more about former Labour Party left wing socialist leader and terrorist sympathiser, Jeremy Corbyn.

Standard of exams has also become a joke. One-third of six-form students received unconditional university entry regardless of A level results, making a complete mockery out of six-form and degree level UK education. On 15th August 2019 A level student pass rate stood at 97 percent, where those that made over 50 percent on the paper received a pass. And with this government blasé attitude towards education attracts even more freedom of piss-take from pupils and students alike. Roaming law-free to cause havoc when they finally leave school and into the real world, protected further still by 21st Century government child rights to extend into an untouchable criminal career.

Racism also remains a hot potato. A study in 2016 unveiled racial abuse has increased since the 2010 UK collision government relaxed yet more rules in schools. In doing so over 4,500 racial complaints by children were made around the country, yet Millennials will have you think that it was previous generations that were racist. And of course will certainly brand me a racist, if not a Nazis and Fascist, maybe demonstrating a touch of ageism, and even a cyclist (see what I did there).

But you only have to look at their own stupendous recorded behaviour on social media sites and see for yourself why young Millennials have become known as the untouchable extremist generation. This includes filming themselves carrying out aggravated racism, hate crimes, bullying, rioting, fighting – including wounding with knives, clubs and iron bars, criminal damage…, the list goes on and on.

Record damage to war graves, military statues, urinating on memorials, unprecedented attacks on military personnel, veterans, and emergency services, including a huge increase of abuse on social media is also on the increase. But this modern hatred on such a large scale has only escalated within the past 20-years. Influenced by musicians, pop groups, synthetic off the peg celebrities, radio and television presenters, left and right wing political persuasion, misrepresentation of religious belief, socialist biased education, loony-left university lecturers, all contributing towards the Millennial social disease, contracted by those easily brain washed shouty lot.

Cambridge University, one of the most prestigious and influential universities in the world, has slowly but surely surrendered to its very own student union by allowing them to pass a notion to ban anything militaristic, including uniforms, from its university colleges. They believe anything to do with the military will trigger anxiety and mental issues amongst students. Astonishingly 55 percent of union members agreed. They also demanded a national ban of Remembrance Day, believing it celebrates war. Classic case of the tale wagging the dog. But there is an irony here. Extinction Rebellion, the pinnacle of student unrest, destroyed their very own front lawn of Trinity College [February 2020] in protest of its contribution towards fossil fuel technology. You have to laugh.

For the rest of society, a social muzzle has been slowly tightened around the mouths of the grown-up moderate over the past few decades. And any hint of discipline has been diluted somewhat by inflicting too much freedom too soon on a young society thwarted by its own self-perpetuated disability growing into adulthood. Whether you're a parent, grandparent, teacher or employer, the newly appointed 21st Century generation has certainly caused a few ripples, not realising they too are nothing more than a passenger on that helmless social ship heading towards total chaos.

Nurtured Millennial arrogance, teased by their very own immature peers, evolved from the revolution of society during the industrial revolution. Consequently over 200-years these darling little angels and their perfect PC world reached crises point in 2020 as it suddenly exploded due to an unforeseen international virus unexpectedly (or suspiciously) caused by someone eating a bat bought from a market in Wuhan, China. If believed, this individual created a global, as well as a Millennial game changer.

November 2019 witnessed a dangerous coronavirus called Covid-19 that quickly spread to become a global pandemic within 4-months, unseen since the Spanish influenza pandemic of 1918-1919. At first, in an attempt to contain the virus, a complete lockdown of all citizens from the streets of Wuhan was ordered by the government. But it was too late. The virus escaped the boundaries of the city and by March 2020 the whole world was infected, causing a global lockdown of almost 7,000,000,000 people. And depending upon the severity of the virus in any given country, lockdown seemed to be on a sliding scale. Good old Blighty, and its liberal approach to society, was a little more relaxed when it came to the individuals need for freedom.

At first, the masses in general took notice of government instruction and behaved themselves. Queuing outside shops with strict shopping rules were also adhered, including the government 2-metre social distancing rule. But as the months unfolded the typical Millennial behaviour soon became apparent by ignoring lockdown protocol. Bored with lockdown and socialising rules, it didn't take long for them to flaunt any restrictions placed upon their precious free and easy lifestyle. And with a typical thought of 'it will never happen to me' carried on regardless.

Although restaurants, café's, gyms, pubs, clubs and other non-essential outlets were closed, and households were forbidden to visit family members or other households, there they were, the untouchable lawless Millennial, having house parties, gathering in public and even arranging rave parties. After all, they would never fall foul to this killer virus, would they? But the risk they created to themselves and others was soon evident with regional spikes of the virus in Bedford, Bradford, Luton, Watford, Oldham, Leicester and Northampton. But it didn't stop there.

It soon became apparent that black and Asian communities were more susceptible to the virus than white communities, to the extent of increasing an infection rate by 8-times. So extra care of isolation would be needed to follow tighter social disciplines. At first, being a tad concerned with their welfare, and rightly so, the news sunk in and kept to their disciplines, with further support from health authorities and the NHS. But an incident in the USA was about to change these disciplines to the point of destroying them altogether.

———

On 25th May 2020 George Floyd, a 46-year old black American from Minneapolis, was arrested for allegedly using counterfeit money. Upon his arrest he was apprehended by a white police officer using force to hold George down with his knee on his neck whilst handcuffing him. But George died of asphyxiation due to the police officer refusing to move, even though George pleaded to let him breathe. Bystanders took video footage of the incident with mobile phones and posted the footage on social media websites. The outcome ignited a social tinderbox that spread world-wide.

Within only a few days black communities from 1000's of towns and cities in the USA gathered in protest of George's death and police brutality against black civilians. A march not seen since the 1960's when Martin Luther King demonstrated against black segregation from white society. These protest were soon influenced in the UK where black and white communities marched in unison, protesting about the outcome of George's death. But why? The USA is thousands of miles away and the story had no influence upon British Society. Only the carefully orchestrated marches weren't arranged just for the death of George Floyd. This was merely a catalyst in the name of racism.

Inevitably these anti-racism marches quickly turned into riots. In London the sacred Cenotaph in central London was graffitied with Nazi slogans and there was even an attempt to burn the Union Flags attached to it. Shop windows were smashed, along with damage to vehicles and other property, and the demonstrators also attacked police officers. Statues such as those of Queen Victoria, Sir Winston Churchill and the Bomber Command memorial statue, all sprayed with Nazi slogans. And yes, it was young Millennials that carried out these callous acts of vandalism and caused further mayhem. And yes, that all self-important student was amongst the ringleaders.

The outcome of these demonstrations will carry on for sometime as the racial equality debate continues, but for the purpose of this book, I reflect upon the Millennial attitude, putting their beliefs and frustration beyond, not only other peoples lives, but their own during a global viral pandemic. And whilst these protests and riots took place the Covid-19 virus continued to rage its death toll amongst the masses. In New York alone, a further 19,000 cases were caused by the ignorance of Millennials, spreading the pandemic by ignoring lockdown rules put in place to supposedly slow down the infection rate.

As the demonstrations subsided, so did some lockdown rules, although still in effect to combat the virus. Nevertheless, Millennials in their hundreds-of-thousands exploited the government relax on lockdown to congregate en-mass at the coast and swarm the beaches. The outcome was shear bedlam, with very little space in between each sun worshiper.

Cars were parked on double-yellow lines, across driveways and grass verges. And with council public toilet facilities still closed due to the pandemic, the crowds simply relieved themselves when and wherever they wanted, including pavements and private front gardens. When the crowds finally went home, Bournemouth beach on the south coast alone had a staggering 40-tonnes of discarded plastic wrappers, paper packets, cartons, bottles and cans, left behind by the very same generation that believes in 'so called' environmental issues and the reduction of global carbon footprints.

But there has to be an underlining reason for all this carefree, anti-everything, do what I want attitude. We cannot only blame the softening of laws, abolition of National Service, television and radio presenters, reality TV or modern comedians – they're all either left-wing loony fruit-loops or lesbians. No, of course not. However, there is one other major ingredient. With a huge influx of pupils staying on at school, and the government extension of child recognition to the age of 21-years of age, Millennials have grown to expect to stay at home considerably longer than those from previous generations.

Subsequently maturity is restricted to the point of developing much, much slower than ever before whilst continuing to be fed, watered, and arse wiped by mum and dad. In other words, a puppy will never mature and become an adult dog whilst fed, watered and kept in captivity. Hence a puppy-state immaturity; easily moulded into obedience by tantalising its own misguided influences, but left to believe they're top dog in a household that allows them to roam without instruction or discipline.

Nevertheless, it has to be said that the majority of Millennials continue to abide by the rules, whilst the younger generation continues to study for that great career. They continue to join the emergency services and Armed Forces to protect our freedom and liberty, even for that shouty know-it-all anti-establishment bunch. Further still, that niggling doubt, impossible itch to scratch, annoying poke in the side, isn't the Millennial Generation, because, like the itch, it doesn't exist.

I know, shock horror. I can almost hear Jeremy Vine fall off his bike in bewilderment as he cycles to his studio in London, only to blame a car driver in Aberdeen for doing so. But it's simply impossible for a single generation to have ever existed over 40-years. As it turns out the generations that make up the 'so called'

Millennial Generation, including Xennials, Generation Y, iGen and Z respectively, exist in there own right. In other words, they're not merely a sub-text to describe younger or older Millennials.

The term 'Millennial', although a brilliant invention at the time to describe the up and coming Millennium born children, should have been just that – a definition to describe Millennial born children. No different from other fads of the time, such as the Millennial bug or Millennial Dome in London, eventually changing its name to the O2 arena once the party of 2000 woke the following morning nursing a hangover. Meanwhile, older generations were forced to grow in the shadow of the 'Millennial'. Abused, raped, and forced to re-invent itself since 1991. Or is it 1999? No, 1979 or maybe 1975 with the Xennials? See, total chaos.

Hang on a second. If that is the case, I have described exactly what any previous generation has said about its successor. To put it another way, a typical description by all predecessors complaining about the next lot, regardless of technological, medical or socially accepted breakthroughs. Yes, it has been considerably worse for older generations, but in many ways we have gone full circle. From a 19th Century coal-using society ruled by employers forcing employees to work all hours god sends, to a 21st Century Lithium mining society ruled by computers, its own achievements, anguish and selfish wants. So in a weird and twisted way we have inadvertently fabricated a worse social deal fuelled by arrogance, greed and ignorance.

On the other hand we no longer starve, at least within our Western society. Have government benefits, excellent health care, upteen choice of different foods, huge amount of leisure time, lazy-style gadgets, instant ordering and delivery, credit on tap, a roof over our heads, even if we fall behind a little on rent and mortgage repayments. Holiday entitlement, cheap travel around the world, employment and human rights protecting us from discrimination and abuse, laws that supposedly protect us from harm, and regulations to save argument. But remember there is a bigger world out there that is still struggling, and couldn't give a toss about your fantastic rules and laws.

Nevertheless, we have Red Dwarf, James May, Richard Hammond and Jeremy Clarkson. Not a bad achievement for 200-years of dispute and determination by the masses. So don't be too down hearted. Actually, give yourself a huge pat on the back. But don't stop here brothers and sisters. Continue the struggle and fight on, otherwise we'll be slipping backwards before you know it. As for those pesky loud students striving to keep us all backwards, and those supposedly grown into adulthood that still believe in their student bullshit rhetoric unfit for the grown-up world, don't be frustrated or angry over their ridiculous childish demands and pathetic rants. Instead, laugh at them. After all, they are nothing but a fad that will eventually burn out, replaced once again with common sense and social ridiculed by the masses.

Yes, most students quietly study hard, knowing what they want to achieve. And most so called 'Millennials' quietly tootle along doing the best they can to make an honest living. Unfortunately, all have been tarnished somewhat by those careless, reckless, self-centred, lazy, arrogant shouty lot that actually portray themselves to be no different to the Brown Shirts in the 1930's – the similarities are uncanny. But one day them shouty lot will have to face the real world we endure day in day out. Hence their need to study subjects not fit for use or ornament so to stay in education for as long as possible, only to be fed and watered by mummy and daddy. Or moan and blame everyone but themselves for their own mistakes. And studying useless subjects because they're too scared to face reality, or blame everyone else, one day their infantile behaviour will be their demise.

After all, with all their puerile and childish demands, insults and publicly throwing toys out of prams when interviewed on breakfast television, caught on social media videos or filmed by film television crews rioting, causing criminal damage or burning the Union Flag, who in their right mind will employ someone poised to cause mayhem and trouble because they're used to getting their own way? Well yes, the BBC. But who else? Okay, the print media, government, schools and universities, but there is no-one else other than the industries that really matter. Those that keep the wheels of commerce turning. So bosses of these companies, do you really want to employ someone from that shouty lot? I certainly won't.

Alpha Generation, it will soon be your turn, and you are certainly not to blame for our social quagmire of problems, issues and arguments. That includes you, Greta. Sure, we've invented some great stuff and achieved countless goals, but made the odd mistake on the way. And yes, some of us older generation folk do find it hard to put up with 21st Century cultures, music (if you can call it that), an incredibly fast moving modern society, everything done on the internet, the outlandish reaction to being offended and the exaggeration of everything and anything. But we grew up in a different, tougher world, so you're going to have to accept that, as we have to learn to accept your world. After all, Generation X is the very last flicker of the old world.

Like you, our world is what made us. You stand fast and refuse to suit our old one, and we cannot simply change to suit your new world. Okay, Jeremy Vine is the exception. But we both have to move forward the best we can. And when the baton is finally passed to you, any change for the 'Beta Generation' (I'm guessing that is the next one) you will no doubt be ridiculed and demanded to suit their generation and it will be just as difficult for you as it was for us – if not worse.

Any future decisions you make on your watch will be down to you and you only – as it was for all previous generations. Taking the blame appears to be a lost art, last employed by Generation X, and you will have no choice but to re-learn it. After all a bunch of so called 'Millennials' were incapable. In the meantime us older lot will be dead or dribbling in the corner of an old folks home next to the sunny window, grinning inanely knowing what you are about to reap should you let your children get their own way. To avoid this please, promise me this, don't ignore past mistakes, learn from them. And stop feeding the puppy!

I may have mentioned Brexit once, but I think I got away
with it.

The Lost Generation	1890 to 1900
The Interbellum Generation	1901 to 1913
The Greatest Generation	1910 to 1924
The Silent Generation	1925 to 1945
Baby Boomer Generation	1946 to 1964
Generation X (Baby Bust)	1965 to 1979
Xennials	1975 to 1985

Millennial era

Generation Y	1980 to 1994
Generation Z/iGen	1995 to 2012
Generation Alpha	2013 to who knows?